YOUR PERSONAL PLAYBOOK
FOR SUCCESS

 Tyndale House Publishers, Inc.
Carol Stream, Illinois

GAME PLAN *for* LIFE

JOE GIBBS

with Jerry B. Jenkins

Visit Tyndale's exciting Web site at www.tyndale.com

Visit Joe Gibbs at his Web site, www.gameplanforlife.com

TYNDALE and Tyndale's quill logo are registered trademarks of Tyndale House Publishers, Inc.

Game Plan for Life: Your Personal Playbook for Success

Designed by Ron Kaufmann

Edited by Dave Lindstedt

Library of Congress Cataloging-in-Publication Data

Gibbs, Joe J.
    Game plan for life : your personal playbook for success / Joe Gibbs with Jerry B. Jenkins.
      p. cm.
    Includes bibliographical references.
    ISBN 978-1-4143-2979-6 (hc)
    1. Christian men—Religious life. 2. Success—Religious aspects—Christianity. I. Jenkins, Jerry B. II. Title.
    BV4528.2.G53 2009
    248.8'42--dc22   2009013139

Printed in the United States of America

15 14 13 12 11 10 09
7 6 5 4 3 2 1

To our grandchildren:

Jackson

Miller

Jason

Ty

Elle

Taylor

Case

Jett

It is Pat's and my hope that one day
they will also be part of
a moral reawakening
in America.

Sincere thanks to my team:

Phyllis Blair
Barry Leventhal
Cindy Mangum
Don Meredith
Chuck Merritt
and all the contributors,
of course.

I am grateful to "my guys," who selflessly
gave their time and effort to this project. Their
friendship and professional teamwork provided
material and spiritual support at critical times.
Special thanks are due to Chuck Merritt of
White Post Media, who so freely gave numerous
hours to help me tell my story.

Thanks to the folks at Tyndale House Publishers,
for allowing me to collaborate with Jerry Jenkins,
and for the creative freedom to do it my way.

We pray that this book will be part of a
moral awakening in America. Thanks be to God,
who causes us to triumph in life.

TABLE OF CONTENTS

Foreword

TONY DUNGY

I was just starting my pro coaching career in 1981, as an assistant for the Pittsburgh Steelers, when Joe Gibbs took over as head coach of the Washington Redskins. Coach Gibbs went on to win three Super Bowl titles in the next eleven years. His teams were always well prepared, but what struck me was that they seemed to thrive in the toughest environments.

Joe's Redskins had a great record in the playoffs, when the pressure is the highest, but they also happened to win championships in 1982 and 1987, both years when we had player strikes and uncertain schedules.

Although I was never privileged to work for Coach Gibbs, he had a tremendous impact on my career. Because of the way his teams played, he intrigued me. I watched him, studied him, and talked to many people who knew him. I wanted to know how he did things, how he was able to get his players to perform with such precision and togetherness—how he was able to get them focused to function so well under pressure and in times of adversity.

Frankly, it didn't surprise me to learn that the Redskins' success under Joe was no accident. I discovered that Joe was a person who believed in God and God's plan for a man's life. Coach Gibbs governed his life that way and led the team that way—with Christian principles learned from the Bible. Though, naturally, his goals as a coach included winning football games, winning was never his sole purpose. His purpose was to let everyone around him see how Christ was leading him, and to let people see those Christian principles in action.

Joe has brought that approach to whatever venture he has undertaken—whether coaching the Redskins or owning a NASCAR racing team. Now he has brought that passion for helping the world see Christian principles in action to a different forum—*Game Plan for Life,* which I believe you will find is a great guide to successful living.

In football, each player gets a playbook at the beginning of the season. It has all the strategy, assignments, and techniques that can make him successful. Our players study that playbook and learn the key parts so they can perform on the field. The job of the coaching staff is to help the players assimilate what's in the playbook for maximum success. As a Christian, I agree with Joe that the best playbook for life is the Bible. It contains all the information we need to lead a successful life and thrive.

Any head coach will tell you that the task of surrounding himself with the best assistant coaches can make or break his season. In addition to telling his own story here, Coach Gibbs has put together the best staff of "assistant coaches" you could imagine to help you understand the playbook. These eleven men have taken eleven fundamental biblical topics and laid them out in a way that brings clear insight into God's thoughts on each one.

You may be a Christian already, or you may be entirely new to this kind of thinking. Regardless, I urge you to give *Game Plan for Life* a fair reading and see what you think. In just talking with Joe, I can feel his passion for this project. He has always been driven, and unwilling to settle for second best. Whatever challenge he's undertaken, he has always delivered championship results. His drive now is to get God's message out and to equip people to handle the tough issues our world throws at us every day.

Once again, he's done it at a Super Bowl level.

CHAPTER ONE

No Game Plan, No Victory

"**J**oe, I've got awful news. Sean Taylor was shot early this morning. He's at Jackson Memorial in Miami." It was 6:00 a.m. on a Monday, and I'd just been awakened by a call from my boss, Dan Snyder, the owner of the Washington Redskins.

Sean Taylor was our superstar safety. He'd played in the Pro Bowl in 2006, and now in 2007 he was tied for most interceptions in the NFC, even though he'd missed the last two games. Some in the media said Sean had the talent to become one of the greatest NFL safeties of all time.

"How bad is it?"

"He got shot in the leg, so I'm not sure."

How bad can that be? I wondered. *Certainly not life threatening.*

Our first-round draft pick in 2004, Sean was having a remarkable season in what was otherwise turning out to be not such a great year for the Redskins. It was November, and we'd just lost to the Tampa Bay Bucs 19–13 at Tampa—our third loss in a row. We were 5–6 on the season, and it sure didn't look like we had a chance to get into the playoffs.

Due to a knee injury, Sean wasn't required to attend the Tampa Bay game. Instead, he was at home with his infant child and her mother in Miami, where he'd grown up.

This was my fourth year back as head coach of the Redskins, and my experience this time around was a long way from what the media had called the "Decade of Dominance," during my first stint as the Redskins' head coach from 1981 to 1992, when we won three Super Bowls.

Now this.

Sean Taylor—nicknamed "Meast" by his teammates because he was "part man and part beast," named by *Sports Illustrated* as the hardest-hitting player in the NFL—shot in the leg. To my horror and the devastation of our whole team, Sean died from his wounds the next day.

A year later, I was in my office at Joe Gibbs Racing in Charlotte, and the incident with Sean still weighed on me. The 2008 NASCAR season had ended, and I was catching up on business with one of our bankers, a good friend.

Out of the blue, he asked if I knew a certain college football coach. I did. "Well," my friend said, "I think you two have the same spiritual father, George Tharel."

I was more than a little surprised to hear George Tharel's name, because he had died seventeen years earlier in Fayetteville, Arkansas. George had taken me under his wing in 1971, when I was an offensive line coach for the University of Arkansas Razorbacks. My wife, Pat, and I had met George just after we'd moved to Fayetteville and began attending the same local church.

Now here I was in my office in Charlotte—a world away from that college town—learning that the same man who'd had a huge influence on me had also inspired this other coach who had passed through Arkansas early in his career.

You might ask, "What's a spiritual father?" For me, he was the guy who took the time to help me understand the spiritual truths I still live by today.

George Tharel had been my Sunday school teacher for two years. He was a man quietly driven to make an impact on other men. As my career took me around the country, I stayed in regular contact with George, because the wisdom he shared kept me grounded and pointed in the right direction.

To anyone else, George might have looked like an ordinary guy. To me, he was extraordinary. He had a great family, managed the local JCPenney store, and served in his church. Here was someone who had lived his life to the fullest, had a big influence on others, and had been gone for years.

That conversation with my banker friend about George Tharel got me thinking.

What had made George's life so significant? Money? No. That he'd worked his way up to manage a local department store? No. That's all forgotten and gone.

That he was some larger-than-life "life coach"? No.

If it was not fame or fortune or reputation, what was it?

What remains of George Tharel is the impact he had on other men's lives. Mine. The college coach my friend was talking about. And every man George took the time to teach spiritual truths throughout the years. His legacy lives through each of us today.

Sean Taylor's death made me realize how fragile life can be. George Tharel's life made me recognize the lasting impact our influence can have on others. As I thought about these two lives, I evaluated the kind of impact I was having on other men. With this book and the project that will follow, I want to pass on some of the truths I've learned and the most important discoveries I've made about life. I hope it will help you avoid some of the mistakes I've made too.

I'll come back to Sean and George again, later in the book. But first, let me set the stage for what's to come.

In the Company of Men

Okay, here's the deal: My whole life has been in the company of other men. I had a brother. I played sports from day one—baseball, basketball, and football in high school, football in college—and I coached in college and the pros. Pat and I have two sons. I now own a NASCAR team.

In short, I know men, and life's not easy for them these days.

Wherever I go—on business or for speaking engagements, sporting events, or whatever—I run into guys who all seem to have the same questions and challenges. I can relate to these men because I've faced many of the same issues in my own life.

Many men see me as a success because of the Super Bowl rings and the NASCAR championships, and I'm not going to pretend I haven't lived what looks like a charmed life. But what guys want to know, everywhere I go, is how they can succeed too. And they're not just talking about becoming rich or famous or winning trophies. They want to be happy. They want to be good husbands and fathers, good people. They want to find true success and relevance in their lives.

Experts tell me that the two sports that have dominated my adult life have about a hundred million fans. Are you one of them? Is that maybe why you picked up this book? Let me tell you right off the bat, I'm gonna be straight with you. I've heard so many questions about life that I gathered a few trusted colleagues and friends, "my guys," and we started talking it through. What is it that men really want to know about, and what do I have to tell them?

See, the bottom line is that I have found something special, something that works, something that has given me a sense of peace and purpose and fulfillment. But despite what a few sportswriters and a kind business associate or two have said along the way, I'm about as far from being an intellectual as you can get. I was a P.E. major. You know, physical education: ballroom dancing and handball!

Sure, there were people who thought I had talent when the college offenses I helped to coach were among the best in the country, and that helped me land an NFL coaching job. And I know it requires some smarts to manage a coaching staff, come up with creative—and successful—game plans, and lead a football team. I'm just saying I'm no scholar. I'm a regular guy who saw his dream come true. I don't apologize for being competitive, striving for excellence, or refusing to quit. But what I want you to know is that it makes sense that my name is Joe. I'm your Average Joe. Forget what you might have seen or read in the media, or anything else you might have heard; I'm not that different from you.

Here's why. Maybe I've got a nice résumé and have created some really special memories, but the best—and hardest—lessons I've learned in my life have come from failures, my own shortcomings, and buying into some of the biggest myths our modern society has to tell. If this book can help you avoid even one of those, I'll consider it a success.

Now, let's get after it.

Winning at the Game of Life

I have thought a lot about life—what is it? Life to me is a game, and you and I are the players. God is our Head Coach, and no one wants to lose in the biggest game of all. I'm going to explain what it takes to win a football game or a car race, but what does it mean to win at the game of life? What is true success?

First, I need to say that when I call life a game, I mean that it's a contest, not that it's trivial or all fun and games. You've learned that by now. But if life is a game, you and I are playing the most important contest of all. All my experience in leading men—as a coach and team builder—has convinced me that to win a game you need a game plan.

If you watch football, you've seen the coach on the sidelines, wearing a headset and carrying a white laminated card. That card is the game plan. While I was with the Redskins, I had thirteen coaches helping me lead the

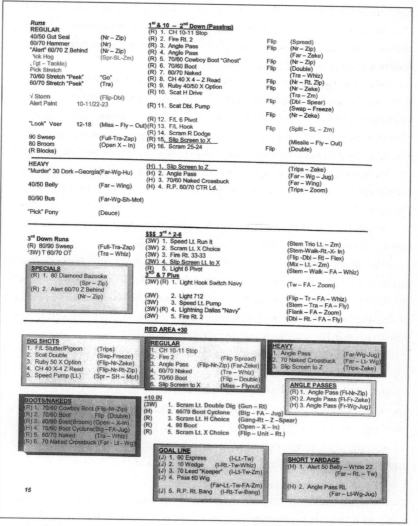

Actual Redskins game plan from 2005 season

team. We had a coach for the running backs, the quarterbacks, the defensive line—coaches for each of the positions and teams. One of the most important things we did as coaches was come to the office on Monday and Tuesday to craft the game plan for the following weekend.

We coaches would spend dozens of hours working through plays and on-field scenarios. We'd watch the films, study the stats, and scrutinize the opposing players for strengths and weaknesses, matching them to our own. In short, we'd develop a specific game plan to win that game. Playing the Cowboys required a totally different game plan than the one we'd use against the Falcons or the Eagles. Each week, we spent many, many hours—whatever it took—to get the game plan right.

When our players came to Redskins Park on Wednesday, we'd hand each one a two-inch-thick binder that would have everything they'd need to know about the other team and the plays and formations we'd be running. Throughout the rest of the week, we'd start to specify certain plays for certain situations—short yardage, goal line, third down priority plays, and so on.

By the end of the week, we'd have the game plan developed down to the exact plays and formations we'd run in every situation. *Nothing was left to chance.*

Maybe you watch a lot of football. If so, you've heard the announcers talking about the "red zone"—referring to the area on the field from the 20 yard line to the goal line. Our game plan was so detailed that it divided those twenty yards into five-yard increments, with specific plays for each segment.

Out of hundreds of plays and dozens of formations, my coaches and I picked the best ones for each game and each situation. That was our game plan. As I said, nothing was left to chance.

The same thing is true for a NASCAR race.

Have you ever seen a crew chief sitting on his box with a white card in his hand? Well, he's the head coach of that team, and he's holding the game plan for that race. At Joe Gibbs Racing, we have a game plan for each of our three cars: numbers 11, 18, and 20.

Let me tell you this: there may not be any sport where a game plan is more crucial to victory than in racing.

The crew chief orchestrates a team of about a dozen "assistant coaches"—from the engine tuner to the shock specialist—and through them, a few hundred race team employees back in Charlotte.

Fuel mileage is a key to a racing game plan. If we think the race is going to come down to fuel mileage, our strategy takes into account when we will pit to take on fuel. We also have a tire strategy. We might change two tires sometimes, as opposed to all four. Obviously, the car gains a lot of track position with a shorter pit stop, but we have to weigh that against tire wear and performance.

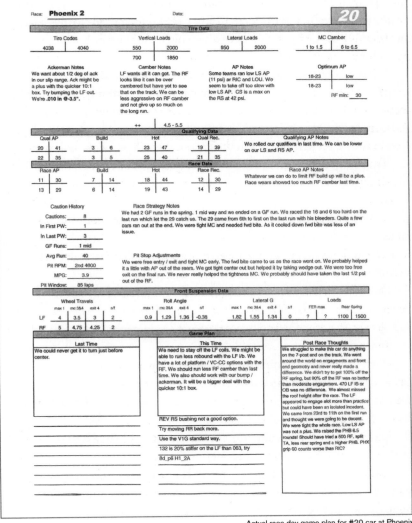

Actual race day game plan for #20 car at Phoenix

There are four basic track types in the NASCAR Sprint Cup Series: short tracks, intermediates, superspeedways, and road courses (which aren't the normal oval and require right- and left-hand turns).

Does that matter? You bet it does. It means a whole different car setup if we're racing at Talladega, a superspeedway with speeds near 200 miles per hour, or at Watkins Glen, a road course where we have to worry about the brakes overheating. Different type of track? Different game plan.

As in football, the crew chiefs build flexibility into the racing game plan to adjust for weather. Is the track likely to get hotter and slicker during the race? Or is it going to get cooler and provide more traction?

Our NASCAR race team even has the equivalent of football's special teams.

Track position is everything in racing, so pit stops are incredibly important. Like a special team unit in football, the seven-man pit crew must perform in the crunch. In twelve seconds, these guys jump the wall, change two or four tires, make wedge and rear track bar adjustments, empty two eleven-gallon fuel cans into the tank—and then get out of the way.

If they blow it, there's a good chance we won't win.

We have a designated outdoor area at Joe Gibbs Racing where our pit crews practice their choreographed stops. Watching the guys train, or running into them in the team weight room, reminds me that they are true athletes and that their contribution to winning is as important as our drivers'.

In football, the postseason playoffs lead to the Super Bowl. In NASCAR, the Chase for the Sprint Cup encompasses the last ten races of the season. Only the top twelve drivers compete for the Series Cup in the Chase.

If you are in the running for a championship at the end of the year, finishing high is more important than risking everything to win. You are not going to take the chance of running out of gas to win a race. On the other hand, if you don't have a shot at the championship, you have nothing to lose. You might say, "We're going to stretch our gas mileage and skip the last pit stop to try and win this race." You get the picture.

Whether it's NASCAR, the NFL, or life, when you're playing to win, you have a game plan. If you're serious about winning, nothing—I mean *nothing*—is left to chance.

You also need a head coach to craft and develop that game plan. He's the one person ultimately in charge of preparing the team to win a game or a race.

That's been my life for more than forty years. As a head coach and team builder I've learned a few things about competition and game plans.

Here's where *you* come in to the *Game Plan for Life.*

I told you earlier that you and I are playing the most important game—the game of life. Well here's the deal: *yes,* there is a game plan, and *yes,* there is a head coach—God.

Now, listen, don't write me off as "too religious" because I say that God is our Head Coach. Yes, I'm a person of faith, and I'm not trying to sneak up on you with this. If my success in sports has earned me any respect, all I'm asking is that you stay with me. If you really want to get a handle on life, I believe I've got something to offer you.

From the questions men ask me at my speaking engagements, to the discussions I have with my friends, and even to my interactions with my grown sons—J.D. and Coy, now husbands and fathers themselves—it's clear to me there are some common areas most of us struggle with at some time in our lives.

There are also some areas in which men are just looking for guidance, hoping to have successful relationships with their friends, wives, and kids. Maybe they feel stuck in a rut at work. Maybe they feel it is too late to change, or they're sorry for the way they've acted toward their loved ones.

I've struggled in some of these areas myself, as you'll see.

So when I talk about a game plan for life, I've got a good idea about the challenges we face. And as you can tell from my NFL and NASCAR experiences, I'm not really one to leave anything to chance, especially something this important.

So, my guys and I hired a research firm to survey a cross-section of American men to find out what was really on their minds and what they wanted to know more about in their search for success and victory in life.

Why do a poll?

Because coaches like player stats?

Yes—to some degree.

You see, we first wanted to validate our notions of what men are interested in, to see if we were on track. Second, we wanted to see if there were any topics men were concerned about that we hadn't considered. (Answer: yes.)

Last, we wanted to have a better understanding of how men viewed spiritual things, so we could talk with them clearly about God and His game plan for life.

To do the survey, we hired a Washington, D.C.–based research firm that does a lot of corporate and political work. In May 2008, the firm surveyed seven hundred randomly chosen men. We asked them seventy-nine questions about what was important to them in life.

About a third of the guys were completely nonreligious, a third had some religion in their lives, and a third were interested in growing spiritually. We also included one hundred pastors, priests, and elders, selected randomly from national church lists.

Frankly, we were a little surprised to find out how deep and spiritual some of the responses were. But the sampling was broad enough to accurately reflect what many men are thinking about, and we hope you'll identify with a lot of these areas.

Think about this: If we're the players and God's our Head Coach, would He put us on the field without a game plan? Absolutely not. He left us His Word, the Bible.

All right, there I go sounding religious again, but hey, I know I'm not going to get anywhere with you if I'm not straight up—especially about the questions you might have about the game plan, which I do believe is the Bible.

Having spent a lot of time with corporate leaders, broadcasters, sports professionals, and other well-educated guys, I know the objections that generally come up when the Bible is mentioned.

They go something like this:

- "Coach, come on, really. The Bible was written two thousand years ago. It's not relevant today."
- "Right, Coach, it's important; but for the life of me I can't find the subjects I'm interested in learning about."
- "Coach, it's just too big and full of confusing language that's a struggle to understand. It's intimidating."

Maybe you have one of these objections yourself. That was my own experience until George Tharel took a little time to help me understand the Bible and how it could change my life. I believe *Game Plan for Life* will provide answers to these objections.

You might be surprised at how many men have learned to turn to the Bible to be successful in the game of life.

Let me tell you that if you hang with me through the end of this book, I think you'll see that the Bible is a lot more relevant than you might think.

Key Things Men Want to Know About

Once we had the results back from the survey, my guys and I identified eleven topics we felt men wanted to understand better. Then we identified eleven scholars widely recognized as experts in their fields and who have spent their lives studying what the Bible says about their particular topic. I asked each of them to write part of a chapter in the *Game Plan for Life*.

Like I said, I'm no intellectual. But I know an expert when I see one.

These guys are experts. One of them, John Lennox, is a professor of mathematics at Oxford University in England and holds three doctorates.

Some of them debate at the top universities around the world.

But don't worry. We asked John and the other experts to make things clear to the Average Joe—to you and me. We have to understand these concepts if we want them to be of any use in real life.

You might say that the eleven authors who helped me lay out *Game Plan for Life* are my team. I will introduce them later. Their goal is to help you understand that the Bible is the game plan and that God is the Head Coach.

When I refer to "my guys," I'm talking about my "assistant coaches," the group of close friends and associates who have helped me develop this project: Don Meredith, who has been a close friend and business associate for thirty years; Dr. Barry Leventhal, academic dean of a well-respected seminary and onetime offensive captain of the UCLA football team; Chuck Merritt, a communications and marketing consultant who has served with Don and me on a board over the years; Phyllis Blair, who works with me at Joe Gibbs Racing and previously at the youth home I founded in Virginia; and Cindy Mangum, my longtime executive assistant, who works with me and my son J.D. and is often the hub between me, Pat, my boys, our sponsors, the media—you get the drift. My "guys" understand me and where we are going with this project.

In the next chapter, I'm going to develop the "life as a game plan" idea. I'll also get a little more into my background to help you understand where I'm coming from. You'll see we have more in common than you might think.

With my own life as evidence, let me tell you this: Following the wrong game plan leads to disaster. Following God's game plan for life led me to success. Believe me, if a P.E. major can do it, you can too.

CHAPTER TWO
My Own Journey

When I talk about the world trying to sell men a bill of goods, believe me, this is one I know from personal experience. I don't know where I got the idea that life was all about getting rich and making a name for yourself. I suppose it was conventional wisdom, but I sure didn't learn it at home.

I was raised near Asheville, North Carolina, in the 1940s by a doting mother who—though we didn't have a lot of money—didn't withhold much from my brother Jim and me. My dad had a drinking problem, so my mother tried to shield us from the negatives. I didn't know I was deprived. I loved that life. We spent most of our time outdoors with our shoes off. Some of my fondest memories are of hunting. I can remember spending afternoons with my shotgun just sitting in the tall grass.

Growing up, I was a pretty good athlete, but not because I was big or strong or gifted. What I had going for me was that I was competitive and determined. I just loved sports and was dedicated, so I worked at it. I wanted to be the best baseball, basketball, and football player on earth. What I lacked in natural ability, I made up for in competitiveness. I have to say, I've never lost that.

I played quarterback in high school after we moved to California, then played on both sides of the line of scrimmage in junior college and finally at San Diego State. My big break was getting to play under Don Coryell, an offensive-minded coach. I wound up on his coaching staff, then moved on to the staffs of Bill Peterson at Florida State, John McKay at USC, and Frank Broyles at Arkansas.

My first pro job came when Coryell was head coach of the St. Louis Cardinals and he brought me on as the offensive backfield coach. Coach McKay hired me as offensive coordinator at Tampa Bay, and I rejoined Coryell when he moved to the San Diego Chargers. It was the high-octane offense there that got me the head job with the Redskins at age forty.

It wasn't hard to see that my good fortune was a result of hitching my wagon to good coaches, some of whom wound up in the NFL. But somewhere along the line, I found myself thinking almost exclusively about making money, gaining position, and winning football games. That doesn't mean I was a bad guy. As a very young man, I made the decision to follow Jesus Christ. I believed in God, and like a lot of other guys, I tried not to get in trouble.

But my faith was certainly not my life. Not many who knew me then would say "committed Christian" when asked to describe Joe Gibbs.

I had met Pat, the girl of my dreams, and we had married, but getting ahead soon consumed me. I believed I needed to make money and gain fame. That meant winning football games, landing a head coaching job, and winning some more. Then I could accumulate things, and things would make me happy. Everybody seemed to agree on that. Besides needing money, fame, and success to be happy, it seemed our culture was also saying, "You've got one life to live, so you'd better make the most of it."

I have to say, that last myth never really reached me; and frankly, my skepticism over that "go for the gusto" mentality may have saved me. I had a nagging feeling in the back of my mind that this life is *not* all there is. Even during the years I spent chasing all those other dreams, I knew there was something deeper, something more important out there than me and my frantic quest to make something of myself. Don't you feel that way sometimes, when you get a minute to stop and think?

The idea that there was a higher purpose to life was planted in me as a child. Like most other kids, even in the Bible Belt, I was taught at school that I was the result of an accidental fusion of amoebas in some primordial ooze two billion years ago. Come on now. I remember sitting there thinking, *I'm not real sharp, but that doesn't sound right to me.*

Call me unscientific, but the whole idea that this world and everything in it is the result of random chance strikes me as nonsense. Think about it: Does any other complex thing in this life ever happen by accident? After what I've shared with you about what goes into a particular NASCAR race strategy or NFL game plan, do you really think that a crew chief is just a glorified mechanic who leads a group of car nuts hoping to be better than the forty other cars on race day? Is the football coach just a cheerleader who assembles a team of great athletes, keeps them in shape, and gives them some rah-rah, hoping they'll do better on Sunday than the other team?

It's kind of funny, but everybody thinks they know something about football. I'll never forget one time flying back to Washington and flagging down a cab in front of the airport. When I got into the cab, I told the driver I wanted to go to the football stadium. If you're a cabbie in Washington, D.C., you ought to at least be able to find the White House and the football stadium—but not this guy. I could tell he was probably new to the country. So I kept telling him where to turn. About five minutes into the ride, he looked over his shoulder and said, in broken English, "You . . . you coach the Washington Redskins!"

Well, I stuck out my chest thinking, *Hey, the guy recognizes the old coach.*

Five seconds later, he turned to me again and said, "You need to throw deep more!"

No question, everybody *thinks* they know something about football.

But the reality is that they don't. Most people have no idea how much effort goes into every game. Like I said, nothing is left to chance.

Oh, sure, good fortune often plays a part in any endeavor, and sometimes the breaks go your way and sometimes they don't. But to think that the universe, and everything it contains, is somehow just a product of time and good fortune goes against every rational part of my brain. I'll let my expert in this area, John Lennox, cover the details in chapter 5, but it seems obvious to me that the evidence for a creator is all around us.

Maybe that knowledge of a creator—instilled in me as a child—was what eventually made it possible for me to recognize my mistakes, and the failures I've had in my life, and get back on track. If I hadn't, I shudder to think of the miserable man I'd be today. Even if I had become the greatest coach in the history of professional football and had seen my teams win Super Bowl after Super Bowl, I'd have missed out on the few things that are really important in this life, and that would have been a tragedy.

I was a slow learner. Though I should have known better, I chased the dream and nearly caught it. That's one of the reasons why this book and the whole *Game Plan for Life* project are so important to me. I don't want for you to make the same mistakes.

As you read on, you'll see that one of our eleven experts, Os Guinness, writing about vocation, asks what kind of life you are living—an examined life or an unexamined life? In other words, do you have a plan, or are you just moving from one thing to the next? Are you living a life of purpose, or are you like the guy who says, "I went to elementary school so I could go to middle school so I could go to high school so I could go to college so I could get a job so I could get married and have kids"? There's some movement there, but often it's going sideways rather than forward.

Guys like that are living an *unexamined* life. I think you're reading this book because you want to live an *examined* life and make the most of it.

God Is Our Head Coach

If you're with me so far and can see the relationship between football and the game of life, I think you'll agree that both games need a head coach. When I came to believe that God had created me, and that I was no accident, I should have been willing to let God be in charge of my life. But that realization came much later for me, as you'll see.

Football players have to let their coach be in charge. For many of them, that isn't easy. One of my favorite guys to coach was quarterback Joe Theismann. He had a passion to succeed, but left to his own wishes, he would have liked to call every play. He was the type of player who would rather kneel in the huddle and draw up a play in the dirt than let the coach call the plays.

At our quarterback meeting before my very first preseason game with the Redskins, I outlined an involved game plan that we had been laboring over all week. Then I made the mistake of asking if anybody had anything to add. Well, Theismann had a million suggestions—things he saw, things he wanted to try. Finally I had to interrupt him and remind him of who was in charge, that there was already a game plan in place, and that it was his job to carry it out.

Everybody's going to follow somebody. In football, it's the head coach. In NASCAR, it's the crew chief. In life, I believe it's God.

Our Coach Cares about Us

As a coach and as a race team owner, I've always felt that the guy in charge has to care about his people. I've had players I loved on game day but could barely stand the rest of the week. I've coached hotheads, egotists, and guys who played their rear ends off on Sunday but wouldn't practice a lick if it were left up to them. I called one guy into my office at Redskins Park and told him, "Hey, I love you on Sunday, but I hate you Monday through Saturday." He was dumbfounded, but I think it made an impression on him. When we run into each other today at different events, he embraces me like a long-lost friend. He knows I cared about him, and that helped bring out the best in him. We'll be friends for life.

In the game of life, our Head Coach loved us enough to send His only Son to die for our sins. "For God so loved the world that he gave his one and only Son, that whoever believes in him shall not perish but have eternal life."[1]

That may be the most famous verse in the Bible, but it never meant more to me than when Pat and I had our sons, J.D. and Coy, and I realized I would do anything for them. I can't even imagine sacrificing one of my sons or one of my grandchildren for anyone, yet God gave His only Son.

A Team Sport

In football, the quarterback counts on his offensive line to protect him. On the other side of the ball, the defensive linemen must do their jobs in order for the linebackers to do theirs. A race car driver is only as good as his crew chief, mechanics, and pit crew. In life, it's the same situation—it's a team sport.

During my early years of success with the Redskins, I was sitting at the breakfast table one morning after a big win, reading the sports page and feeling pretty good about myself. We were getting ready for the divisional championship game in Dallas the next Sunday, and of course the papers were pumping my tires and saying how smart I was. You might say I was beginning to believe it myself. I was strutting around the house, getting ready to go to the office, when Pat said, "Would you mind picking up your bathrobe and socks?" (Isn't it great how God gives a guy the perfect wife to keep him down to earth?)

I picked up after myself as requested, but in the back of my mind I was thinking, *The nerve of her, talking to such an important man that way!*

And then she started in on our sons and how I needed to keep them in line on some matter or another.

Doesn't she realize what I've got to do this week to get ready for Dallas?

So of course I stormed out of the house—and even slammed the door. (Hey, listen, if you're a married guy, don't tell me you've never done that!)

I make it a practice to pray during my drive to work, and that morning was no exception. About halfway to the office, it dawned on me what had just happened. I said to myself, "Is life about winning football games, or is it about my kids and the family?"

As soon as I got to Redskins Park, I called home and told my wife, "What you're taking care of at home, our two boys, is more important than what I'm taking care of at work." From that day forward, I began to strive for a better balance between my work and my family.

Like I said, I'm a slow learner. But I've come to realize that despite everything nice that's come with my career—the privileges and the honors, the most important thing Pat and I are going to leave on this earth is the influence, good or bad, we've had on others—and in particular, on our two sons, their wives, and our grandkids.

Regardless of your profession, some days everybody's cheering for you, and the next day they're booing. Then they're cheering again. You might climb the ladder, reaching, striving, and before you know it, fifteen or twenty years have passed and your kids have grown up without you. You've missed out on the most important things in life.

I'm firmly convinced that someday I'm going to be sitting around in an old-folks home with a bunch of other old guys, and I'm going to be bragging to them, "Hey, I coached the Washington Redskins!" And they're going to call the nurse and tell her, "Get this nut out of here. He thinks he coached the Washington Redskins."

Philippians 2:3-5 says, "Do nothing out of selfish ambition or vain conceit, but in humility consider others better than yourselves. Each of you should look not only to your own interests, but also to the interests of others. Your attitude should be the same as that of Christ Jesus."

Remember, life is a team sport.

The Clock

In some sports, the clock seems to come into play only near the end of the game. Let me tell you: I was always aware of that ticking clock, from the opening kickoff onward. Sure, it really weighs on you the deeper you get into the game; but from the very first play, there are things we need to do, things we want to accomplish. And whether it's preserving our time-outs, clock management before halftime, or taking time off the clock late in games when we have the lead, that clock is a big part of the picture. It affects everything we do on the field. That's one thing I love about football.

In between my two coaching stints, I did some TV analyst work for NBC, and I enjoyed working on the air with my buddy Mike Ditka, former coach of the Bears and the Saints. He was bigger than life. At the end of a show, we'd be walking off the set and I'd say, "I wonder how we did?"

Mike would say, "I don't know, but there's probably somebody in a back room somewhere writing us up." In TV analyst work, there is no clock and there is no scoreboard.

Frankly, Mike Ditka didn't much care what anybody else thought about his performance. In football, it's what the scoreboard says at the end of sixty minutes that matters. There's no guesswork. No opinion. No judges with flash cards. You either won or you lost. You've got to love that.

That's true about car racing too—not the clock, but the outcome. First car legally across the finish line wins. That's it, pure and simple.

You know where I'm going with this. In the game of life, the clock on our lives is definitely ticking. The difference is that we don't know how much time we have left. My dad was seventy-two years old when he passed away, not that much older than I am right now. My spiritual father, George Tharel, died at seventy-one. Robert Fraley, my former agent and close friend, lost his life in the same plane crash that killed pro golfer Payne Stewart and four other people in 1999. Robert was forty-six. Payne was forty-two.

We used to kid Robert that he had a perfect life. The perfect car. The perfect wife. The perfect business. He represented a bunch of NFL coaches, Payne Stewart and several other golfers, Orel Hershiser and other baseball players. His firm occupied a whole floor of a large building in downtown Orlando. Fortunately, Robert had his priorities straight and was a man of faith. In Robert's house, above his treadmill, was this statement: "We must care for our bodies as though we were going to live forever, but we must care

✈ for our souls as if we are going to die tomorrow." Robert surely didn't know, nor did he expect, that he had only forty-six years on this earth to play the game of life. None of us knows how much time we have.

In the first chapter, I talked about Sean Taylor, our safety who was shot and killed at the young age of twenty-four. It's never too early to put your house in order.

NASCAR can be a dangerous sport. Even with all the safety precautions, when a 3,450-pound race car, traveling 200 mph, loses control and hits another car or a retaining wall, there are no guarantees. Dale Earnhardt was only forty-nine when his spectacular career and life ended suddenly in a racing accident.

It would be nice to be able to look up at the clock on our game of life and know exactly how much time we have left. That might change a lot of what we do, the decisions we make, the actions we take. Short of that, we need to live every moment as if it could be our last. James 4:14 in the Bible says, "You do not even know what will happen tomorrow. What is your life? You are a mist that appears for a little while and then vanishes."

Human Nature Doesn't Change

I've tried to impress upon you that I'm a practical guy. I like stuff to make sense. I don't read the Bible like a theologian. I've heard all the arguments about how the Bible is a long, hard-to-understand book of fables and myths, written thousands of years ago. But you know what? Some things never change. Even with all those stories in the Bible about people making huge mistakes and paying for it later, we still do the same things today.

We live in a fast-paced world, and I noticed big changes upon my return to the NFL after being out of coaching for twelve years. There had been major shifts in both offensive and defensive styles and game plans; even differences in how we went about getting players, with free agency and a shorter draft. So, yes, a lot had changed. What hadn't changed was human nature.

Down through history, what motivates or discourages men has remained the same. We're still driven by the same things: money, fear, greed, self-interest, and praise. What I've learned from my daily Bible reading all these years is that nothing has changed in the last two thousand years. We may invent new ways to sin, but the fact is we all want our own way. We don't want anybody telling us what to do or not to do. But when we screw up, we pay the consequences—if not now, then someday. As the Bible says, you reap what you sow.

The Bible makes the perfect playbook for the game of life because it works. For one thing, it's miraculous—especially when you think about how it all came together. More than forty authors over a period of 1,500 years, are you kidding me? And yet it remains perfect, makes sense, and is relevant.

That's more than I can say about my annual playbooks for the Redskins. My coaching staff and I worked hard on those babies until we had them just so. But they weren't even close to perfect. Seven or eight coaches would sit in a closed room until well after midnight, night after night, hammering out an offensive game plan. If all those authors of the Bible, over all those years, could somehow get it right, wouldn't you think we could too?

But no. Our differences of opinion almost brought us to blows sometimes.

Here's my point with all this talk of playbooks and game plans: If it was so important to me and my staff to have everything in place, and to work on our game plans all hours of the day and night, how much more important is it that we have a playbook and a plan for the game of life?

That's why when we get into the eleven chapters by my all-star contributors, we're going to start with a discussion of the Bible and why we can believe it and trust it. Maybe at this point you don't think you can. If you can't, the rest of this game plan isn't going to work, because it's all based on the Bible.

If you're a skeptic—and that's perfectly fair if you are—I'm going to count on you to give me the benefit of the doubt and let my Bible expert, Josh McDowell, show you what an outstanding, miraculous, and perfect book the Bible really is.

I learn by doing, by trial and error (mostly error). When I've let the Bible guide me, I've succeeded. When I haven't, I've failed. It's as simple as that.

Need to be convinced? Want some examples of how I messed up? Sure you do. We all love to read of other people's failures. I've got plenty, and I don't think it's a coincidence that a lot of them line up with the very topics we discovered men want to know about. I built the *Game Plan for Life* team just like I built my NFL and NASCAR teams over the years—by finding the best people I could to play each position. For this book, I asked my team of knowledgeable experts to present the truth about the Bible, God, Creation, Sin and Addiction, Salvation, Relationships, Finances, Vocation, Health, Purpose, and Heaven. If that list contains some areas you're curious about, that's no accident. Like I said, this wasn't a matter of sitting around trying to guess what men might be interested in. This is the result of a professional survey and my four decades of experience as a team builder and coach.

Now, let's get started.

CHAPTER THREE
The Ultimate Playbook

I mentioned that we start *Game Plan for Life* with the Bible because if you can't come to accept the Bible for what it is, you're going to have trouble with the rest of the game plan. I'm not naive. I know some people have a real hard time understanding why the Bible is so important.

The story is told that when the great evangelist Billy Graham was just starting out, even he had a crisis of faith about the Bible. He was about to burst onto the national scene with a long series of very successful meetings in Los Angeles in 1949 when a former colleague and fellow preacher left the faith because he could no longer accept the Bible as the inspired Word of God.

The preacher's intellectual arguments and questions really troubled Mr. Graham, and he sensed that his own doubts would affect his preaching if he didn't get the whole thing straight in his heart and mind. Finally, pacing in the woods and crying out to God for proof that the Bible was true, he put his Bible on a tree stump and knelt before it, deciding to accept it by faith. If you know anything about Billy Graham's ministry over the last sixty years, you know that complete faith in the trustworthiness of the Bible has been his hallmark. I have had the honor of participating with him in several of his crusades.

When I think about the statistic I quoted in the previous chapter about the Bible being written over 1,500 years by more than forty authors, it makes me wonder what the odds are against it fitting together and making sense, let alone being the literal Word of God and perfect in every respect.

Have you ever played one of those party games in which a person pulls a sentence out of a hat and reads it to the next person? The next person is expected to recite it from memory—just one sentence—to the next person, and so on. I'm sure that, like me, every time you played the game you've laughed out loud at the difference between the original sentence and the way the last person recited it. Sometimes not more than two or three words are the same and the original meaning has been lost.

So how did the Bible get translated and copied down through the centuries and yet remain the same as it was in the beginning? I'm guessing God had a hand in it, aren't you?

Speaking of how everyday conversations get messed up, I'll never forget what happened in Tampa Bay when John McKay hired me to be the offensive coordinator of the Buccaneers in 1978. I'd been the running backs coach for the St. Louis Cardinals under Don Coryell for four years before that, so I was really looking forward to what I considered a promotion. The thing was, McKay had always called his own plays. I came in hoping to make a name for myself as an offensive coordinator so I could get myself in position for a head coaching job. But I was helping design a game plan and calling the plays for a head coach who had always done it himself.

Back in those days, we didn't have electronic communication between the sidelines and the quarterback, so we developed a system of hand signals from the sidelines to tell our quarterback out on the field which play to call. He would then tell the team in the huddle. It was an effective way for me to call the plays and communicate them to the team.

Unfortunately, we lost the first two games of the season.

When reporters asked Coach McKay what he thought of his team's execution, he said, "I think it'd be a good idea."

Finally, McKay came to me and said, "Joe, I'm not comfortable with these hand signals. I want you to tell a player on the sideline, who'll go in and tell the quarterback, who'll tell the team. That way, I'll be able to hear you and it'll be better than using these signals I don't know anything about."

When we lost a couple more games, Coach McKay came to me again and said, "Joe, I don't think *you're* comfortable being on the sidelines calling these plays. I want you to go upstairs to the press box and call the play down to an assistant coach on the sideline, who'll tell a player, who will go in and tell the quarterback, who'll tell the team."

Now I'm here to tell you, when you send a play call like "trips-right-zoom-liz-585-F-cross-sneak" to a receiver who has already been hit in the head three or four times, you shouldn't be surprised if you have some trouble recognizing the play when the ball is snapped.

To paraphrase the immortal words of the warden in *Cool Hand Luke*, what we had was a failure to communicate.

And that was just pro football. Imagine trying to communicate the inspired words of God to humanity, which is certainly a much more complicated task. Yet the Bible remains the best-selling book, year after year, inspiring new generations of people just as it has for centuries.

Yes, the Bible talks about men and women and their purpose, but I've also learned that when you are a believer, it has an unusual ability to speak to you directly.

A little farther into the game plan, I'm going to share about a financial disaster I fell into. The long and short of it is that it took me years to overcome. One of the most important lessons I learned from this debacle was that the Bible can be real to me in times of need.

During this period, I would get on my knees every morning and pray before opening my Bible. One day I might be praying, "Dear Lord, I have a major financial mess on my hands—I am getting ready to visit some of the banks—I need a game plan."

Well, guess what? I'd pick up the Bible, and I'd get clear insight—a strategy to help me get through that *very* day—specific guidance to help me deal with the bankers or whatever issue I happened to be facing at that time. I'm telling you, it was as if God were speaking directly to me from His Word.

That may sound like fantasy to you. I understand. I don't like mysteries and things that are not clear. Like I've said, I'm a practical guy, maybe like you, and I'm reporting to you my own experience. Here's the deal: My experiences are like those of millions of other men and women. It's just that you have to give the Bible a chance.

Earlier, I mentioned that one of the objections I hear about the Bible is that it is hard to understand and relate to. That can especially be the case when it comes to the books in the Old Testament. Jesus and the parable of the Good Samaritan? We get that. We even have "Good Samaritan" laws today that protect someone from being sued for helping a person in need. Everybody knows what a Good Samaritan is. But the Old Testament? That can get a little dicey.

I began this book with the story of Sean Taylor, our Pro Bowl safety who was killed during the 2007 season. He died on a Tuesday, and the following Sunday we had to play the Buffalo Bills. The Redskins were shaken to their foundation. It was an emotional time for all of us. And to add to it, I made one of the worst decisions of my entire professional career during the Buffalo game.

Here's how Jason Reid of the *Washington Post* described it the next morning:

> In the final, frantic moments of another close game after the most diffi-cult week the Washington Redskins could remember, Coach Joe Gibbs sought help before making a key decision yesterday against the Buffalo Bills. . . .
>
> Unsure about the rules regarding the use of time-outs in an attempt to "freeze" a place kicker, Gibbs said he consulted an official along the sideline, asking whether he could call another time-out after the one he had used a moment earlier, before Buffalo's Rian Lindell sent the ball through the uprights from 51 yards away. Regardless of what the official told Gibbs, his decision to call consecutive time-outs in that situation led to a 15-yard penalty. "To be quite truthful, I made a decision there at the end that very likely cost us the game," Gibbs said. "That's on me."
>
> Put in position to make a shorter kick in the rain because of Gibbs's gaffe, Lindell connected again, this time on a 36-yard field goal with only four seconds remaining on the clock. The Bills rallied for a 17–16 victory in front of 85,831 at FedEx Field. . . .The Redskins got the ball back with three seconds left and ran two plays. Quarterback Jason Campbell's final pass landed incomplete and the Redskins had a four-game losing streak for the first time since Oct. 10, 2004.[1]

The game had been tight all the way. I knew the players wanted to win it for Sean, but when I looked in their eyes I didn't see the competitive fire I was used to seeing. We were leading 16–14 with about a minute left, and the Bills stopped us and forced us to punt. Now a field goal could win it for them.

Sure enough, they moved the ball to just within their kicker's range, and I called a time-out to ice him. To this day I still don't know why I did this, but when the time-out was over, I asked the ref if I could call another one. I should have gotten a clue from the fact that he didn't respond. Here I had been coaching all my adult life. I know the rules. I know you can't call two time-outs in a row.

I asked the ref again, and he said, "Do you want it?"

"Yeah, time out!"

I still wince when thinking about that mistake. That was all Joe Gibbs. No shading the truth and no one else to share the blame with me that day. It was my failure, for all the world to see, courtesy of national television. But I've told you that a great deal of what I've learned in my life has come through my failures and mistakes. I'm taking the time to share these with you, so maybe you'll learn something with me.

How could I be so stupid?

The resulting fifteen-yard penalty definitely put them in range, and a few seconds later, the field goal gave them the 17–16 win. The walk to the locker room was the longest of my life. It was the worst feeling I've ever had as a coach.

Whenever the Redskins struggled, the writers and pundits speculated that the game had passed me by. Well, now they really had ammunition.

I gathered the team. "Guys," I said, "I cost us this game. I was responsible for this loss."

Dejected, I moved all the way to the other side of the locker room to be alone. To his credit, owner Dan Snyder came over and told me, "You're my coach. Don't worry about this." I appreciated it, but all I could do was shake my head. Next, I had to go to the pressroom and own up to it.

As Pat and I sat in the car for the ride home, I was as low as I've ever been after a game. She tried to encourage me, but I was having none of it. Finally she said, "It really disappoints me that you're taking this that way."

"I can't help it," I said. "It's how I feel."

I went into a tailspin, questioning myself and my judgment. It was a terrible time for me, especially in light of what we'd been through with Sean. I was trying to lead the team through a crisis, and this was what I did for them?

The reality was that I didn't have time to dwell on my mistake. The following Thursday night, the Chicago Bears were coming to town, and I had a job to do.

I had to regain my composure and focus.

Here's where the Bible got real for me. In my Bible study during this period, I happened to be reading in the Old Testament.

Second Kings 3 tells a great story about a leader named Jehoshaphat. He leads an army on a march to a battle. As they are going through a desert, there is no water for the soldiers or animals. After seven days, they are out of water.

Jehoshaphat goes to the prophet Elisha and says, "What does God say about this?" Elisha says, "This is what the LORD says: Make this valley full of ditches. For this is what the LORD says: You will see neither wind nor rain, yet this valley will be filled with water, and you, your cattle and your other animals will drink. This is an easy thing in the eyes of the LORD"[2]

The message to me? "This is an easy thing in the eyes of the LORD."

Yep, I had made a huge mistake and let my guys down. I had damaged my reputation. But getting through that was going to be an easy thing in the eyes of the Lord. This story helped me see that as a believer in God, I'd get through this mess. That 2,500-year-old word was a comfort to me. It helped me put away my mistake and get focused on the future.

Like Elisha predicted for the king in the verses above, I saw nothing to indicate that things would get better. But no matter what the outcome, God was in control. All I needed to do was be faithful and plow forward as best as I could, continue to dig ditches like Jehoshaphat's army did and leave the outcome to the Lord.

And what was the outcome? The Redskins went on a four-game winning streak against four of the NFC's toughest opponents—including a game in New York against the eventual Super Bowl–winning Giants, which resulted in the Redskins making the playoffs.

What I am pointing to is how the Bible came alive for me in one of the most crucial times in my life and helped me to navigate a personal crisis. If you believe the Bible is the inspired Word of God, you will get the impact and benefit of it today in your own life.

The whole premise of *Game Plan for Life* is that God is in charge and that His plan for your life can be found in the Bible. The logical question then becomes, can you trust the Bible? That's where my friend Josh McDowell comes in.

My first exposure to Josh McDowell came when I read his book More Than
a Carpenter. *I'm not a big reader, so something has really got to grab me,
and that book did. Josh has authored or coauthored more than sixty books and
workbooks, with more than thirty million in print worldwide. He has spoken
to more than seven million young people in eighty-four countries, including on
more than seven hundred university and college campuses. Josh has my respect.
I faced a lot of tough crowds when playing games away from home in the NFL,
but I can't picture a bigger challenge than speaking on college campuses
about the validity of the Bible.*

Can I Believe the Bible?

JOSH McDOWELL

When I was a kid, I didn't care about things like the Bible, God, Jesus, or
church. I was too busy fuming with hatred inside most of the time. Mostly
I didn't show it, but hatred ground away at me. Everything—people, things,
issues—made me mad.

One person I hated more than anyone else was my father. He was the
town drunk, and my friends at school joked about him. I laughed, but I
was crying on the inside. I remember one time finding my mother lying in
manure behind the cows in the barn after my father had knocked her down
and she couldn't get up. I wanted to kill him.

By the time I went off to college, I wanted just three things: I wanted to
be happy (something my hatred had stolen from my childhood); I wanted
to find meaning for my life; and I wanted freedom—the ability to do what
I knew I should do but didn't have the power to do.

As I started looking for answers, it seemed that almost everyone I talked
to was into religion. So I went to church. But I must have gone to the wrong
one, because I felt worse there than anywhere else.

So I chucked religion.

I tried all kinds of other things, but no matter what I chose, the thrill quickly wore off. I felt like a car in a demolition derby—getting bashed from all sides and going nowhere.

Then I noticed a group of students and two professors who seemed to soar above their circumstances. They talked about happiness, purpose, and freedom in life. They seemed to have everything I was searching for, so I began to hang out with them.

One afternoon, as we sat around a table in the student union, I said, "Why are you guys so different from everybody else here?"

One of the students, a young woman, looked me straight in the eye and said, "Jesus Christ."

"Don't give me that garbage," I said. "I'm fed up with religion."

"I didn't say 'religion,'" she replied. "I said 'Jesus Christ.'"

My new friends challenged me to seriously examine the claims that Jesus Christ is the Son of God and that the Bible is the Word of God. I accepted their challenge, determined to prove them wrong. I was confident I would drown them in evidence and show them that the Bible was nothing more than fiction and fantasy, especially the parts about Jesus, who was supposedly the reason for their happiness, purpose, and freedom.

I'm here to tell you that I completely failed. Instead of finding evidence that would discredit their faith, I discovered that the Bible is fully accurate and reliable and that Jesus Christ is exactly who the Bible says He is. Best of all, in the process I found what I really wanted—happiness, meaning in life, and true freedom.

Where did I get that? From the God revealed in the Bible. To say that I love Him, and that He loves me, may sound like the craziest thing you've ever heard. But stay with me; I once thought so, too. If you buy even halfway into Joe Gibbs's idea that you need a game plan for your life, I'm sure you'll agree that you're going to need a playbook. And what better playbook could you find than the one that God has provided?

But maybe you still have some questions—not the least of which may be, is the Bible a reliable source?

Can You Trust What the Bible Says about God?

What do you believe about the Bible? Do you trust what it tells you about God and His Son, Jesus Christ? Can it really be what it claims to be—God's love letter to humanity? How can you know for sure?

In order to live in right relationship with God, you need an accurate picture of Him. I'm convinced the Bible provides that picture. However, a lot of people today have convinced themselves that the Bible can't be trusted. So they don't even read it. As a result, they have no idea what God is really like or how they can get to know Him. The difference with me was that, even though I initially approached the Bible with skepticism and even hostility, I really studied it. Maybe my motives and intentions were wrong, but I dug deep.

Here's what I discovered: We *can* trust the Bible, and we *can* know God personally through its pages. This reality changed my life as a university student, and I've been traveling the world ever since, telling the truth about the Bible to everyone I can. In this chapter, I want to share this great news with you.

Most people dismiss the Bible because they have accepted a number of false assumptions about it. Here are six of the most popular, which I will answer with six liberating facts that will help you anchor your confidence in who God is and what He tells you in His Word, the Bible.

False assumption #1: The Bible is just another man-made book.

If you want to liven up the conversation at your next tailgate party, throw out this question: What is the Bible? The answers you get could be all over the map:

- It's a book of great literature, like the writings of Shakespeare.
- It's stories and nice thoughts about life.
- It's the rulebook for the Christian religion, as the Koran is for Islam.
- It's the big black book passed down through our family with great-grandma's china.
- It's one of a number of different versions of truth.

Some people view the Bible as just another book about philosophy, ethics, and how to live a meaningful life. But calling the Bible just another book is like calling the great Vince Lombardi just another football coach. The Bible is in a class by itself.

Fact #1: The Bible is God's unique message about who He is and how you can know Him.

Consider what I discovered about the Bible's unique qualifications:

- It was written over a span of 1,500 years—forty generations.
- It was penned by more than forty authors from different walks of life, including kings, peasants, philosophers, fishermen, poets, statesmen, scholars, military leaders, a doctor, a tax collector, and a rabbi.
- The authors wrote from three continents: Asia, Africa, and Europe.
- The authors wrote in three languages: Hebrew, Aramaic, and Greek.
- Its prophecies have proven 100-percent accurate.

Key evidence for the accuracy of the Bible is in the scores of specific prophecies about nations and events that were fulfilled hundreds of years later. The Bible takes the accuracy of these prophecies very seriously. The prophet's very life was on the line! One single prophecy that did not come true would be disastrous for a prophet: He was to be stoned to death on the spot.[3] During the days of the Old Testament, people were not recklessly jumping onto the prophetic bandwagon. They knew they had to be right 100 percent of the time.

So let's take a look at just some of the hundreds of biblical prophecies that have been fulfilled.

The most amazing and convincing prophecy fulfilled about the nation Israel is her very survival and ultimate return to the Promised Land in the modern state of Israel, founded in 1948. Although there has always been a Jewish presence in the land of Israel, God promised unconditionally that the descendants of Abraham, Isaac, and Jacob would return from the four corners of the earth to the land of Israel, never to be taken into exile ever again.[4]

Normally when a nation is conquered, overrun, and scattered, it takes only three or four generations (120 to 160 years) for the people to lose their national identity. Not so with Israel. They were overrun by the Roman legions in AD 70 and scattered throughout the Roman Empire. In accordance with biblical prophecy, for generations (nearly two thousand years) Israel languished in exile yet never lost her national identity and purpose.

Then, in accordance with biblical prophecy, the people of Israel returned to their ancient land. No other nation in the history of mankind has ever accomplished such a feat.

It is said that Napoleon was once asked why he believed the Bible. He answered, "Because of the Jews!" Think about it: When was the last time you saw a Hittite in New York City? or an Amorite? When those ancient civilizations were conquered, they disappeared from the face of the earth. Not so with the Jews—just as the Bible predicted. So one of the most powerful proofs from prophecy is the survival of God's ancient people, the Jews.

The Bible contains even more specific predictions about who would be the Messiah. Scholars have demonstrated that some three hundred Old Testament predictions were literally fulfilled in the life of Jesus Christ. Dr. Peter Stone, in his book *Science Speaks,* says that by applying the science of probability to just eight of those prophecies, "we find that the chance that any man might have lived down to the present time and fulfilled all eight prophecies is 1 in 10^{17}."[5] That's one chance in 100,000,000,000,000,000.

Here is an example of eight (out of more than three hundred) messianic prophecies and their fulfillment in Jesus Christ:

THE PROPHECY	THE FULFILLMENT	THE TIME SPAN
Born of a virgin Isaiah 7:14	Luke 1:26-38	700 years
Born in Bethlehem Micah 5:2	Matthew 2:1; Luke 2:4-7	700 years
The time of His appearance Daniel 9:24-27	Luke 19:44; Galatians 4:4	538 years
Abandoned by His disciples Zechariah 13:7	Matthew 26:31; Mark 14:50	520 years
Pierced in His side Zechariah 12:10	John 19:34, 37	520 years
His resurrection and exaltation Psalm 16:10 Isaiah 52:13; 53:10-12	Acts 2:25-32	1,000 years (Psalms) 700 years (Isaiah)
His ascension into heaven Psalm 68:18	Acts 1:9; Ephesians 4:8	1,000 years
A forerunner prepares His way Isaiah 40:3-5; Malachi 3:1	Matthew 3:1-3; Luke 3:3-6	700 years (Isaiah) 450 years (Malachi)

If you agree that these fulfilled messianic prophecies bear the stamp of the divine, you should seriously consider the Bible as the Word of

God—a book worthy of your investigation, especially as it makes claims about your eternal destiny.

The Bible treats hundreds of controversial subjects with harmony and continuity from Genesis to Revelation and focuses on one consistent theme: God's love and plan for His human creation.

One of the New Testament writers, known as the apostle Paul, writes, "All Scripture is God-breathed and is useful for teaching, rebuking, correcting and training in righteousness, so that the man of God may be thoroughly equipped for every good work."[6] God is not trying to restrict you or bully you with His instructions. He always has your best interests at heart, and His Word is intended to protect you and provide for you.

If the Bible is really God's written message to the human race, it *must* be accurate and reliable. If it were just a collection of nice thoughts, it wouldn't matter if parts of it had been left out or changed over the centuries. If it's only one of many versions of truth, who cares whether it's accurate? But if the Bible is really what God wants to tell you about Himself and your relationship with Him, it is extremely important for you to know that it was recorded exactly as God gave it and has been accurately passed down to you today.

False assumption #2: The Bible is full of myths and legends.

When people claim that the Bible is full of myths and legends, they are usually referring to the New Testament—especially the accounts of the life, death, and resurrection of Jesus Christ recorded in Matthew, Mark, Luke, and John. The arguments typically sound something like this:

- The virgin birth of Jesus is just an invention to explain away Mary's getting pregnant before the wedding.
- The miracles of Jesus, such as walking on water, are explainable natural events that got exaggerated over time.
- Jesus' resurrection was made up by His grieving followers after His brutal death.

Because Christians base their faith on these so-called incredible and unbelievable stories, skeptics assume that nothing in the Bible can be accepted as truth.

Fact #2: The Bible can be trusted because Jesus' disciples staked their lives on its truth.

If Jesus' followers made up the "legend" of His resurrection, they paid for that lie with their lives. History tells us that ten of Jesus' original twelve disciples suffered violent deaths as a result of boldly proclaiming that He was the risen Son of God.

Would these men have died for a lie? Though it's true that thousands of people throughout history have died for a lie, they did so *only* if they thought it was the truth. If the resurrection of Jesus was a lie and the disciples knew it, certainly one or two at least—and probably several—would have cracked under the pressure and confessed the conspiracy to save their lives.

But it wasn't a conspiracy based on a lie. The disciples saw Jesus alive after His death and burial. Luke writes, "After his suffering, he [Jesus] showed himself to these men [the disciples] and gave many convincing proofs that he was alive."7

Why did the followers of Jesus need "many convincing proofs"? Because when Jesus died, they thought it was all over—the movement, the cause, the kingdom. When Jesus was arrested, they ran and hid.8 And when they were told that His tomb was empty, at first they didn't believe it.9 They needed serious convincing, especially a guy by the name of Thomas.10 Can you identify with him? I sure can.

What was the result of their seeing Jesus alive? The disciples were transformed from cowardly to courageous—overnight! They could not have faced torture and death unless they were totally convinced of Jesus' resurrection. Jesus' life, death, and resurrection form the central theme of the Bible. The boldness and courage of His once cowardly followers is powerful evidence for the reliability of the Bible as a whole.

False assumption #3: The Bible was written by people who had little firsthand knowledge of the events.

In 2003, Jayson Blair, a reporter for the *New York Times*, was fired for inventing sources, making up facts, and stealing material he used to write nearly seven hundred stories. Some highly regarded authors from the ancient world were in the same boat as Blair. A survey of ancient nonbiblical writings shows that many writers reported events that took place many years before they were born, in countries they never visited. Though their information may have been close to factual, wouldn't you have greater trust in writers who wrote with firsthand knowledge?

A lot of people mistakenly assume that the authors of the Bible are among the ancients whose sources were distant and doubtful. They rightfully argue, "How can you place confidence in documents where the facts may not be accurate?"

Fact #3: Most of the Bible was written by eyewitnesses or from eyewitness sources.

When we examine the sources of the New Testament, for example, overwhelming evidence confirms that the accounts of Jesus' life, the history of the early church, and the letters that form the bulk of the New Testament were all written either by eyewitnesses to the events or by people who knew eyewitnesses. Here's what some of them wrote:

> **Luke:** "Many have undertaken to draw up an account of the things that have been fulfilled among us, just as they were handed down to us by *those who from the first were eyewitnesses* and servants of the word."[11]
>
> **Mark:** We know that Mark relied largely on the account of the apostle Peter, a direct eyewitness.
>
> **John:** "We proclaim to you what *we have seen and heard.*"[12]
>
> **Peter:** "We did not follow cleverly invented stories when we told you about the power and coming of our Lord Jesus Christ, but *we were eyewitnesses* of his majesty."[13]
>
> **Peter and John:** "We cannot help speaking about what *we have seen and heard.*"[14]

These primary sources are evidence of the credibility of the New Testament record. And they are all the more convincing because these men appealed to the knowledge of their readers—even their most critical opponents—who could easily have contradicted any false accounts or claims. These authors *invited* correction by other eyewitnesses:

> **Peter:** "Men of Israel, listen to this: Jesus of Nazareth was a man accredited by God to you by miracles, wonders and signs, which God did among you through him, *as you yourselves know.*"[15]

Paul: "What I am saying is true and reasonable. The king is familiar with these things, and I can speak freely to him. I am convinced that *none of this has escaped his notice, because it was not done in a corner.*"[16]

These disciples were saying, in effect, "Check it out"; "Ask around"; "You know as well as I do that this is true!" Such challenges demonstrate supreme confidence that what they spoke and recorded was absolutely factual.

"Come on, Josh," you may say, "that's only what the writers *claimed.* Someone writing a century or more after the fact can claim *anything.*"

Yes, if the accounts recorded in the Gospels were dreamed up long after the disciples themselves were dead and gone, then the credibility of the New Testament record could be called into question. But the fact is, the books of the New Testament were written during the lifetimes of the people whose lives they record, not a century or more after the events they describe.

William F. Albright (1891–1971), an archaeologist and professor of Semitic languages at Johns Hopkins University, writes, "We can already say emphatically that there is no longer any solid basis for dating any book of the New Testament after about AD 80, two full generations before the date between 130 and 150 given by the more radical New Testament critics of today."[17]

Ample evidence exists to show that, for the most part, the men who wrote the Bible had firsthand knowledge of the events they recorded or had access to people who had witnessed those events. We have no reason to deny that the words of the Bible are true.

False assumption #4: The Bible was written and copied by hand, so it is full of mistakes.

Imagine this: Writing longhand, you copy word-for-word an article from the Internet about your favorite football player or race car driver. Then you ask a friend to copy your version by hand. She in turn gives her copy to someone else to copy by hand, and so on, until there are fifty handwritten copies in the chain.

Now, how far down the chain could you go before you would find a copying mistake, such as someone writing *this* instead of *the*? Or before you noticed something missing, such as a phrase or sentence left out by mistake?

Or what if one of the copiers purposely changed the content because he liked another athlete better than yours?

What are the chances that you and your forty-nine friends could copy the article without any mistakes? I'd say zero! Many people assume that the Bible we have today can't be trusted for the same reason: copying mistakes.

The documents included in the Bible were originally written with pen and ink on papyrus, many centuries before the printing press was invented. As the ink faded and the papyrus deteriorated, copies were made of the original manuscripts, and copies were made of the copies.

None of the original manuscripts of the Bible has been found. What we have are copies of copies ranging in size from scrolls to scraps of papyrus. The Bible today is a translation of the most reliable existing manuscript copies, but how can we be sure that the words in our modern-day Bibles are the same as what God originally said?

Fact #4: Overwhelming evidence proves that the Bible has been accurately preserved.

To determine the reliability of the Bible manuscript copies we have today, we can ask two questions that historians ask to test the reliability of any ancient literature:

1. *How many manuscript copies still exist?*

   Like the Bible, other ancient writings have been passed down through the centuries as manuscript copies. Checking multiple copies against each other allows scholars to find copying mistakes and determine the author's original words. Obviously, the more copies you have of a manuscript, the closer you will get to the original.

   Modern editions of classic ancient books are often based on just a handful of existing copies. Yet scholars are confident that the present versions accurately reflect the authors' originals.

   By comparison, trusting that the Bible has been preserved and passed down to us accurately is a slam dunk. Take the New Testament, for example. We're not talking about mere hundreds or even a few thousand handwritten manuscript copies still in existence. Libraries and museums around the world today hold close to twenty-five thousand copies of portions of the New Testament.

2. *How much time passed between the original writing and the earliest copies we have?*

Obviously, the closer the copies are to the originals, the more reliable the copies will be. The earliest copies of most classic ancient writings are 400 to 1,400 years removed from the originals. The earliest copies we have of New Testament documents, however, are only 50 to 225 years removed from the original documents.

The following chart illustrates the stark contrast in reliability between several volumes of ancient literature and the New Testament.[18]

Author/Book	Date Written	Earliest Copies	Time Gap	Number of Copies
Homer, *The Iliad*	800 BC	ca. 400 BC	ca. 400 yrs	643
Thucydides, *History*	460–400 BC	ca. A.D. 900	ca. 1,300 yrs	8
Caesar, *Gallic Wars*	100–44 BC	ca. AD 900	ca. 1,000 yrs	10
Livy, *History of Rome*	59 BC–AD 17	ca. AD 400 (partial)	ca. 400 yrs	1 (partial)
Livy, *History of Rome*	59 BC–AD 17	ca. AD 1000 (most)	ca. 1,000 yrs	19 (most)
Pliny the Elder, *Natural History*	AD 61–113	ca. AD 850	ca. 750 yrs	7
The New Testament	AD 50–100	ca. AD 114–325	ca. 50–225 yrs	24,000+

The evidence is overwhelming. "In the variety and fullness of the evidence on which it rests, the New Testament stands absolutely and unapproachably alone among ancient prose writings,"[19] writes New Testament scholar F. J. A. Hort. Theologian Norman Geisler adds, "The abundance of manuscript copies makes it possible to reconstruct the original with virtually complete accuracy."[20] Christian apologist Ravi Zacharias (see his chapter in this book) writes, "In real terms, the New Testament is easily the best attested ancient writing in terms of the sheer number of documents, the time span between the events and the document, and the variety of documents available to sustain or contradict it. There is nothing in ancient manuscript evidence to match such textual availability and integrity."[21]

Caretakers of the Old Testament

The reliability of the Old Testament is strongly supported by what we know about the methods used by the Jewish scholars, called scribes, who were the caretakers of the manuscripts from generation to generation.

From around 500 BC to AD 900, the scribes were in charge of preserving the ancient manuscripts and producing new copies when necessary. They considered these responsibilities sacred and performed them reverently.

Talk about meticulous! The scribes followed so many rules for how copies were to be made that it would make the most particular neat freak you know seem like a slob. Here are just a few examples:

- Not even the shortest word could be copied from memory; everything had to be copied letter by letter.
- The scribes had to count the number of times each letter of the alphabet occurred in each book and make sure it matched exactly the count in the original.
- If a copied manuscript was found to contain even one mistake, the whole manuscript was discarded.

In light of the overwhelming evidence, Frederic G. Kenyon, director and principal librarian of the British Museum and second to none in authority for evaluating manuscripts, concludes, "The Christian can take the whole Bible in his hand and say without fear or hesitation that he holds in it the true word of God, handed down without essential loss from generation to generation throughout the centuries."[22]

False assumption #5: The Bible's reliability cannot be proved from outside sources.

Many people assume that the Bible's claim to be the inspired, reliable Word of God is hollow because the only evidence for such a claim is the Bible itself. It would be kind of like claiming to be the world's number one authority on anything. If you're the only one saying it, who's going to believe you?

Fact #5: The Bible's reliability is substantially supported by external sources.

Mountains of persuasive evidence *outside* of the Bible confirm the truth of what is *inside* the Bible. I'll give you just a few examples of the evidence, and these barely scratch the surface.

The writings of early Christians

Extensive quotations of Scripture by leaders, writers, and theologians in the early church confirm the reliability of our modern-day Bible. We can document approximately thirty-six thousand quotations from these sources, and these range from single verses to entire passages. All but eleven verses of the New Testament can be verified from these secondary quotations.

Norman Geisler writes, "Early Christian writers provide quotations so numerous and widespread that if no manuscripts of the New Testament existed today, the New Testament could be reproduced from the writings of the early Fathers alone."[23]

Clement of Rome (AD 95) quotes from Matthew, Mark, Luke, Acts, 1 Corinthians, 1 Peter, Hebrews, and Titus.

Ignatius (AD 70–110) quotes from thirteen New Testament books, including Matthew, John, Acts, Romans, Galatians, James, and 1 Peter.

Clement of Alexandria (AD 150–212) quotes 2,400 times from all but three books of the New Testament.

Cyprian (died AD 258) quotes 740 times from the Old Testament and more than 1,000 times from the New Testament.

The writings of early non-Christians

Even many non-Christians from early centuries of the modern era authenticate the people, places, and events of the New Testament in their writings. Their records help substantiate that the world at large was well aware of the events of the New Testament and the claims of Scripture.

Tacitus, a first-century Roman historian, wrote about the death of Jesus and alluded to a "mischievous superstition" (likely a reference to Jesus' resurrection).

The writings of Josephus, a first-century Jewish historian, contain many statements that verify the historical validity of both the Old and New Testaments.

In a letter to Emperor Trajan in about AD 112, Pliny the Younger, a Roman author and administrator, describes early Christian worship practices, which confirms that Christians worshiped Jesus as God from an early date.

The evidence of archaeology

Archaeological discoveries, especially in the last half century, strongly attest to the reliability of the Bible. "Discovery after discovery has established the accuracy of innumerable details, and has brought increased recognition to the value of the Bible as a source of history," archaeologist William F. Albright has written.[24]

For example, for centuries, no archaeological evidence existed to support that Pontius Pilate ever lived. Then in 1961, two Italian archaeologists uncovered a Latin inscription referring to Pilate by name as a Roman governor.

It would take many books to list all the archeological discoveries that confirm the historical reliability of the Bible, but here is a sampling:

- Archeological discoveries have confirmed numerous historical details of Luke's record of the birth of Jesus, including the existence of a list of taxpayers and a periodic census.[25]
- During the excavations of Jericho (1930–1936), British archaeologist John Garstang stated, "The walls of Jericho fell outwards so completely that the attackers would be able to clamber up and over their ruins into the city."[26] This discovery is noteworthy because the walls of besieged cities typically fell inward, forced by the attackers.[27]
- The destruction of Sodom was long regarded as religious legend—until archaeological discoveries confirmed the existence of the city mentioned in the Old Testament and the fiery judgment that destroyed it.[28]

Evidence from outside the Bible resoundingly supports the Bible's historical reliability. It is the most thoroughly documented collection of writings in all of history. Thus, you have every reason to trust the Bible.

False assumption #6: The Bible doesn't make any difference in how people live.

Sometimes it seems that people who claim to follow the Bible really aren't any different from anybody else. We've all seen headlines like these:

- "Pastor admits link to prostitute, resigns"
- "Fundamentalist Christian sentenced in abortion clinic bombing"

- "TV evangelist bilks donors of millions"
- "Bible-toting athlete arrested in drug sting"
- "Divorce rate same for churchgoers and non-churchgoers"
- "Denomination in bitter dispute over articles of faith"

Chances are, you know some people whose behavior doesn't live up to the faith they claim to practice. This apparent hypocrisy has caused some skeptics to claim that the Bible is powerless to make a difference in a person's life.

Fact #6: God changes the lives of those who take His Word to heart.

I am walking evidence that the Bible is true and that Jesus can dramatically change a person's life. I'm not saying I'm perfect—far from it—or that I don't screw up from time to time. But thanks to the power of God's Word, I continue to enjoy the happiness, significance, and purpose that the Bible promises to those who trust in Jesus Christ.

I became a Christian during my second year of college. That means I accepted the fact that Jesus died on the cross for my sins, and I believed that God had raised Him from the dead. You've probably heard people talk about a "bolt of lightning" conversion experience. Well, nothing that dramatic happened to me. But, in time, there were some obvious changes in my life.

First, I *experienced mental peace.* My mind had always been in a whirlwind of conflicts. I couldn't concentrate to study or think. In the first few months after I decided to trust Jesus for the forgiveness of my sins and for my salvation, peace of mind began to quiet my thinking. I'm not talking about an absence of conflict—that was still there—but now I had a growing (and I would say *supernatural*) ability to cope with it.

Second, I *gained control over my temper.* I used to blow up at people for no reason. I still have painful, guilty memories of almost killing a man during my first year in college. But one day, after my decision to trust Jesus, I met a conflict head-on, only to find that my foul temper was gone!

Third, I *found freedom from resentment.* About five months after I became a Christian, a love for my father—clearly from God—flooded my life. It turned my resentment upside down. It was so strong that I was able to look my father in the eye and say, "Dad, I love you"—and really mean it!

How could this happen? I had *hated* my father. He had caused me no end of shame and embarrassment. He had abused my mother. And he was still a drunk. Yet the God whose story is told in the Bible had so deeply changed my life through the power of Jesus Christ that my hatred for my father turned to love.

Shortly after that, I was in a serious car accident and lay in bed with my neck in traction. I'll never forget my father standing over me and saying, "Son, how can you love a father like me?"

I said, "Dad, six months ago I despised you." Then I shared with him my conclusions about Jesus Christ and how He had changed me.

My father said, "Son, if God can do in my life what I've seen Him do in yours, I want to give Him that opportunity."

Often, a new Christian's life changes gradually over several days, weeks, or years. But my father changed right before my eyes. He touched alcohol only once more after that, but he got it as far as his lips and put it down. He didn't need it anymore.

It's overwhelming to me to realize that the God of the universe supervised the writing and passing down of His words from generation to generation so that you and I could have an accurate picture of Him. It's amazing to hold in our hands a book that we can confidently believe is an accurate transmission of God-breathed words. And it's thrilling to know that God gives us His Word so we can know Him intimately and be changed by His power.

After more than forty years of watching God change thousands of lives—just like he changed mine and my father's, I've come to this conclusion: The Bible is true, alive, and powerful, and a relationship with Jesus Christ changes lives. If you ask Him to take control of your life, just watch how your attitudes and actions will change, because Jesus—the one who is at the center of everything in the Bible—is in the business of forgiving sin, removing guilt, changing people from the inside out, and healing relationships.

Will you give him that opportunity in your life?[29]

JOE'S TWO-MINUTE DRILL
The Ultimate Playbook: Can I Believe the Bible?

As I have studied the Bible over the years, I have become convinced that it is the inspired Word of God and has application in every area of our lives. It is God's playbook for the game of life and the key to finding true purpose, meaning, and freedom. Let me recap several truths about the Bible that Josh pointed out for us:

- ✓ The Bible is more than a book; it is a specific message to us from God.
- ✓ The Bible is not just a collection of myths; many men have died defending its truths. Ten of Jesus' original twelve disciples suffered violent deaths because of the faith they boldly proclaimed.
- ✓ Most of the Bible was written either by firsthand eyewitnesses or by individuals who personally knew eyewitnesses to the events described.
- ✓ There is overwhelming evidence to prove that the Bible has been accurately preserved over time (more accurately than any other ancient classic). Nearly 25,000 copies of portions of the New Testament are available today, some of them copied just 50 to 225 years after the original documents were written.
- ✓ The reliability of the Bible is upheld by many external sources. These sources include writings of early Christians and non-Christians, and the findings of archaeologists.
- ✓ The God of the Bible changes the lives of individuals who take His words to heart.
- ✓ Further evidence for the accuracy of the Bible is found in many Old Testament prophecies that find their fulfillment hundreds of years later in the New Testament.

CHAPTER FOUR

The Coach

I had always hoped to have a chance to coach at the University of Southern California. After my family moved to California, I played high school football and followed USC with great interest. In 1960, John McKay took over as head coach at USC, and he soon became the king of college football. He won two national championships in his first eight seasons (and later won two more) and led one of the best football programs in the country. So, in 1969, when I got an opportunity to interview for a coaching position with Coach McKay, I was excited and nervous.

I spent the first half of the interview wondering if I was going to have a chance to be one of his coaches. Halfway through the interview he started saying, "If you take this job . . ."

What? He's gonna offer me the job? You can bet your life I was going to take it if he did. And he did! Pat and I were thrilled. We were going back home to southern California to live the dream, with me as an offensive line coach for USC.

My first year at USC, we had a great team. We won the 1970 Rose Bowl and were at the top of the college football food chain. I remember thinking, *This is it!* I was on my way up the ladder toward being a head coach. Yet something was nagging at me inside. I really wasn't at peace.

You know, I've never worked with products or goods. My whole life has been working with people. I've either recruited them to play ball for me at colleges or with pro teams, or I've hired them to work with me on a coaching staff. I've analyzed, decided upon, and wooed people, and then tried to mold them into a team. I like people.

I find people's lives interesting. It's exciting to find out how people got to where they are in life. I like to know how and why they made their decisions. And people have had a tremendous impact on my life, as well. I watch them and study them, and I try to learn from them.

A man who deeply impressed me was the great Hall of Fame receiver Raymond Berry. He and I coached on Frank Broyles's staff at Arkansas in 1971–1972, just after I left USC. Raymond was a committed Christian, and it was obvious. He had a peace about him that commanded respect. He was soft-spoken, but his players listened to every word. He was self-effacing and gentle, but he always told the straightforward truth. (In that respect, he's a lot like Super Bowl–winning head coach Tony Dungy, who wrote the foreword for this book, and who has also been described as powerful but soft-spoken.)

I have to admit, back in my early coaching days I was an egotist. I was rigid. I wanted my own way, and I didn't have much time for people who disagreed with me. Raymond Berry was the opposite. I didn't let it show, but his life was working on me.

Another guy whose life has had a huge effect on mine was Don Breaux (pronounced Bro)—not just because he was like Raymond, but because he had once been like me and then became like Raymond. I first met Don by phone when he called after the 1966 season when I was coaching at San Diego State. He was a slow-talking Southerner, and it was hard for even a North Carolina native like me to understand him. He said he'd heard good things about me and wondered if I'd be interested in coaching at Florida State under Bill Peterson. Bigger school. More money. Where do I sign?

Now, a few years later, Don and I were coaching at Arkansas together. I was having a great time, and except for becoming a head coach, I couldn't imagine wanting anything more from life. I was getting paid to be involved with a sport I loved. I traveled all over the country recruiting players. Pat and I had a son and another on the way. Life was good. We lived in Fayetteville and were attending church. I was even enjoying that more than I thought I would.

For years, church had been just an obligation for me, but now with the birth of my first child, J.D., I was starting to think more seriously about life. My heart still burned for a head coaching job, and I was still as competitive as ever, but I had begun thinking about what kind of a person and father I really wanted to be. Major changes were in the wind for me, but I didn't know it.

Don Breaux had been a lot like me when we coached together at Florida State: self-centered, rough around the edges, always looking for some fun. At that time his life was all football and fishing. I rode with him to work, and he and his wife, Harleen, would sometimes squabble in the front seat as if I weren't even there. They loved each other, but like a lot of couples, they could be hard on each other.

Don and I played cards, chewed tobacco, and drank, and I have to say my language wasn't what it should have been for a guy claiming to be a Christian. I really hadn't changed much from my college days when I had drifted from the Lord. I'm embarrassed to say that, back in school, my friends and I had stolen some hubcaps and car batteries and even cheated on tests.

The coaching life is really tough on wives, and Pat has always rolled with the punches. But the one thing she wanted when the season was over was *me*. I remember at the end of one season at Florida State, we had just played our bowl game, and I had not been home more than fifteen minutes before Don stopped by the house. I had just settled into my recliner to talk to Pat about what we wanted to do in the off-season when I heard a car horn outside. I stepped outside, and there was Don in his Nash Rambler with a fishing boat hanging out the back. He hollered, "Wanna go drown some worms?" That was Don, always pushing the envelope, looking for something fun to do. One look at Pat told me I had to decline.

Now, just three years later, Don and I were together again on the staff at Arkansas, and after two or three days I realized I hardly recognized the man. Where was the foulmouthed rounder? He now treated his wife and daughters with love and respect, and even his language had changed. Finally I had to ask, "Don, what's happened to you, man?"

"You know, Joe, I gave my life to Christ, and it totally changed my outlook on everything."

One thing I knew was that a man couldn't change *himself* like that. Sure, a guy can turn over a new leaf, change a bad habit or two. But what I was seeing here was a whole new person. It rocked me. Pat had become excited about her faith through our church. Raymond Berry had impressed the heck out of me. And now Don?

Seeing God working in other people's lives made it a whole lot easier to take Him seriously.

I was further impressed that year by a young man named Mike Kirkland, one of the high school seniors I was recruiting. He was only eighteen years old, but his Christian walk and the loving relationship I witnessed in his family really caught my attention. That's what *I* wanted. I wanted to be a good father, and I knew Pat wanted that of me too. Yet I was the odd man out. If our family wasn't like the families that impressed me, *I* would be the reason.

Somehow, God had put all these people in front of me as a mirror, and I didn't like how it was reflecting on me. They had what I wanted, but I was not where they were. I believed in God, but I was not committed to following Him. They were, and that made all the difference.

Let me just say that the way God has become real to me is a practical matter. I look for commonsense proof of God's existence, and I've found it in four areas:

1. The profound changes I've witnessed in other people's lives
2. The complexity of the universe and the way it was created
3. The miraculous existence of the Bible and the way it has been scrutinized down through history and remains error free and relevant today
4. The changes God has made in my life

At this point in my life, I was beginning to see God at work in other people's lives.

By most standards, I was measuring up to the world's idea of success— except for not yet having landed the head coaching job I wanted. But I was not a success on God's scale. I was empty and unhappy.

What was it about these people that made them so at peace? My Sunday school teacher, George Tharel, told me that too many people, even those who believe in Jesus Christ, don't understand that He loves them even when they make mistakes.

I believed in Jesus, admired Him, and respected Him. I thought I was paying homage to Him when I went to church. Fact was, I was pretty much ignoring Him. Sure, I went to church and kind of knew the drill. I could talk the talk with others and sound religious enough if I needed to. But that's about all I did. Most of my focus was on me and what I wanted to do. That's why I did not have what these other people had: that supernatural peace.

I was convinced that God had made me to be a football coach. He'd given me the desire, fire, competitiveness, and a mind for the game. Football was not the problem. *I* was the problem. I was looking at my life through the world's eyes. The world said I had to do well at my work in order to be admired and successful. I had to be a winner; always call the right play; always make the right move.

God was trying to impress upon me that, in His eyes, I was forgiven and loved no matter what—win or lose. He wanted to show me that His love would feel more real to me in the bad times than the good, because that was when I needed Him most. In the bad times, the down times, he would be molding me and shaping me in the way I needed, knocking off my rough edges to make me the kind of man He wanted me to be. I could actually be improved through adversity if I committed myself to Him.

I was thirty-two years old, and one thing was clear: I had not been living for God. I had been living for myself. I had been chasing all the things I thought were important, and I had been missing the point of life. The end-all mission in my life—to land a head coaching job—was backward. I thought a job like that would make me a better person: financially comfortable, respected in the community, loaded with friends.

The kind of guys I had looked up to were macho men, motocross and race car drivers, football players, people who knocked other people down and made their own way in the world. Now I found myself drawn to a quiet, peaceful, loving man like George Tharel, who was clearly trying to please God.

It was time to get things straight.

At first, I didn't talk to George about it. I didn't even talk to Pat about it, though she says now she saw things changing in me and knew it was coming.

As I sat in church one night, I felt God really working on me. I knew that "living right" was not what got anybody into Heaven. Ephesians 2:8-9 says, "For it is by grace you have been saved, through faith—and this not from yourselves, it is the gift of God—not by works, so that no one can boast."

I wanted more than just assurance I was going to Heaven. I wanted to please God. I wanted to know Him. I wanted to be a loving person who was at peace with his family. I wanted to be a man who had something to offer his children. It was time to live by God's standard rather than the world's.

I prayed silently in that church pew, telling God I was ready to commit myself to Him. Then I went before the congregation to make it public. I meant business. In my church, we called it a "re-dedication to Christ."

My relationship with George Tharel deepened to the point where I considered him my spiritual father until the day he died. Though we moved away from Arkansas, and I coached four different teams after that, I heard from George nearly every week by phone or letter, encouraging me and admonishing me to continue my daily relationship with the Lord.

The Bible came alive for me, and more than once I've been astounded to find that it seems to speak to whatever situation I find myself in. To me, that's evidence of God too. It's like when I hold one of my grandchildren and feel the unconditional love I know could only come from God.

When I re-dedicated my life to Christ, I felt a great weight lift from my shoulders. I had more joy and happiness, even though no one had told me that life would get any easier. If anything, my life became more difficult after that. My life has never been the same, but it would be a lie to say it's all been easy and happy. It hasn't.

Believe it or not, our survey research showed that men are curious about, or confused about, the nature of God. That's why I asked Ken Boa, an Oxford-trained theologian, to tackle the subject in this book. As I have already said, I believe there is undeniable proof that God exists. It is evident in Creation, in the Bible, and in changes I've seen in my own life and in the lives of others.

I think you will find Ken Boa's chapter on God as fascinating as I did. Once you've determined that you can believe and trust the Bible, what's more important than really getting to know God? Ken's chapter details who God is and why He wants to have a relationship with you.

No question, Ken Boa is a bright guy. He is an award-winning author with more than forty books to his credit, including 20 Compelling Evidences that God Exists, Conformed to His Image, *and* Faith Has Its Reasons. *He is also a contributing editor to* The Open Bible, *from Thomas Nelson Publishers, and consulting editor to the* NASB Study Bible, *from Zondervan. Ken has doctorates from New York University and Oxford University and a master's of theology from Dallas Theological Seminary. If you want someone to take on the daunting task of explaining God in five thousand words, it had better be someone with smarts. Ken is the guy.*

Who Is God?

KEN BOA

There are two kinds of people—those who seek to know God, and those who seek to avoid Him. Both will succeed in the end.

Which are you?

Life is short, and people too often put their hopes for fulfillment and self-worth in their own performance, possessions, position, or power. But this approach fails on all counts. Not only are they left feeling empty, but they have also failed to account for their eternal future. If you're one who doesn't believe in an afterlife, you had better be right, because depending on your own resources and accomplishments will assure you of nothing but everlasting separation from the God who loves you.

As you consider formulating a game plan for your life, your view of God will be crucial. As the great Christian writer A. W. Tozer said, "What comes into our minds when we think about God is the most important thing about us."[1]

How you see God will determine the course of your life. It will affect the most important decisions you make: who you marry, how you raise your kids, how you spend your time and your money, and (according to the Bible) where you will spend eternity.

Four Realities about God

Here is what we need to accept when considering the God who loves us:

- We each have a personal view of God, but there is only one correct way to know and understand Him. Considering a matter so important, we cannot settle for an each-to-his-own-idea God.
- The Bible teaches that each person is made in the image of God; therefore, we were created to love and to be loved.
- God is three persons in one—Father, Son, and Holy Spirit; and it is through our relationship with each member of the Trinity that we are able to relate to God and experience His love and guidance. (I know that may sound cryptic and overly religious if you're new to this kind of thinking, but I will clarify as we go along in this chapter.)
- We each must *accept* God's love in order to live a truly successful and relevant life.

Understanding and experiencing these four realities about God are essential to God's game plan for your life.

Let me tell you why I think it's so important for you to realize that there is only one correct way to know and understand God, and why you must bring your personal view of Him into alignment with what the Bible teaches. The words of three notable men will help to illustrate my point.

The first, Albert Camus, was a French author and philosopher who won the Nobel Prize for literature in 1957. He contributed to a philosophical movement called existentialism, which describes humanity as living without purpose in an absurd and meaningless world. Camus did not believe in God, but he visited a local church occasionally to listen to the beautiful organ music. Eventually he and the minister became friends.

Near the end of his life, Camus shared his innermost thoughts with the pastor. He said, "The reason I have been coming to church is because I am seeking. I'm almost on a pilgrimage—seeking something to fill the void that I am experiencing—and no one else knows. Certainly the public and the readers of my novels, while they see that void, are not finding the answers in what they are reading. But, deep down, you are right—I am searching for something that the world is not giving me. . . . There is something that is invisible. We may not hear the voice, but there is some way in which we can become aware that we are not the only ones in the world and that there is help for all of us."[2]

Camus was brilliant, but clearly he did not have all the answers. He felt something, or someone, beyond his five senses, and he gravitated toward church in an attempt to find it.

David Servan-Schreiber has a doctorate in medicine and another in neuroscience. In his 2007 book *Anticancer—A New Way of Life*, he tells that an MRI scan revealed a walnut-sized tumor in his brain. Following treatment, he appeared to be healthy—until his cancer reappeared a few years later. He describes his response:

> Finding out you have cancer is a shock. You feel betrayed by life and by your own body. But finding out you've had a relapse is crushing. It's as if you've suddenly discovered that the monster you thought you'd vanquished was still there. It had gone on tracking you in the shadows and wound up catching you again. . . . I still remember the tumult that gripped me. I would have liked to talk to God. But I didn't believe in him. I finally managed to concentrate on my breathing, calm the turmoil in my thoughts, and turn inward. In the end, it was a form of prayer: "O my body, my being, my life force, speak to me! Help me sense what's happening to you. Help me understand why you couldn't cope. Tell me what you need."[3]

Can you imagine a lonelier existence than longing to talk to a God in whom you don't believe? But Dr. Servan-Schreiber "prayed" anyway, saying to his body what he would have liked to say to God.

The third man addresses why people—like Albert Camus and David Servan-Schreiber, and like you and me—think of God when we are confronted by the enormity of life. C. S. Lewis, a British author and committed Christian who wrote many books, including the popular Chronicles of Narnia series of children's books, said, "The great thing to remember is that, though our feelings come and go, [God's] love for us does not. It is not wearied by our sins, or our indifference; and, therefore, it is quite relentless in its determination that we shall be cured of those sins, at whatever cost to us, at whatever cost to Him."[4]

Albert Camus concluded that his intellectual pursuits were insuffi-
cient to satisfy the longings of his soul, and he found himself in church—
searching for more.

Dr. Servan-Schreiber, when facing a physical crisis for a second time,
confessed that it would make sense to talk to God—if only he believed
in Him.

C. S. Lewis, a follower of Jesus, discovered that God is love and that He
pursues us.

Do you identify with any or all of these three men? If you believe in
God and have a relationship with Him through Jesus Christ—which is the
basis for *Game Plan for Life*—you may have progressed through the experiences of Albert Camus and Dr. Servan-Schreiber on your way to that faith.
Like Camus, you may have realized a need that could not be met within the
bounds of this world. Or, like Dr. Servan-Schreiber, you may have suffered
a crisis and tried to call out to God, even though you weren't sure you
believed in Him.

It has been my experience that most people progress through stages of
wondering and unbelief before they arrive at a place of certain belief in God.
It seems to me that when we truly understand what we ultimately desire, it is
God Himself.

Knowing God Is What We Were Created to Do

Everyone seems to have an idea about God. If you doubt that, just listen to
celebrities and politicians and scholars. But only one view of God can be
correct. It doesn't make sense that He can be something different for every
person. If that were true, we would be guilty of creating God in our own
image, rather than the other way around. The Bible, which we saw in chapter
3 is a reliable source, teaches that man is created in the image of God.[5]

Beyond the needs for food and shelter—the need to stay alive—
mankind has two needs that set us apart from the rest of Creation: the
need to be loved and the need to love. Why? Because we are made in the
image of the God, and God is love. Once we have a personal relationship
with God, and are therefore loved in the truest sense of the word, we are
able to genuinely love ourselves and other people.

But let me ask you a question: Is it as obvious to you as it is to me that
most people don't love others in the truest sense? What masquerades as love

today is anything but the unselfish, sacrificial love of God. People seem to give only in order to get. Human lust has displaced divine love. No wonder society seems lost and out of joint.

We need to know and understand that God loves us unconditionally with a love He demonstrated once and for all when He sent Jesus Christ to die on the cross for the sins of all humanity. That's what Jesus meant when He said, "For God so loved the world that he gave his one and only Son, that whoever believes in him shall not perish but have eternal life."[6] That's why Jesus called God's love "good news."

Making It Personal

But enough about the world. What about *you?* By now, I hope it's clear that once you have received this kind of love for yourself, your life will change forever. You will be able to love those around you with the same kind of unconditional love that God has for you.

Saint Augustine, a fifth-century church bishop, wrote: "You have made us for yourself, O Lord, and our hearts are restless until they rest in you" (author's paraphrase).[7]

Albert Camus was a restless man. No doubt he was loved and appreciated by family and friends, but that wasn't enough. His heart was restless because it hadn't yet found its ultimate resting place in God. As human beings, we were created to be loved, first and foremost, by God. No other love is sufficient to satisfy who we are as people created in God's image.

Once we are at rest in God's unconditional love, we are free to love others without preconditions. Most human conflict arises when one person demands something of another that the second person is unable to provide. We tend to look to others to provide for us the peace, satisfaction, and contentment—that is, the love—that only God can give. A man will sometimes say to his wife, "If you really loved me you would . . ." And when she fails to provide that love (in whatever form), he holds her responsible for a failure that is really his own—a failure to rest in the love that God offers him.

Knowing God and receiving His love are the most important things we can do. They are the keys to loving ourselves (being content with our gifts, abilities, and purpose in life) and therefore being able to love our wives, children, and others. Our failure to live in the reality of God's love creates a restlessness that will show itself in all kinds of hurtful ways.

The Three-Part Puzzle of the Trinity

Now we come to what may be the most difficult to understand part of God's unchanging character: that He is a Trinity, a three-in-one being. But because we are created in His image, we need to understand who He is.

The Old Testament emphasizes the unity of God. The great Jewish confession of faith known as the Shema begins with these words: "Hear, O Israel: The LORD our God, the LORD is one."[8] But even though the Old Testament was written before Jesus came to earth in the flesh and before the gift of the Holy Spirit was given to all who put their trust in Jesus, we still see glimpses of these two at work alongside God the Father. The Holy Spirit (or Spirit of God) is mentioned more than fifteen times in the Old Testament, and many scholars believe that "the angel of the Lord" refers to pre-incarnate appearances of Jesus Christ.[9]

Finally, in the New Testament, the idea that God is one and yet is seen in three distinct persons—Father, Son, and Holy Spirit—comes more clearly into focus.[10]

Now, the truth that God is three persons does not mean that He is merely expressing Himself in three different forms (like water, which is sometimes liquid, sometimes ice, and sometimes steam). Rather, all three persons are fully God, yet distinct, and united as one. In at least one instance, recorded in Matthew 3:16-17, all three persons of the Trinity appear in the same place at the same time—as individuals. When Jesus was in the Jordan River being baptized, the Father's voice was heard from Heaven, and the Spirit descended "like a dove" from Heaven.

The Trinity may seem like an abstract theological concept best reserved for study by seminary students and pastors. But it's not. It's an important concept for you and me to understand, because it helps us recognize how God works in our lives.

Though Father, Son, and Spirit are each fully God (and none is less God than the others), they are distinct in their respective roles. According to the Bible, God shows Himself as *love* (through the Father), *light* (through Jesus, the Son), and *leadership* (through the Holy Spirit). Let's take a closer look at what this all means.

God's love for us

The Bible clearly teaches that "God is love."[11] The apostle John wrote those words to people who claimed to know God but were not very loving people.

His point was this: If you claim to know God, but don't love others, then something is wrong—because God is love. When you think of love, you should think of God. I like the way author Wayne Grudem puts it: "God's love means that God eternally gives of himself to others."[12]

The greatest expression of God's love is seen in His plan of salvation for sinful people. The apostle Paul says that it was "the God and Father of our Lord Jesus Christ"[13] who set in motion this plan, the ultimate expression of His love for the human beings He had created in His own image. "God decided in advance to adopt us into his own family by bringing us to himself through Jesus Christ."[14]

Many verses in the New Testament illustrate the working out of God's plan to show His love:

This is love: not that we loved God, but that he loved us and sent his Son as an atoning sacrifice for our sins.[15]

... But God demonstrates his own love for us in this: While we were still sinners, Christ died for us.[16]

... For God so loved the world that he gave his one and only Son, that whoever believes in him shall not perish but have eternal life.[17]

Note the active verbs in those verses: God *sent,* God *demonstrates,* God *gave.* God's love for us is not theoretical; it is practical and evident. God proved that He loves us by what He did for us. And in every case, at the center of God's love was His Son, Jesus Christ, the second person of the Trinity.

Jesus, the light of the world

Jesus said, "I am the light of the world. Whoever follows me will never walk in darkness, but will have the light of life."[18] He also said, "While I am in the world, I am the light of the world."[19]

We know from science that darkness isn't a color in the spectrum of light waves. Rather, darkness is simply the absence of light. So when light invades a dark setting, it doesn't drive darkness out; it fills the space. That's what Jesus did when He came into the world—He filled a spiritually dark and empty space with the light of God.

When we say something like, "Joe shed light on the subject," we convey what light does. It makes things clear, visible, understandable, and usable.

That's what Jesus did by coming as the "light of the world." He made known the love of God. Up and down the dusty roads of Israel, Jesus put sandal-leather to God's love. He shined the light and love of God into the dark corners of the world so that we all might know how much we are loved by God. Then He went so far as to offer His own life as a sacrifice to pay for our sins.

Jesus declares in John 15:13, "Greater love has no one than this, that he lay down his life for his friends." He went on to say to His disciples, "I have called you friends, for everything that I learned from my Father I have made known to you."[20]Jesus explained what He learned in both words and actions.

The Bible says that nature reveals the presence of God and something about His creativity, power, and majesty.[21] But Creation cannot explain the nature of man's sin, nor can it provide a solution. The Son of God came to earth in the person of Jesus of Nazareth to do what only someone who is both God and man could do: communicate the love of God to us in a way we could understand.

The Holy Spirit, our leader

You've perhaps heard the story of the little guy in a Sunday school class who was hard at work on a drawing. When the teacher asked him what he was doing, he said, "I'm drawing God."

"But no one knows what God looks like," the teacher said.

"They will when I'm finished," the boy replied.

The truth is, we don't know what God looks like. "No one has ever seen God."[22] But beyond that, there is another reason, given by Jesus Himself: "God is spirit."[23] The word *spirit* is not capitalized here, because Jesus is not referring so much to the Holy Spirit as to the being of God Himself. Also note that the text doesn't say, "God is *a* spirit."

In referring to the Holy Spirit, I have chosen to use the word *leader* (to go along with *love* and *light*), because it illustrates perfectly the Spirit's role in the work of God. Jesus told His disciples that it was better that He should return to Heaven, so that the Holy Spirit could come to live within every individual Christian from that point on.[24] "When he, the Spirit of truth, comes, he will guide you into all truth."[25]

The way the Holy Spirit makes the love of God real is by leading God's people into truth, into serving others, into comforting, helping, and providing. Every time someone comes into the light of Jesus by faith and experiences the love of God, the Holy Spirit takes up residence in that person's life.

The Holy Spirit also acts as "a seal . . . a deposit guaranteeing our inheritance,"[26] which identifies us as belonging to God and guarantees our ultimate eternal inheritance with God.

But the Holy Spirit does even more. Even though God is perfect and His love never fails, we don't always receive His love as it is given, because we ourselves are imperfect.[27] Yet the Spirit speaks to us, reminding us of the truth found in the Bible and prompting us to rest in the promises of God regardless of our circumstances.

The Father sent the Son into the world to make Himself and His love known. The Son (Jesus) sent the Holy Spirit into the world to lead God's people into the experience of His love.

Even if we come to the correct perspective on who God is, including understanding that we are made in His image, and also that God is a Trinity, we must personally accept His love into our lives.

Finding True Success and Relevance

In chapter 1, Coach Gibbs tells the story of Sean Taylor, the All Pro safety for the Redskins who lost his life at the age of twenty-four. But there's another important part of Sean's story he didn't tell.

When Sean Taylor first came to the Redskins, after leaving college early to enter the NFL draft, he ran into trouble on and off the field. He was fined $25,000 for leaving early from a required NFL symposium for new players, and he was penalized and fined a number of times for late hits and uniform infractions. He also had a couple of brushes with the law. As Joe Gibbs has noted, "Sean was focused on himself and at times rebelled against authority. He was clearly struggling as a new guy."

Nevertheless, in 2006, Sean Taylor was named to the NFC Pro Bowl team. In 2007, *Sports Illustrated* said, "Taylor has the speed of a cornerback but the strength of a linebacker. That combination and his tendency to be near the ball make him one of the hardest hitters in the league and a constant defensive threat."[28]

According to Coach Gibbs, "Sean Taylor had an amazing ability to be where the ball was on the field. He would practically appear out of nowhere to be in the middle of a play. In thirty years of coaching, Sean stands out to me as one of the most gifted athletes I have worked with."

Tied for most interceptions in the NFC in 2007, even though he had missed two weeks of the season, number 21 looked like he would once again be in the Pro Bowl. More important, his teammates and coaches had noticed that Taylor was more at peace with himself, less self-centered, more considerate of others. This all seemed to coincide with the birth of his daughter, Jackie. Something had changed in Sean Taylor.

When Sean was shot and killed, the entire NFL community was stunned. A great player had been mindlessly gunned down, leaving behind his eighteen-month-old daughter and her mother. At first, some in the media speculated that Taylor's violent death was just part of the pattern of his life. But those close to him knew better. They'd seen the change in his life from being focused on himself to being focused on those around him.

Redskins chaplain Brett Fuller believed that after some tough years, Sean Taylor had finally accepted the love of God. He had started to come to chapel at Redskins Park. He had begun reading his Bible. He was focused on his new daughter and her mother.

"Sean Taylor gave his life protecting his family," Joe Gibbs said. "To me, Sean's life exhibited the change that can only take place when we accept the love of God. His loss was devastating to his family, our team, and me personally. But I believe someday I will get to see Sean Taylor playing safety on God's team."

For the rest of the 2007 season, the Redskins wore a black 21 on their uniforms. Sean Taylor was posthumously elected to his second Pro Bowl. His life, though cut short, continues to affect those who knew him.

What about You?

No matter your situation in life—whether you're a high achiever like Sean Taylor or not—you were made in the image of God to love and be loved. You can know a lot about God, but unless you accept His love, you will not be able to love others the way you were meant to.

Accepting God's love is the beginning of a great journey that will lead to eternal rewards and blessing for you and everyone in your life. Remember, how you view God is the most important thing about you. It will determine the course of your life and will affect all your major decisions, including where you spend eternity.

Consider God as your Head Coach, the one who has created your game plan for life. The question you need to ask yourself is whether you are fully experiencing God's love, as demonstrated by Jesus Christ and applied by the Holy Spirit. That, in a nutshell, is God's wonderful game plan for your life.

Attributes	Description	Reference
Eternal	He is not bound by time	Psalm 90:2
Immutable	He is unchanging and unchangeable—He can be trusted	James 1:17
Omnipresent	He is everywhere	Psalm 139:7-12
Omniscient	He knows all actual and possible things	Matthew 11:21
Omnipotent	He is all-powerful	Revelation 19:6
Just	He is fair in moral judgments	Acts 17:31
True	He is in agreement and is consistent within the Trinity	John 14:6
Free	He is independent from all His creatures	Isaiah 40:13-14
Holy	He is separate and free from all sin	1 John 1:5
Sovereign	He is Supreme Ruler over everything at all times	Ephesians 1:3-14

JOE'S TWO-MINUTE DRILL
The Coach: Who Is God?

In the Bible's game plan for life, the Head Coach is God. In order for us to get on God's team and experience the blessings that come with being a player, we must first get to know the Coach. Let me recap the truths about God that Ken points out for us:

- ✓ We all have a personal view of God. However, there is only one correct way to know and understand Him.
- ✓ God is love. He loves mankind unconditionally and pursues a relationship with us. His greatest expression of love to us was sending his Son to die for our sins.

✓ We are all made in God's image; therefore, we all have the need to be loved and to love others. Only after we have experienced God's love for us can we truly love others the way God wants us to.

✓ God is a Trinity (three-in-one) of Father, Son, and Holy Spirit. These three are distinct persons, with distinct roles, but one in nature and purpose. It is through the Trinity that we best relate to God and experience His love for us.

✓ We each need to accept God's love in order to live a truly successful and relevant life.

CHAPTER FIVE

Creation

I'm really going to have to count on my expert, John Lennox, to cover the scientific evidence for this topic; but from a strictly practical point of view, I think there's more evidence for creation than for evolution. Were you created, or did you evolve? I know there are a lot of smart people on both sides of this argument; but again, I'm just a commonsense kind of a guy. I look at the world and nature and things like the human body, particularly the eye, and I wonder how anybody thinks that came about as the result of an accident or chance.

Look at your own wristwatch. Maybe you have an idea of what's going on inside that complicated thing to make those simple second, minute, and hour hands keep accurate time. But what if someone told you that all those parts were put in a shoebox and shaken for a few weeks—hey, say a few million years—and your watch resulted from that. You'd laugh in his face.

Another complex process that I've come to have some firsthand knowledge of is the building of high-performance race cars. Most people can't even imagine how complicated it is to build a race car.

We're told that one of the most popular tours in the Charlotte area is the tour of our race shop at Joe Gibbs Racing. Often I'll see groups going through the shop, and I always get a kick out of their response. They can't believe the technology and sophistication that goes into making race cars.

We build our race cars from scratch, starting in our engineering design department with computer models. The engineers work directly with our chassis fabricators because we are constantly upgrading our components. Once the fabricators and welding specialists put it all together, the chassis moves down to the body fabrication shop. There it is put on a plate and our specialists assemble the rest of the body, beginning with the roof, deck lid, hood, and front fascia.

Keep in mind that the entire car—front to back, top to bottom, side to side—must correspond perfectly to the NASCAR template for Toyotas. The templates must never deviate more than 1/16 of an inch anywhere on the car!

Next, the car rolls to the paint shop. We then send it to the assembly area for suspension, electrical system, oil system, interior, and steering system. Our main assembly area is a football field in length, and each of our approximately thirty-six cars is placed in its own individual bay.

Here the engine is installed. Our engine department will have spent up to two weeks preparing all of the components for our race motors. Before an engine is allocated to a race car, it undergoes extensive testing on our AVL dynos (an engineering device that helps us develop our engines) to ensure it is generating the desired horsepower.

We currently design and manufacture more than two thousand parts for our cars.

Now, do you think those two thousand parts in that $200,000 machine fall together by accident? "No way," you say—yet you'd allow someone to tell you that a wondrous machine like the human body is the result of millions of years of chance through evolution? What human invention even comes close to the sophistication and precision of the human mind? The Bible puts it this way:

> The heavens declare the glory of God; the skies proclaim the work of his hands.[1]
> Since the creation of the world God's invisible qualities—his eternal power and divine nature—have been clearly seen, being understood from what has been made, so that men are without excuse.[2]

Here's another commonsense problem I have with evolution: What creates the soul in a man? A dog feels pain when he is hurt and joy when he is fed, but does he worry about his purpose in life, how to be the best dog he can be, or how to help feed the other poor dogs of the world? No. Can he create a great work of art that speaks to other dogs' souls for centuries to come? No. He's just a dog. A great companion? Absolutely. But as far as we can tell, he's not worried about the great questions of life, such as where he'll spend eternity. He doesn't have the soul of a human.

Along these lines, in Darwin's survival-of-the-fittest story, where does human love factor into the equation?

Okay, you're going to have to indulge me as a proud grandfather for a minute. I still remember standing in the waiting room while my first grandchild was being delivered. J.D. and Melissa had named him after me, Joe Jackson Gibbs. I couldn't wait to see him. After about fifteen minutes, the nurses brought little Jackson out. As soon as I took him in my arms, his eyes made contact with mine—I couldn't believe it. It was like he was saying, "Here I am, Coach. Let's get it on!" Today, he's all boy, but he'll still come up to me and say, "Coach, I love you," and give me a hug for no reason at all. That's a result of evolution?

I recently watched another one of my grandsons, Ty, age six, race his BMX bike at a local competition. He has a gift for racing anything with two wheels. He actually has made me and his dad, Coy, a bit nervous, because his aggressive nature has led to some pretty bad spills.

After he won this particular race and received his trophy, Ty did an amazing thing. Sweating like crazy from the competition, he walked over to me in the stands and sat on my lap. For about ten minutes, he sat there watching the other races. I was thinking, *Hey, he just decided on his own to come over and sit with me.* Now, if you're a parent or a grand-parent, you know what I'm talking about and why that connection is so special.

To say that the ability to love each other and experience the emotion I felt is just an accident of nature makes no sense to me. I believe love is a gift to us from God.

Now on to John Lennox...

To tackle the question of origins, I wanted a scientist with impeccable credentials. John Lennox fills the bill. Maybe you've seen him debate atheists Richard Dawkins or Christopher Hitchens. With his mild Irish brogue and gentle manner, John is as gracious as he is brilliant. He has a master's in bioethics and three doctorates, and he serves as professor of mathematics at the University of Oxford. He is also a fellow in mathematics and philosophy of science at Green College, Oxford, where he serves as pastoral advisor. He has published more than seventy peer-reviewed articles on mathematics, coauthored two Oxford mathematical monographs, and worked as a translator of Russian mathematics. He speaks Russian, French, and German and is the author of several books on the relationship of science with religion and ethics. John may have a lot of fancy degrees, but between the two of us, I'm the only one with a master's degree in physical education from San Diego State!

How Did Life Begin?

JOHN C. LENNOX

You may be familiar with the board game called *Life*, which dates back well over a hundred years. Players make their way around the game board, making investments, getting married, changing jobs, etc., in the hopes of ending up in a millionaire's mansion and not in bankruptcy.

What about real life, though? We call it a game, but it's anything but trivial, and you only get one shot at it.

What is life for or about, if anything? Are there any rules, or do we just make those up as we go along?

The Big Question

Is our "playing field," the universe, all that exists, or is there also a God who created it? It clearly matters which answer you choose: Either God doesn't exist (atheism), or He does (theism). Your answer determines who you think you are and where you think you fit in the grand story, the big picture, of life.

Atheism naturally holds that humanity is simply a freak of nature, a chance product without ultimate significance. To the atheist, matter and energy are the ultimate realities, and they have made you and me what we are. We are reduced to physics and chemistry.

Francis Crick, who won the Nobel Prize (along with James Watson) for discovering the double-helix structure of DNA, draws this bleak conclusion: "'You,' your joys and your sorrows, your memories and ambitions, your sense of personal identity and free will, are in fact no more than the behavior of a vast assembly of nerve cells and their associated molecules."[3]

Columnist David Brooks describes it this way in a 2008 op-ed piece in the *New York Times:* "To [some] self-confident researchers, the idea that the spirit might exist apart from the body is just ridiculous. Instead, everything arises from atoms. Genes shape temperament. Brain chemicals shape behavior. Assemblies of neurons create consciousness. Free will is an illusion. Human beings are hard-wired to do this or that. Religion is an accident."[4]

Is that it?

Or were we created in the image of God and made for a purpose?

In the atheist's view, human life has no ultimate value, meaning, or purpose. Human life "has no more meaning than the life of slime mold," says John Gray, professor emeritus of the history of European thought at London University.[5]

On the other hand, according to the Bible, human beings have incalculable dignity and value.

That's why questions about God and Creation are crucial to our sense of identity and self-worth. That is also why there is such a public battle raging about Creation these days. Phrases such as "belief in Creation is irrational," and "evolution proves God doesn't exist," are bandied about with such ferocity that often more heat is generated than light.

We must choose between God and science, says the world's most famous atheist, Richard Dawkins. In his best-selling book *The God Delusion,* Dawkins claims that science has shown it is impossible to believe in a Creator God. Religion, in his view, is a childish fantasy, even if one is sincere about it. Regardless, he says, we don't need religion, because science is the only real way to truth.

Now, you may sincerely think that belief in God as the Creator is not a fantasy. But you don't want to just go along blindly if there's evidence to the contrary. Dawkins's kind of talk can knock your confidence. The question then becomes, Are there solid grounds for believing in God as Creator?

You know it's not enough just to be sincere. A doctor might sincerely prescribe aspirin to treat a headache, but if the real trouble is brain cancer, the aspirin will do no good at all. The doctor's sincerity would be fatally wrong. Nowadays, when it comes to God, if you have any faith at all you may feel pressured to keep quiet. No one wants to be taken for an idiot, and many of these scientists can seem much cleverer than we are. The problem is that, when we get intimidated by science, God gets squeezed out of the public square and is soon eliminated from consideration altogether.

I am a scientist *and* a Christian, and I think Richard Dawkins is wrong. The choice is *not* between God and science. Science has not shown (and cannot show) that belief in God the Creator is absurd. In fact, I believe that science *confirms* the biblical view that there was a Creation.

Science and the Bible Agree That There Was a Beginning

"In the beginning, God created the heavens and the earth." These majestic words form the introduction to the most translated, most printed, and most read book in history. I can well remember the profound effect they had on me as a student at Cambridge University when they were read on live television by the crew of Apollo 8 from their lunar capsule on Christmas Eve, 1968.

Those words are a challenge to anyone who thinks that science has proved Genesis wrong. For here is one place, at least, where the Bible and science agree: There *was* a beginning. The universe has not always been here. What is striking about this fact is that for centuries the Bible has said that there was a beginning, whereas scientists only began to think seriously about it relatively recently. Ironically, when scientific evidence that the universe has not existed forever (as scientists had believed for centuries) began to appear, some leading scientists put up fierce resistance because they thought it would give too much support to those who believed in Creation. They did not get their way, however, as the evidence for a beginning was too strong. And so the big bang theory of the origin of the universe was born.

It is important for us to realize that the expression *big bang* is one used

by scientists (and everyone else) to describe their belief that the universe—
or more accurately, space-time—had a beginning. Arno Penzias won a
Nobel Prize in physics for discovering a trace of that beginning—an echo of
Creation—the so-called cosmic microwave background. He later told the
New York Times, "The best data we have . . . are exactly what I would have
predicted, had I nothing to go on but the five books of Moses, the Psalms,
and the Bible as a whole."[6]

We Do Not Have to Choose between Science and God

As science advances and discovers more and more mechanisms, atheists
tell us with great authority, there is less and less space for God. In particular,
they say, evolution has made it impossible to believe in God.

Not true.

Natural selection and mutation form a mechanism that does something.[7] Gravity also does something. But when Newton discovered gravity,
he did not make the mistake of many atheists and say that because he now
had a scientific explanation in terms of law and mechanism, he no longer
needed God. That would have been as foolish as saying that because you
understand the mechanisms and laws by which a Ford car works, you don't
need to believe in the existence of Henry Ford.

The existence of a mechanism does not prove that no one designed the
mechanism. The more Newton understood about the universe and its work-
ings, the more he worshipped God for the genius of His work. As the book
of Psalms puts it: "The heavens declare the glory of God; the skies proclaim
the work of his hands."[8]

If the choice were really between God and science, as Dawkins
suggests, no real scientist would be a believer in God. But that is simply
not so. William Phillips, who shared the Nobel Prize for physics in 1997,
and Francis Collins, who directed the Human Genome Project, are both
Christians—and there are many more. Botanist Sir Ghillean Prance, a
Fellow of the Royal Society and former director of the Kew Royal Botanic
Gardens in England, says, "For many years I have believed that God is the
great designer behind all nature. . . . All my studies in science since then have
confirmed my faith. I regard the Bible as my principal source of authority."[9]

Prance was not suggesting that the Bible is a science textbook. The Bible and science deal with essentially different issues. Science deals mainly with the *how* questions, whereas the Bible deals mainly with the *why* questions. Let me try to illustrate this.

Imagine we are in a room full of brilliant scientists. At the front, a man stands beside a table on which rests a magnificent gold cup. I introduce him as an expert goldsmith and then invite the scientists to analyze the cup. A chemist explains *how* the cup is composed of atoms of gold of great purity. These atoms are unbelievably small and yet are held together by powerful forces. A physicist takes it further and explains *how* the atoms are themselves composed of elementary particles—and so on, until we have the best scientific description available.

I then ask the experts to tell me *why* the goldsmith made the cup. The goldsmith, of course, knows why he made it, but not even the most brilliant scientific mind can answer the question. Unless the goldsmith reveals it to us, we will never know that he made the cup to honor the outstanding quarterback of the year.

In this way, as Nobel Prize winner Peter Medawar says, it is easy to see that science has its limits. Science cannot even begin to answer the questions of a child: Why is the universe here? Why are we here? What is the meaning of life?

We must turn elsewhere for answers to those questions. The Bible claims to be God's answer.

Faith in the Creator Inspired Science

Atheists such as Richard Dawkins tell us that the trouble with religion is that it is based on faith, and science does not involve faith. But he is wrong. Science involves faith in its very foundations. Every scientist, from the start, must believe that the universe has order and can be understood (at least in part) by the human mind. Einstein once said he could not imagine a scientist without such faith.

But what justifies this faith that every scientist has in the human mind? Atheism cannot justify it. Atheism teaches that our beliefs are the product of our brains, which in turn are the product of mindless, unguided processes. If that is so, why should we believe anything our minds tell us, including scientific theories? Atheism thus undermines the validity of the very human reason on which science depends.

Belief in God does not.

The great pioneers of science, such as Galileo, Kepler, and Newton, expected to find law in nature because they believed in a Lawgiver. They believed the universe could be understood (at least in part) because they believed that both the universe and the human mind were created by God. Their faith in God, far from hindering their science, inspired it. The biblical teaching about Creation was the cradle in which modern science was born.[10]

Who Created the Creator?

One of the key statements about Creation is found in the New Testament, at the beginning of the Gospel of John. Introducing his biography of Jesus, John writes, "In the beginning was the Word, and the Word was with God, and the Word was God. . . . All things were made by him."[11]

This statement may strike you as strange at first. What does John mean by "the Word was God"? In Greek, the language in which the New Testament was written, the word for "word" is *logos,* from which we get terms such as *logic, logical,* and *logistics.* It conveys ideas of reason, command, speech, and information. Writers in ancient Greece used it to describe their belief that an eternal reason was behind the universe. John fills the word *logos* with a deeper significance to tell us that the reason behind the universe is a personal God. He tells us that God did not come to be, but has existed eternally. The universe, by contrast, has not existed forever. It did come to be. This means that God the Creator is distinct from His creation.

It is important to grasp that God is eternal, because one of the most common atheist arguments these days is that if you believe God created the universe, then you will have to ask who created God, and so on forever. Atheists Richard Dawkins, Christopher Hitchens, and Sam Harris believe that this is the killer question that makes belief in God impossible. Yet it isn't hard to see that they are wrong. If you ask who created God, it plainly shows that you are thinking of a created God. Created gods are a delusion—we call them idols! But the God of the Bible was not created—He is eternal.

Now, here is the odd thing. The atheists have to believe that they themselves were created by the fundamental mass or energy of the universe—for they do not believe there was a creator God. But then we are entitled to ask, "If mass or energy created you, who created mass and energy?"

The reality is that, no matter your belief system, the questions must stop somewhere. For Christians, the questions stop with God; for atheists, they stop with the universe (or matter and energy). For Christians, God is the ultimate reality; for atheists, matter and energy are the ultimate realities. The real issue, then, is this: Which makes more sense—that an intelligent God created the universe and human beings, or that somehow the universe exists and its mindless matter and energy gave rise to human beings?

The Origin of Words

The whole business of origins becomes even more fascinating when we turn from the structure of the universe to look inside the cell. Our bodies contain about ten trillion cells, and each one contains one of the longest "words" known to science. We call it DNA. It can be thought of as a tape on which is a string of letters in a chemical language that contains just four letters: C, G, A, and T. So a bit of the string might look something like this: CAATGGCTAGT. The sequence of letters is like a computer program in that it contains coded instructions (information) that the cell uses to make the proteins that are essential to life. It is incredibly long, containing roughly 3.5 billion letters. Not surprisingly, the task of writing it out has been enormous. Nevertheless, in 2003, the Human Genome Project, one of the great triumphs of modern science, was completed. When its director, Francis Collins, announced its completion in the presence of the president of the United States, he said, "It is humbling for me, and awe-inspiring, to realize that we have caught the first glimpse of our own instruction book, previously known only to God."[12]

Suppose you received in the mail a piece of paper on which was written: TICKET FOR SUPER BOWL. If you were not expecting it, you would probably be very excited. But my point is this: When you look at the ticket, you know that printing it would have involved many processes, some of which you may not understand. But because it contains information, you also know that intelligence must have been involved. The mechanical processes involved in printing, however complex, are not themselves enough to explain the words on the ticket.

What is more, the words on the Super Bowl ticket are just eighteen letters long, yet we know without question that an intelligent author was involved. How is it, then, that so many people can look at a DNA word that is more than three billion letters long and conclude that no intelligence was involved?

Philosopher Antony Flew, for much of his life, was Richard Dawkins's predecessor as the world's most famous atheist. He frequently and vigorously debated Christians. However, in recent years, he has become convinced that biologists' investigation of DNA "has shown, by the almost unbelievable complexity of the arrangements which are needed to produce life, that intelligence must have been involved."[13] He insists that his change of mind was due to obeying Socrates' famous command: "We must follow the argument wherever it leads."

I hope you are beginning to see why the statement *In the beginning was the Word. . . . All things were made by him* makes far more sense to me as a scientist than the atheists' idea that the origin of life involves nothing more than unguided, mindless natural processes.

So important is the idea that God is the Word that this emphasis is to be found in many places where the Bible discusses the Creation. In Genesis 1, for example, each step of the Creation is prefaced by the statement *And God said . . .* , underlining the idea of creation by the *Word* of God. Furthermore, the letter to the Hebrew Christians in the New Testament makes a fascinating statement: "By faith we understand that the universe was formed at God's command, so that what is seen was not made out of what was visible."[14] God, as we have seen, is the source of the information and energy that created the world. But this statement reminds us of something very interesting: *information is invisible.* The carriers of information are often visible—such as the writing on the page you are reading at this moment. But the information itself is not visible. Indeed, it is not even material. Is it not ironic that atheists, who are often materialists, now have to face the fact that information, which plays such a central role in science, is not material? The carriers of information are usually material—like paper and ink. But information is not. So information cannot be reduced to matter and energy.

The bottom line, in the words of Nobel Prize winner Roger Sperry, is this: "The meaning of the message will not be found in the chemistry of the ink."[15] Matter and energy are therefore not all that exist. This is further confirmation that it is God, the Word, who is the creator and sustainer of the universe. As the New Testament says, "Since the creation of the world God's invisible qualities—his eternal power and divine nature—have been clearly seen, being understood from what has been made."[16]

Intelligent Design and Creationism

You've no doubt heard something on the news about the controversy over Intelligent Design (ID), and you may be wondering how it fits into the picture we've drawn here. Parents and school boards have been fighting over whether to teach ID either alongside or instead of evolution.

The notion that there is an intelligent cause behind the universe, far from being recent, is a highly respectable view that is as ancient as philosophy and religion themselves.

Why then all the fuss today? Because the meaning of the term *intelligent design* has changed dramatically and is now loaded with so many misunderstandings that it has become almost useless for discussion.

The original idea was to distinguish two issues: (1) the simple recognition that there is some sort of design behind nature, and (2) the identity of the designer. The problem is that these are separate questions. The first is scientific, and the second is theological—and thus is assumed by most to be outside the realm of science. The point of distinguishing between the two issues is to clear the path to the question of whether there is any way in which science can help us with the answer to the first question; namely, can we acknowledge that there is evidence of design in nature?

Nowadays, this original intention is all but lost, and ID is assumed by many to describe "crypto-creationists"—that is, people who are closet creationists and don't want to admit it. To make things more difficult, the term *creationist* has also changed its meaning. It used to denote someone who believed in a Creator, plain and simple. Now, however, it has come to mean someone who not only believes in a Creator, but who also adheres to a particular interpretation of Genesis in which the earth is seen as only a few thousand years old. This narrowing of the term obscures the fact that there is a wide divergence of scholarly opinion on the interpretation of the Genesis account, even among Christian thinkers who ascribe final authority to the biblical record.[17]

The Goal of Creation

One of the striking things about the Genesis account is that it tells us that God did not do everything at once. "In the beginning God created the heavens and the earth."[18] That was the start. But then we are told that the earth was "without form, and void."[19] So God undertook a series of steps (each one prefaced by *And God said . . .*) and formed and shaped the world, eventually filling it with life. The last step God took was to create human beings, both male and female, in His own image. Clearly, according to the Bible, God had a plan in mind for the earth. Our planet is special in that it was created with an ultimate purpose—to have human beings on it.

Actually, the Genesis account fits well with what science tells us. You probably learned in elementary school, as I did, that if the earth were a little nearer the sun or a little farther away, life as we know it would be impossible because of the increased heat or cold. If it spun faster, we would have no atmosphere and be catapulted into space. If the earth rotated more slowly, it would be too hot during the day and too cold at night for life to survive.

And that is only the start. So many things have to be just right for life to thrive on Earth. In recent years, physicists and cosmologists have discovered that the fundamental constants of nature—those special numbers on which everything depends—have to be precise to an unbelievable degree of accuracy for life to be possible. For instance, theoretical physicist Paul Davies tells us about two of these numbers—the electromagnetic force constant and the universal gravitational constant. Don't worry if you don't understand what these terms mean. The important thing is simply to grasp that if you increase the ratio of one to the other by an incredibly tiny amount—one part in 10^{40} (1 followed by 40 zeroes)—then only small stars can exist; if you decrease it by the same amount, there would be only large stars. The fact is, we must have both large and small stars in the universe: large ones to produce elements in their thermonuclear furnaces, and small ones that burn long enough to sustain our planet with life.

To use Davies's illustration, that is the kind of accuracy a sharpshooter would need to hit a one-inch target at the far side of the observable universe, twenty billion light years away.[20]

Nobel Prize winner Arno Penzias says, "Astronomy leads us to a unique event, a universe which was created out of nothing, one with the very delicate balance needed to provide exactly the right conditions required to permit life, and one which has an underlying (one might say 'supernatural') plan."[21]

So, both Genesis and science say that the earth is a very special place. But Genesis tells us more. It says human beings were created in the image of God. Now consider this stunning message of the Bible: The stars declare (show) the glory of God, yes, but they are not made in God's image. You are. That gives you incalculable value.

Why Do You Exist?

John, the disciple of Jesus who wrote the Gospel of John, also wrote the last book of the Bible, Revelation. One of its scenes describes the worship of God as Creator: "You are worthy, our Lord and God, to receive glory and honor and power, for you created all things, and *by your will* they were created and have their being."[22] Our staggering universe in all its beauty—from the Milky Way to the tiniest flower—was created as a free act of God, just because He wanted to. That means that you and I ultimately exist *because God wanted us to.*

We all know the feeling of being left out of a group, whether not being invited to play with others as a child or ignored at a party or in a meeting as an adult. We feel as if we're not wanted. Not so with God the Creator. He wanted us to be, or we wouldn't exist. To Him, we have infinite value. That leads us to our next question.

For What Were We Created?

Suppose a golfer wins a sport utility vehicle for a hitting a hole in one. Six months later you visit him, and there is the SUV sitting in the sun. Through its windows you can see that it is full of plants. He says, "I'm really pleased with this marvelous greenhouse I won. It is ideal for my plants."

Besides asking if he really doesn't know what an SUV is for and suggesting he read the manufacturer's handbook, you might also call a psychiatrist.

A silly story, yes, but it illustrates an important truth. You have a body and a mind—what are they for? What is your life for?

In the atheist view, human beings have no ultimate purpose. The Christian view is very different. God created us for a purpose—and there is a Maker's handbook, the Bible, that helps us to understand our purpose. In Genesis 2, we get a second account of Creation that, far from contradicting the account in Genesis 1, gives it a different perspective. It tells us about the nature and purpose of life.

It starts with the fact that we were formed from the dust of the ground. There is a material basis to human life—carbon, iron, and so on. However, we are more than simply inanimate material. We are alive. "God formed the man from the dust of the ground and breathed into his nostrils the breath of life, and man became a living being."[23]

Next, we are told that God made "trees that were pleasing to the eye and good for food."[24] We human beings have an aesthetic, artistic sense; even if we have no ability to draw or paint or sculpt, we all were created with the capacity to enjoy beauty—whether the beauty of flowers, trees, animals, mountains and oceans, or human creativity: magnificent art and enthralling music, the elegance of scientific results, the skill of a brilliant athlete, even good food.

Our sense of beauty is so strong that it can sometimes dominate our lives. For many people, life is just a game in which the object is to get as many beautiful things as possible into their corner. But is that all there is?

The Genesis record tells us that human beings were placed in a garden, out of which flowed a river that led to a land rich in resources. Since time immemorial, mankind has explored the earth by following rivers. We are curious, inquisitive beings—we want to find things out. That is what also drives scientific research. For some, it can become an obsession; they will even forgo food and sleep in their consuming passion to explore.

God gave the first humans work to do; namely, looking after and developing the garden. We all know that work of any kind (paid or voluntary) is an important aspect of life that contributes to our sense of fulfilment. But we also know work can easily dominate our lives and lead to burnout.

Interestingly, God also instructed the first human, Adam, to name the animals. Naming things is the very essence of science, and we can see that Genesis, far from being anti-science, gives us a strong mandate for naming things.

Genesis also tells us that there is more to life than work. God has made men and women to complement each other. We are relational beings. Marriage, family, and friends are an important aspect of human life, and the family forms the fundamental unit of society.

No doubt you can see from even this very brief summary that the Creation story defines life for us by describing many things that make life meaningful: our family life, work, curiosity, and even our aesthetic sense that loves beauty—not to mention food.

Is this all? The question may seem strange, because your life may be filled with these very things. Atheist Richard Dawkins certainly thinks they are enough. He dedicated his best-seller *The God Delusion* to the memory of Douglas Adams, author of *The Hitchhiker's Guide to the Galaxy*. Quoting Adams, he writes, "Isn't it enough to see that a garden is beautiful without having to believe that there are fairies at the bottom of it too?"[25]

But those are not the only alternatives. Dawkins offers us either the garden on its own, or the garden with fairies. But, as anyone knows, including Dawkins, you don't have a garden without a gardener (and, what is more, an owner). The work of a gardener is what distinguishes a garden from a wilderness. Dawkins may well have done a good job of showing that fairies don't exist—but then most of us don't believe in them anyway! What Dawkins has *not* done is to show us that there is no Gardener or Owner of this world.

Created for the Creator—the Origins of Morality

We were created not simply to have relationships with other human beings, wonderful as that can be, but also to have a relationship with the Creator and Owner of the universe. This is what being made in God's image ultimately means. Imagine! You were designed to enjoy the friendship and fellowship of your Creator as you go about the business of life. That is ultimately what you were created for—and why you need a handbook to tell you what it is all about.

Now, a relationship without boundaries is scarcely a relationship. A marriage in which the partners are not loyal to each other is not a true marriage. The boundary of legal commitment is there to protect the relationship. Likewise, God set boundaries for man's relationship with Him by forbidding him to eat of the tree of the knowledge of good and evil.[26] That shows that humans were created as moral beings.

The very fact that we are moral beings is powerful evidence for the existence of a Creator. Immanuel Kant, the famous German philosopher, confessed, "Two things fill the mind with ever new and increasing admiration and awe, the oftener and more steadily we reflect on them: the starry heavens above and the moral law within."[27]

Atheists argue that there is no need for God when it comes to morality. They disagree with the assertion, often attributed to the famous Russian novelist Fyodor Dostoyevsky, that "if there is no God, then everything is permitted."[28] But that statement doesn't mean that atheists cannot do good things. After all, the Bible clearly teaches that all men and women are created in the image of God and so are moral beings with a conscience—whether they believe in God or not. Therefore, of course atheists can behave well; too often they put to shame those who profess to believe in God.

To say "If there is no God, then everything is permitted" means that atheists have *no ground* for morality. Listen to Richard Dawkins: "It is pretty hard to defend absolute morals on anything other than religious grounds." He is right. In fact, it is pretty hard to defend any morality whatsoever on the basis of what he says elsewhere: "In a universe of blind physical forces and genetic replication, some people are going to get hurt, other people are going to get lucky, and you won't find any rhyme or reason in it, nor any justice. The universe we observe has precisely the properties we should expect if there is, at the bottom, no design, no purpose, no evil and no good. Nothing but blind, pitiless, indifference. DNA neither knows nor cares. DNA just is. And we dance to its music."[29]

So good and evil don't exist? If terrorists choose to fly airliners into office buildings and kill thousands of people, they were simply dancing to their own DNA? Dawkins's atheism delivers no explanation for morality—it destroys it.

What Has Gone Wrong with Creation?

When God finished creating the universe, the Bible says that He saw that it was very good.[30] Yet it is obvious that creation has been damaged, that there is something badly wrong with our world and with us. Human beings cheat, exploit, terrorize, fight, maim, and kill each other; disease, famine, and catastrophe stalk our planet. God seems distant and alien, and many have even given up on Him. Something has clearly gone wrong—but what?

The problem, according to Genesis, is not any lack of evidence for God's existence. It arose in the area of man's relationship with God. The humans in the Garden of Eden had not yet encountered evil and had to rely on God's authority to know what was evil. That does not mean that God was determined to keep them in a state of innocence forever. Consider the way we treat our own children.

A farmer, for instance, keeps his gun locked in a cupboard, forbidding his eleven-year-old son ever to play with it. The boy is not yet capable of handling the gun properly; he has no real idea how easily he could misuse it with deadly consequences. When he is older, he will gradually be trained how to handle the weapon safely, under his father's strict supervision.

But say one day the boy disobeys his father, takes the gun, and accidentally shoots his sister. He suffers two evils: the guilt of having killed his sister, and alienation from his father for having rejected his authority.

So it is in the Genesis story. Instead of learning to trust God's authority and waiting for Him to prepare them to learn what evil is and to face it without being overcome by it, the man and woman reject God's word and attempt to learn good from evil, independent of God. They immediately experience both guilt and alienation from God for having rejected His authority, and the anguish of having to face a lifelong struggle against evil. They had not been prepared to stay within the boundary, and therefore they break the relationship with God that was meant to be the highest and most fulfilling thing in life.

Yielding to the temptation to become independent of God has spread like a virus down the centuries, and it has led to many people even denying God's existence.[31] One telltale result is that we no longer tend to be grateful for the wonderful gifts of life. We are, of course, glad for them and enjoy them, but our natural human instinct to express gratitude to the giver of all good things has died. Denying the Creator, we have no one to be grateful to. Denying the true God, we make ourselves gods instead, deifying the forces of nature, or human reason, or passion.

There is, however, good news. Very good news. It is that God, who created the universe and upholds it, became human in the person of Jesus Christ. By His death on the cross for human sin and rebellion, He offers to heal the alienation between us and God. Because we went wrong when we stopped trusting God, the way back to God will involve learning to trust Him again. In the words of the apostle John, "He [Jesus] came to that which was his own, but his own did not receive him. Yet to all who received him, to those who believed in his name, he gave the right to become children of God."[32]

That means that you, too, can become a child of God by accepting that Jesus died for your sins, believing that God raised Jesus from the dead, and confessing to others that Jesus is Lord.

God's loving, sacrificial response to our sin gives the lie to the widespread misrepresentation that He is a tyrant.

God a tyrant? Hardly. He loves you. Those who trust in Jesus, the Son of God, receive the very life of God and become His children.

JOE'S TWO-MINUTE DRILL
Creation: How Did Life Begin?

A lot of people assert that a Christian view of Creation is unscientific. But, as John Lennox shows us, there is no conflict between science and the Christian faith. Let me recap several truths about Creation that John points out for us:

- ✓ Science and the Bible agree that there was a beginning to the universe (i.e., it was created). The universe has not always been here.
- ✓ Science and the Bible deal essentially with different issues, and therefore can coexist. We do not need to choose between one and the other. Many scientists today believe in the existence of God.
- ✓ Scientists believe there is order to the universe and that it can be understood by human minds. This takes faith.
- ✓ God was not created. He is eternal.
- ✓ The complex design of the human body points to a Creator. Each of the body's ten trillion or so cells contains DNA, on which 3.5 billion letters of genetic code are written. These letters contain instructions that the cells use to make the proteins essential to life.
- ✓ God created us in His own image and with a purpose in mind. Our lives are of great value to Him. Ultimately, we were created for a relationship with God.

CHAPTER SIX

Sin and Addiction

"**Y**ou let this boy go unsupervised. He was driving somebody else's car. You're just lucky he didn't kill someone!"

The superintendent of juvenile hall was yelling at my dad. The man didn't get one more word out before my dad lunged across the room—not at him, but at me!

As my dad and I tumbled over my chair, he growled, "Raised under the arm of the law! I'm gonna kill you!"

My dad had spent his entire professional life in law enforcement—and it took every bit of strength my mother and the superintendent had to keep him from strangling me.

Talk about putting the fear of God in a sixteen-year-old boy.

After Dad had calmed down, the superintendent backpedaled a bit. "Well, listen, Mr. Gibbs, what your son did certainly wasn't good, but it could have turned out a lot worse. No one was hurt. Let me ask you, are you sure he's gonna be safe if he goes home with you this afternoon?"

Truth was, I had it coming.

You see, a couple of buddies and I had borrowed a friend's mom's car to go to the grocery store. We raised a little Cain, picked up a few things— including some oranges—and hauled out of there.

As I drove us back to our friend's house, we saw a boy up ahead of us on a bike. My buddies keep telling me to get closer and closer to him. I wasn't sure what they were up to, but as we drew near, they started pelting him with the oranges. I got distracted, swerved, and brushed the kid with the car.

As we passed by, I looked in the rearview mirror and saw the boy fall. Then, like some teenagers you might know, I floored it and got out of there. We made it back to our friend's house and parked the car, but I was really worried about the kid we had hit. I decided to go back and check on him.

When I arrived, the scene looked terrible. There was an ambulance, the bike, a bunch of onlookers, and some police cars. It was time to fess up.

That's how I ended up in juvenile hall that afternoon.

Thank God the boy was not injured, but I sure got into a lot of trouble.

Later that night, at home, my dad—after taking a lot of heat from my mother for his performance at juvenile hall—had a few words for me. "Son," he said, "you'll probably get into a few more messes while you're under my roof. I'm not going to let you off the hook, but I will stick with you, no matter what."

He meant it. And you can believe I did my best never to be in that kind of situation again.

God is also like that to us. He knows our human nature—we are sinners and are going to keep falling short—but he never leaves us, no matter what.

Interestingly, as we conducted our research for *Game Plan for Life,* the topic of sin came up as very important to men. They wanted to know how to overcome sin—from anger, to lying, to destructive addictions like pornography or drugs. This surprised me and my guys because today it's rare to hear much about sin or personal accountability. It's always something or somebody else's fault.

It's rare today that we see sin for what it is—selfish, destructive behavior that hurts us, hurts others, and is offensive to God.

In fact, sinful behavior is often rewarded today—like the celebrity who made an infamous sex tape and became even more popular. Some people are even dumb enough to tape their own crimes to share with their friends.

The truth is, sin and addiction are no laughing matter.

Dexter Manley played defensive end for me on the Redskins. He was a man who lost a lot in life because he couldn't overcome the demons inside himself.

At 6' 2" and 270 pounds, Dexter ran like a deer and had enormous natural strength. I can remember him as a rookie at practice, chasing running backs down the field thirty yards or more while dragging a 150-pound blocking bag. Talk about strong! He once got into a fight in the locker room and picked up a lineman and slammed him into a bulletin board. Metal prongs sticking out of the board left holes in the guy's back.

If you had lived around Washington during that time, you would know that Dexter was also a cutup. Just a great guy, always joking, always smiling.

At our summer camp practices in Carlisle, Pennsylvania, we had our Wednesday night scrimmages under the lights. Dexter would line up across from our 300-pound Pro Bowl tackle and yell in a high-pitched voice, "Run it over here!" Sure enough, they would, and—*whomp!*—Dexter would make a great play for no gain.

Dexter also had a drinking problem. This led to a drug addiction, and he eventually lost just about everything. He ended his career early, even though I think he still had a few more seasons of great play left in him.

A couple of years after he left the Redskins and was back in his home city of Houston, Texas, I heard Dexter was in real trouble. I decided to visit him. I wanted to put in a good word with the judge who was getting ready to sentence him.

There in the courthouse, fun-loving, larger-than-life Dexter Manley was chained to a chair. He greeted me with tears in his eyes. Here was a great talent who had lost everything to his addictions. As his coach, I was heartbroken.

Dexter eventually turned his life around, and he now does everything in his power to motivate young people to avoid the temptations that brought him down. He is also an advocate for literacy. When he was growing up, he was such a great athlete that he kept getting pushed through schools. By the time he left college for the NFL, he was reading at only a second-grade level. Now he works to help others learn to read.

Some people think they are above sin, but most know they're sinners. I sure do. Anybody who tells you he or she came to faith in Christ and became perfect is deceived. "If we claim to be without sin, we deceive ourselves and the truth is not in us. If we confess our sins, [God] is faithful and just and will forgive us our sins and purify us from all unrighteousness."[1]

I don't need to lay out all my sins and shortcomings before you, any more than I would expect you to do the same for me. But if you're honest, you know we're a lot alike. I still fight the temptation to want the spotlight, to want to get ahead, to be self-centered and want my own way, among many other shortcomings.

It took me thirty-two years to recognize that the sin in my life was hindering me and my family and keeping up a wall up between God and me. The Bible says in 2 Corinthians 5:17, "If anyone is in Christ, he is a new creation; the old has gone, the new has come!" But we still battle our old nature and need to constantly be on guard against temptation. And we need to ask God for forgiveness when we fail. That's what Ravi Zacharias writes about in this chapter.

Ravi Zacharias is widely regarded as one of the great thinkers of this generation. He was educated at Trinity International University and Cambridge University and is currently a visiting lecturer at Wycliffe Hall, Oxford. He has authored or edited more than twenty books, several of which have been translated into many languages. His most recent book is titled The End of Reason: A Response to the New Atheists. *Ravi's weekly radio program,* Let My People Think, *airs on more than seventeen hundred radio outlets worldwide. Ravi debates at many of the world's top universities, yet he has an amazing ability to speak to the Average Joe. Recently he addressed the employees of Joe Gibbs Racing and had a profound impact. If you want to be intellectually humbled, just spend a few hours with Ravi!*

How Do I Deal with Sin?

RAVI ZACHARIAS

An incident when I was seventeen years old still causes storms of emotion to well up within me. Even with the passage of time, the memory throbs like a reinjured wound.

When I was young, my aimless life immensely frustrated my father. As committed as he was to a brilliant career for me, I was just as desirous of living for the sports field—a love of my life in which he had no interest.

He had a point, of course. Every young boy in New Delhi wanted to become a cricketer and play for India, just as every youngster in Texas wants to play for the Dallas Cowboys. But I thought for me it was more than just a dream. I showed promise in sports. At my college, I played cricket, field hockey, tennis, and table tennis. Yet never once did my dad come to see me play, even in a big game. We were marching to different drumbeats.

The most wrenching words I ever heard my father say were, "You will never make anything of your life!" Frankly, it seemed he was right, and he was trying only to jolt me into reality.

Our strained relationship was only made worse by a depth of emptiness that welled up within me. The imposing figure of my father represented to me that life should have purpose—and my life clearly had none. Inside myself, all I saw was failure. When I assessed my life, I thought there was nothing ahead for me.

Worse yet, I had nowhere to turn for answers. I didn't even know if the answers to my deepest hungers actually existed. Life had simply stopped making any sense to me. And if my life had no purpose, why try to work it out anyway? I had no idea where to look for hope.

Then one day I attended a cremation service for a Hindu friend of mine. When the service was over and the body had been reduced to ashes, I asked the Hindu priest where my friend was now.

"Young man," he said, "that is a question you will be asking all your life, and you will never find a certain answer."

If that is the best a priest can do, I thought, *what hope is there for a novice like me?*

As the months went by, I calmly yet firmly came to a tragic decision: A quiet exit would save my family further shame, and it would spare me further failure. In an effort to take my own life, I poisoned myself and was soon rushed to the hospital.

While I was recuperating, a man who knew me came and gave me a Bible.

I was so weak I could not hold it, and because I was in intensive care and the man was not a family member, he was not allowed to stay. So he flipped through the pages until he came to John 14:19. "Here," he said, pointing it out to my mother. "This is for Ravi."

After he left, my mother read it aloud, "Because I live, you will live also."[2]

The words hit me like a ton of bricks.

Live?

"Mom," I managed, "please read it again."

I had no idea what it meant, nor any idea of the context. All I knew was that the "life" it mentioned sounded very different from mine.

She read the verse again.

Somehow I knew it was the truth, and it overwhelmed me. In that moment, with a simple prayer of trust, my desperate heart found meaning. God reached down to a teenage boy in India, caring enough to hear my cry.

How incredible that God has a personal interest in the struggles of our lives! The broad reach of the gospel, in its implications for history and for all of humanity, ought never to diminish the truth that it is also intensely personal. God loves you. God wants you to know Him.

"But," you say, "you don't know me, who I really am, all the things I've done." Maybe you've allowed alcohol to enslave you, or you've become addicted to drugs. Maybe, like the disciple Peter, you've actually cursed and lied in denying that you even know Jesus. Talk about sin! Yet Jesus forgave Peter, and He'll forgive you.

No one knows the restoring power of God like someone who has walked the road to destruction. God is not just the God of power in Creation; He is also the God who is present even in our affliction—or our addiction.

The story is told of a man who took a job in a zoo impersonating a monkey. The zoo's last monkey had just died, and busloads of children were expected to visit the next day.

A perfect costume was designed for him, and he was given a crash course in tree-swinging and monkey sounds. By midday the next day, he was encouraged by the appreciation of the children and really got into playing the monkey. But while swinging from branch to branch, he suddenly slipped and fell into the lion's den.

"Help!" he shouted, fearing for his life.

The lion raced over to him and whispered urgently, "Shut up, or we'll both lose our jobs!"

That's funny, but isn't it true that we often play games of pretense? It's one thing for a spy to fool the enemy. It's quite another thing to fool ourselves with the games we play. In trying to deceive others by appearing to be something we're not, we deceive ourselves.

It has been said that we've attempted to build civilizations when we don't even know what it means to be civilized. We philosophize without knowing the very source of reason. We attempt to create without knowing the Master Artist. We moralize on life, but we do not know the Moral Lawgiver. We try in vain to build utopias, which fail when ideas become more valuable than people. On the verge of tragedy, we shout, "Help!" only to discover that the person we're appealing to is playing the same delusional game we are.

Once, early in the twentieth century, the *London Times* asked several famous authors to submit essays on the topic, What's Wrong with the World? The response of writer G. K. Chesterton was directly to the point:

> Dear Sirs:
>   I am.
> Yours Truly,
> G. K. Chesterton

Can you identify with that?

I certainly can.

I'm what's wrong with the world. The way the world was intended by its Creator and the way I am living are at odds.

My friend Joe Gibbs has titled this book *Game Plan for Life*. That will work only if it points to the Book of books, the Bible. The Bible clearly reveals what's wrong with us—and what's right with us. That most valuable book in the world diagnoses our problem and prescribes the God-given cure.

One of the more profound letters in the Bible was written by a man named Paul, a Jewish scholar who became a believer in Jesus after gaining a reputation as a persecutor of Christians. In this letter to his fellow believers in Rome—a city known for its glory and pomp; a city that was all about human power and show—Paul writes,

> God shows his anger from heaven against all sinful, wicked people who suppress the truth by their wickedness. They know the truth about God because he has made it obvious to them. For ever since the world was created, people have seen the earth and sky. Through everything God made, they can clearly see his invisible qualities—his eternal power and divine nature. So they have no excuse for not knowing God.

Yes, they knew God, but they wouldn't worship him as God or even give him thanks. And they began to think up foolish ideas of what God was like. As a result, their minds became dark and confused. Claiming to be wise, they instead became utter fools. And instead of worshiping the glorious, ever-living God, they worshiped idols made to look like mere people and birds and animals and reptiles.

So God abandoned them to do whatever shameful things their hearts desired. As a result, they did vile and degrading things with each other's bodies. They traded the truth about God for a lie. So they worshiped and served the things God created instead of the Creator himself, who is worthy of eternal praise! Amen.[3]

Very simply, Paul is saying that everything that needs to be known about God has already been revealed by Him. We see His imprint even in the way He has made us. We know that something cannot come from nothing. God is the starting point. God is the Designer.

Jesus' critics once came to Him, hoping to pit Him against the ruling powers of Rome:

Watching for their opportunity, the leaders sent spies pretending to be honest men. They tried to get Jesus to say something that could be reported to the Roman governor so he would arrest Jesus.

"Teacher," they said, "we know that you speak and teach what is right and are not influenced by what others think. You teach the way of God truthfully. Now tell us—is it right for us to pay taxes to Caesar or not?"

He saw through their trickery and said, "Show me a Roman coin. Whose picture and title are stamped on it?"

"Caesar's," they replied.

"Well then," he said, "give to Caesar what belongs to Caesar, and give to God what belongs to God."

So they failed to trap him by what he said in front of the people. Instead, they were amazed by his answer, and they became silent.[4]

Jesus had trapped them in their own craftiness. Had they been sincere, they would have followed up by asking, "And what belongs to God?"

Jesus' answer would have been unequivocal: "Just as Caesar put his own image on the coin, so God has stamped His own image on you."

God is revealed not only in Creation itself, but also in each of us. It is no accident that you have the power of perception, that you can think and reason. This comes from God, so we cannot escape Him. Try as we might to shake Him off, we can't run far enough. Part of what He has stamped on us is our need for essential worth, as well as an awareness of our own weaknesses and shortcomings.

We simply cannot gloss over the reality that we are sinners, hard as we may try to deny it. This shows itself in bad habits, addictions, selfishness, greed, and all manner of other moral failures. Our problem is not the absence of evidence for God's existence; rather, it is that we try to suppress that evidence. We hate to admit this about ourselves, but the fact is we have a natural bent toward evil because we have suppressed the evidence of God within us. Though we see clearly, again and again, the evil and selfish intent of our actions, we use every rationalization we can think of to deny what we know to be true.

Famed theologian Dr. John R. W. Stott says that many of the things we take for granted in our everyday lives would not be necessary if it were not for human sin.

> Nearly all legislation has grown up because human beings cannot be trusted to settle their own disputes with justice and without self-interest. A promise is not enough; we need a contract. Doors are not enough; we have to lock and bolt them. The payment of fares is not enough; tickets have to be issued, inspected and collected. Law and order are not enough; we need the police to enforce them. All this is due to man's sin. We cannot trust each other. We need protection against one another. It is a terrible indictment of human nature.[5]

Even as I write this, numerous wars are raging across the world. It is ironic because in the last two centuries, mankind supposedly "came of age." All the World Expositions and Exhibitions boasted of how far we have come in human progress. Yet the twentieth century was the bloodiest in history, with more people dying in warfare than in the previous nineteen centuries combined.

But let's get personal. You and I know the root of all this, and it has a name, a word we resist saying, a word that applies to us individually and not just to nations and mankind. The Bible uses the term repeatedly and without apology. We all suffer from what God calls *sin*. Oh, how we hate that word!

The S Word

Actually, the word *sin* has two clear meanings. The first—"to miss the mark"—seems less damning, but its sense is still strong. It's the soccer ball hitting the goalpost instead of the net. It's the one spike on the runner's shoe that drifts outside the racing lane and leads to disqualification. It's the running back's foot stepping out of bounds by a fraction of an inch.

If it's true that football is a game of inches, there's no question that life is too. When we miss the mark of who or what we were meant to be, the consequences are significant.

You're likely more familiar with the second meaning of the word *sin*: a deliberate violation, a transgression, breaking the rules. Sin is knowing what is right and choosing to do otherwise; saying no in the face of God.

Born and raised in India, I was a latecomer to the American sporting scene. I grew up playing cricket, soccer, and field hockey. I well recall watching my first American football game. It didn't take long to figure out that one of the objectives of the offense was to move the ball ten yards, preferably in three tries. A fourth attempt was an option, but if the risk was greater than the gain, it was better to punt and give up possession of the ball.

What befuddled me was that gaining ten yards didn't seem that difficult. Think of all the ways they could move the ball thirty feet! But I had overlooked two fundamental realities: First, what stood in the way was an array of big, tough defenders, who all looked capable of shattering bones with a single blow; and second, there were rules. So, the goal was to gain the yardage *within the rules of the game*. A player couldn't take the ball up into the stands and wait until he saw an opening on the field. Nor could the quarterback throw a forward pass after he crossed the line of scrimmage. And that was just the beginning.

Once I understood that *the rules were made to protect the game* and not the other way around, the game became a delight to watch. It didn't take long before I understood the thrill of tossing a touchdown pass and the heartache of losing a fumble.

If you're an avid football fan, you may remember, or have read about, an embarrassing play made by defensive lineman Jim Marshall of the Minnesota Vikings more than forty years ago. Marshall was no slouch. He is second all-time for most consecutive games played, with 282 (behind punter Jeff Feagles's 336), and still holds the NFL record for most consecutive games started, at 270.

Marshall also holds the career record for most recovered fumbles—which is ironic because of what happened after one such recovery on October 25, 1964, against the San Francisco 49ers. During that game, Marshall recovered a fumble and raced sixty-six yards. The wrong way. Into his own end zone. Worse, before he realized what he had done, he tossed away the ball in celebration, resulting in a safety and two points for the 49ers. Luckily for Marshall, the Vikings went on to win the game, and he contributed a quarterback sack and forced a fumble as redemption for his own mistake.

Roy Riegels, nicknamed "Wrong Way" after a similarly botched fumble recovery, wasn't as fortunate as Marshall. In the 1929 Rose Bowl, while playing for the University of California, Riegels made an errant run of just under seventy yards. After he was stopped by his teammates at California's 1 yard line, a blocked punt resulted in a safety, and California ultimately lost the game, 8–7.

We could say that humanity fumbled the ball in the Garden of Eden and headed the wrong way, right into the mess of lawlessness we have created for ourselves. But viewing the Fall only as a historic event in the ancient past keeps us from seeing our own roles as sinners.

In the early days of Disneyland, evangelist Billy Graham visited as a personal guest of Walt Disney's. As he was leaving, he said, "Walt, you have a great fantasy land here."

"Oh, you preachers get it all wrong," Disney replied. "This is reality in here. Out there is fantasy."[6]

The world of reality that God made and the world of fantasy we have created are diametrically opposed; we are reaping the consequences of the fatal decision to choose our own world over God's. How did it all happen? This is the story of our fumble and God's plan for our recovery and ultimate victory.

Seeing Yourself for Who You Really Are

As you develop a game plan for your life, you must start by seeing yourself for who you really are. You may not be prepared yet to refer to yourself as a sinner, but if you have bad habits, if you disappoint yourself or others with your selfishness, addictions, temper, or any number of other weaknesses, perhaps you'll see yourself here. And I hope you'll see the cure.

Following are four steps to understanding the story of human depravity and the consequences of breaking the rules: rejection, alienation, domination, and condemnation.

Rejection: Ruling out the rules

As much as we resist the word *sin,* seeing how we got to where we are can help us to find the way back. The first step away from God for each of us was that of *rejection.* Intentionally or not, we rejected God's plan for us—the blueprint, the script, the rules He had set in place. Instead of accepting the rules that made God's game plan for life something to be enjoyed, we rejected them, substituting our own rules and our own plans. The resulting chaos has ruined the game for everyone.

I don't like restrictions any more than you do. In human terms, I love catchphrases such as "No rules," "A world without boundaries," "Do as you please," "If it feels good, do it," or "It can't be wrong when it feels so right" (my personal favorite).

All these enticing clichés appeal to our pride and personal independence. Wouldn't you enjoy being a law unto yourself? But imagine a world in which each person made his own law. The chaos would be unimaginable! Such turmoil would take the enchantment out of life, just as it would take the thrill out of a game. It would be like a recent television commercial for TheLadders.com, in which a professional tennis match is interrupted by spectators who come out of the stands and onto the court, each attempting to play tennis, but instead crowding each other out and knocking the actual players out of the game.[7]

We all know the Ten Commandments. We might not all be able to recite each one, but we have a basic understanding of what they are: God considers life sacred or set apart. Holy. Our worship of Him is sacred. Our very lives are sacred. Our word should be sacred, as well as our bodies, our property, our time, and our relationships—and the rights of our neighbors to the same.

At first glance, this may seem heavily theological, but stay with me. When we violate sacredness, it makes for a profane world.

The word *profane* originally meant "outside the temple." So if we violate God's plan for sacred—or holy—living, we move our lives outside the temple into what we would have to admit is a godless world.

No doubt you've heard the word *holy* applied to the Bible and to God. But what does it mean when it's applied to you and me? It simply means we are separated (or set apart) because we rightly belong to someone else. Our lives belong to God. Therefore, we are expected to live for Him.

Now here's the point we too often miss. If our lives are sacred and are intended to be lived for God, our ultimate fulfillment will come only if we live according to that purpose. But if we choose to violate our purpose and live according to our own interests and desires, the result will be emptiness. We will have missed the mark and broken the rules of the game. We will have sinned.

Are you familiar with the writings of Oscar Wilde? Perhaps in high school or college you read something by Wilde, who is best known as the poster child for the "life has no boundaries, pleasure at all costs" mentality. Yet one of his most famous works is *The Picture of Dorian Gray,* the story of a young man whose pursuit of pleasure becomes his own undoing. Dorian's matchless attractiveness inspires an artist, Basil Hallward, to paint his portrait. After the painting is finished, Dorian becomes quite taken by his own beauty.

Under the influence of a certain Lord Henry, who counsels him about the value and the fleeting nature of youth and beauty, Dorian wishes he could live in any way he desires and that the consequences of a pleasure-driven life would leave his looks unaffected and mar the painting instead. When his wish appears to be coming true, Dorian hides the picture under lock and key in the attic.

As the years unfold, Dorian lives life to the hilt, experiencing anything he desires. To his amazement, no debauchery or evil ever affects the perfection of his face. Though he indulges himself in lust, greed, and pride, his appearance remains youthful and handsome.

After some years, Basil Hallward pays him a visit and asks about rumors he's heard about Dorian's wayward lifestyle—rumors the artist is not able to believe, based on his knowledge of Dorian as a young man. In response, Dorian takes Basil into the attic and undrapes the painting. To Basil's horror, the face in the portrait is disfigured and hideous, a countenance totally marred by sin. He looks directly at Dorian and says, "If it is true and this is what you have done with your life, why, you must be worse even than those who talk against you fancy you to be!"

The artist pleads with Dorian to confess his sin and repent, but Dorian says it's too late.

"It is never too late, Dorian," the artist says. "Let us kneel down and try if we cannot remember a prayer. Isn't there a verse somewhere, 'Though your sins be as scarlet, yet I will make them as white as snow'?"[8]

Rather than repent, Dorian becomes enraged and stabs the artist in the neck, killing him. Later, after cleaning up all evidence of the murder, Dorian notices a red stain, like blood, on one of the hands of the man in the portrait. Over time, the stain grows larger and spreads—to the hand that hadn't held the knife, and onto the feet, as if the artist's blood had dripped from the knife. Concerned now that the portrait might become evidence against him should it ever be seen, Dorian decides to destroy the painting. Brandishing the same knife with which he had killed the artist, he stabs the portrait.

A dreadful scream brings Dorian's servants running up the stairs. When they finally gain access to the attic, they find a grotesque man lying dead on the floor beside the pristine portrait of the beautiful, young Dorian Gray.

The disfigured, repulsive face of the real Dorian was the result of the self-centered fantasy he pursued. So too our own lives can be disfigured by the choices we make. Sin exchanges reality for fantasy, destroying the sacredness of life. Once we understand the reality of what God has made us for, we will recognize that our pursuit of the unreal world of our own fantasies violates and rejects our true purpose.

But sin is not just an act; it is also an attitude. The offense is not only in what we do, but also in the attitude of our hearts. Jesus made this clear in His famed Sermon on the Mount when he said that lust itself is adultery. He said that hateful anger is murder, even if blood is never spilled. Sin resides in the heart before it is ever translated into action.

We need to be careful here. Maybe we don't violate all of the commandments. Maybe we're proud of the ones we keep and see ourselves as virtuous compared to others. But as far as the condition of our hearts, we are all on equal ground before God.

A classic story illustrates this. Two brothers were known to be vile to the core. When one of them died suddenly, the other went to his pastor and said, "I will pay you anything to officiate the funeral of my brother. But I have one request—that you refer to him as a saint."

The pastor, knowing both brothers well, hesitated but finally agreed.

At the packed funeral, the pastor looked down from the pulpit and said, "The man you see here in the coffin was a hooligan. He was a liar. He was an adulterer. He committed every conceivable evil act. But compared to his brother, he was a saint."

Alienation: A Stranger to Yourself

If *rejection* of God is where the slide begins, *alienation* is where it picks up speed. I realize that *alienation* may not be a word you use every day to describe your life, but its meaning will soon become clear.

In rejecting God by trading away His plan for our lives for the ugliness of our own selfish desires, we become *alienated* from the very persons God intended us to be. We become strangers to ourselves. There is an ironic twist here. This may sound strange, but are you aware of an inner need to worship? We are attracted to certain people, certain personalities, certain teams, certain quarterbacks, certain race car drivers, even certain fictitious personas. For example, there are people who so admired John Wayne—or at least the macho roles he often played—that they nearly worshiped him.

Believe it or not, we have an inner need to worship. I believe this need was planted in us by God so that we could worship Him, but when we choose our own way and become strangers to even ourselves, we still have that urge to worship.

Human beings are incurably religious. When we turn away from the true God, we end up making ourselves into gods or finding other substitutes, such as those mentioned above. We cannot shake off the longing to worship, but we direct our worship to things that are not worthy. As the Old Testament prophet Habakkuk says, "What good is an idol carved by man, or a cast image that deceives you? How foolish to trust in your own creation—a god that can't even talk! What sorrow awaits you who say to wooden idols, 'Wake up and save us!' To speechless stone images you say, 'Rise up and teach us!' Can an idol tell you what to do? They may be overlaid with gold and silver, but they are lifeless inside. But the LORD is in his holy Temple. Let all the earth be silent before him."[9]

In Psalm 135, King David writes of idols that are blind, deaf, and dumb.

And then he adds this rather pointed comment: "And those who make idols are just like them, as are all who trust in them" (verse 18). You may enjoy a self-centered life for a season, maybe even for years, but when you look back on your life, will it be with contentment and satisfaction? How futile the pleasures and things we pursue! How sad to become alienated from ourselves and from what God meant for us to be.

The word *individual* means "one that is indivisible." Yet, when we distance ourselves from God and pursue our individual desires, we create division within ourselves and violate our very nature. We cannot find meaning because we have strayed from and become strangers to our intended purpose. We're left chasing poor substitutes to try to fill the void that we ourselves have created.

In the Old Testament, Isaiah describes worshipers of idols and those who deify themselves as like "a vision in the night—as when a hungry man dreams that he is eating, but he awakens and his hunger remains; as when a thirsty man dreams that he is drinking, but he awakens faint, with his thirst unquenched."[10]

In the Sermon on the Mount, Jesus says, "Your eye is a lamp that provides light for your body. When your eye is good, your whole body is filled with light. But when your eye is bad, your whole body is filled with darkness. And if the light you think you have is actually darkness, how deep that darkness is!"[11]

Domination: The Enslavement of Pleasure

From *rejection* and *alienation,* we move to *domination.* We become slaves to the habits and ideas we have come to revere in place of God; so, instead of giving us freedom, they actually shackle us. Think of all the ways mankind has sought to be free. Political theory was supposed to free us. Technology has freed us. Industry has freed us. Science has freed us. Chemistry has freed us. Education has freed us. Some think drugs can free us. Civilized people have supposedly broken a thousand tyrannies, but look where we are now. We're merely restless people, drunk with a sense of freedom.

But let's keep this personal. Don't you often feel that if you just keep searching, somewhere out there something will lead you to Utopia, that perfect blend of freedom and satisfaction? But Utopia is a mirage, because we are too obsessed with ourselves and with doing things our own way.

Some years ago, I met Elvis Presley's stepbrother, Rick Stanley, who had also served as Elvis's bodyguard. I asked him how it was possible that a man with so much ended up needing drugs to perform, to go to sleep, to wake up, to merely get by every day. "How did he become such an addict?"

Rick said, sadly and profoundly, "Elvis was not addicted to drugs. He was addicted to fame."

I have never forgotten that simple epitaph.

The worst effects of sin are seen not in war or pain or scars, but in the impact of sin on the human spirit—the impact of chasing inappropriate and unworthy loves, the low ideals, the brutalized and enslaved conscience. The apostle Paul says, "Their lives became full of every kind of wickedness, sin, greed, hate, envy, murder, quarreling, deception, malicious behavior, and gossip. They are backstabbers, haters of God, insolent, proud, and boastful. They invent new ways of sinning, and they disobey their parents. They refuse to understand, break their promises, are heartless, and have no mercy. They know God's justice requires that those who do these things deserve to die, yet they do them anyway. Worse yet, they encourage others to do them, too."[12]

Condemnation: Payday Someday

No one likes the term *condemnation*. We know what it means, and we don't like to think of the judgment to come. We have become so accustomed to running our own lives that anything that smacks of punishment seems like a primitive threat to keep people in line. But just as there is no free lunch, there is no free ride through life. Someday the moment of reckoning will arrive. It'll be payday someday.

The idea of eventually facing judgment reminds me of the sad story of disgraced sprinter Marion Jones. Remember her? She is a tall, lithe, beautiful African-American woman, with a bright smile and an engaging personality, who was flooded with adulation for winning three gold medals and two bronze at the 2000 Summer Olympics in Sydney, Australia.

She defeated her competition by such margins that many had to raise the steroid question; but she just didn't seem the type. And she denied it to everyone, including the press, the public, and even two grand juries. But eventually, the evidence, and her conscience, caught up with her. When she could no longer run from the truth, she confessed to the deceit she had foisted on the world. Her admission of guilt was sad but powerful. Following is part of a letter she wrote before being sentenced to prison for perjury:

Dear family and close friends,

I hope this letter finds all of you well. . . .

I write this letter to all of you for a few reasons. The first is simply because I love you all. Some things will be happening in the next week that I want you all to know about from me FIRST. . . .

The fact [is] that I have made mistakes in my life, made bad decisions, and have carried a great amount of pain and hurt throughout my life.

I want you all to understand that I have constructed what I thought was this impenetrable wall to protect me from hurtful and harmful people and things. . . .

Having said this, I realize the need to be up front and honest with you about several things that have transpired in my life. I will not candy coat the following statements, as I have done this and tapped around the truth for too long. . . .

I lied for a few reasons. I lied because I panicked.

I lied to protect my coach at the time. I lied to protect all that I had worked so very hard for in my life and career. And lastly, I lied to protect myself. It was an incredibly stupid thing to do.

I made the decision to break the law and have to take full responsibility for doing so. All of this was after my attorneys had specifically told me several times the need to be totally truthful with the agents. . . .

Although it is extremely hard to fathom being away from my family for any length of time, I have to put the rest in God's hands and pray that this horrible chapter in my life be resolved as soon as possible. . . .

. . . The next several months will be very difficult for me and my family, and all of you as well. With all of this happening, though, I want you to know that I feel a huge relief already being lifted as I will finally be able to tell the truth, as hard as it might be.

. . . I am sorry for putting you all through this after you have been there for me through everything. I want to apologize to you, in advance, for the questions that you will be asked about me and about your relationships with me.

And lastly, I am sorry for disappointing you all, in so many ways. My intent was never to hurt any of you.

I hope that one day I will be able to share with you, and the world, my struggles with certain things in my life—and in addition use my story to help direct, motivate, and possibly even inspire young people to make better decisions in their lives.

Please keep me in your prayers.

Love, Marion[13]

It is difficult not to feel sorrow for one who has squandered such a gift. The double loss is that we will never know whether Marion Jones could still have been a champion without these banned substances. There is some evidence that she was the fastest woman in the world even before she began taking performance-enhancing drugs.

Lessons are built into life. Love and truth must go hand in hand. Love and deceit are contradictory. There is no such thing as love without cost. God's love to us came at the price of the death of His Son, and we can't appreciate that forgiveness and receive that love while substituting our own will for the plan He has for our lives.

Think about it: A world without ultimate justice would be a very cruel world. It is here that the Good News of Christ shines in its greatest brilliance. Sin is bad news, but it remains bad news only if we stop short of the remedy. It is good news when we recognize sin for what it is and understand God's offer of forgiveness.

If we think of our mistakes and our wrongs only in terms of how they affect us, and don't consider what they mean to God, there really is no hope. Just feeling guilty does not get to the heart of the problem. We make a huge mistake if we think of sin as just unethical or immoral. We are not just unethical; we are lost in sin and spiritually dead.

But this is the Good News! When I recognize sin—whether it be an addiction, greed, lust, gluttony, drunkenness, hatred, jealousy, or any number of other failings—when I can say, "I'm not just *guilty*, I'm a *sinner*," then someone can say to me, "Ah, I have a Savior for you who has paid the price and offers forgiveness because of His grace and mercy."

The Bible warns us of the judgment of God if we reject Him and alienate ourselves from Him. (See, for example, Matthew 18:8; 25:41, 46; Mark 3:29; 2 Thessalonians 1:9; Hebrews 6:2; Jude 1:7.) Look these verses up for yourself and you will see that to leave your sin unacknowledged is to choose a destiny of eternal separation from God, cut off from His love, beauty, and purpose for your life. That's the bad news of ignoring the Good News.

Even more passages in the Bible reveal that forgiveness and restoration come from the heart of God. First John 1:9 states it most clearly: "If we confess our sins to him, he is faithful and just to forgive us our sins and to cleanse us from all wickedness."[14] In this strange way, sin is part of the Good News of the gospel.

The biggest difference between Jesus Christ and the ethical and moral teachers who have been revered by man is that the teachers tried to make bad people good, but Jesus came to make dead people live. East or west, north or south, ancient or modern, the problem is the same and the solution is the same. Once we understand the heinousness of sin, we will gain a deep and lasting gratitude to God.

I was seventeen years old on a bed of attempted suicide in Delhi when I gave my life to Jesus Christ. I was not a bad man becoming a good man; I was a dead man who was now going to live for a cause greater than himself. Someone has said that sin scorches us most when it comes under the scrutinizing light of God's forgiveness. All of us who are forgiven know how scorching sin can be. That's why we can truly appreciate what the converted slave trader, John Newton, wrote: "Amazing grace, how sweet the sound that saved a wretch like me. I once was lost but now am found, was blind but now I see."[15]

JOE'S TWO-MINUTE DRILL
Sin and Addiction: How Do I Deal with Sin?

To be on the winning team in the game of life, we need to understand our true standing before God. The fact is, He is holy and righteous and without sin. We, on the other hand, are sinful and unworthy of His love. However, as Ravi shows us, we have hope in the person of Jesus Christ. Let me recap several truths about sin and addiction that Ravi points out for us:

- ✓ God loves us and is interested in our struggles. Without God, we have nowhere to turn for answers to explain the emptiness we feel inside, nowhere to turn for hope.
- ✓ We must see ourselves as we really are—as sinners. We have all deliberately run from God and rejected Him. Our sin is the root of our suffering and struggles.
- ✓ We were made for God. Ultimate satisfaction and fulfillment in life will come only by living for Him and according to His playbook, the Bible.
- ✓ We have chosen to be enslaved by our sinful habits and pleasures. We are lost in sin and spiritually dead. One day we will stand before God in judgment for the choices we've made.
- ✓ The message of the Bible is that God offers forgiveness for sin and freedom from the habits and addictions that hold us. Jesus died on the cross to restore our broken relationship with God.

CHAPTER SEVEN

Salvation

Let me talk to you about courage.

Working in the NFL and NASCAR, I've had the chance to see courage up close and personal.

NASCAR driver Tony Stewart grew up in Indiana with the dream of one day racing in the Indy 500. After he had worked his way up through the ranks, a respected team owner allowed him to take the first step toward his dream—testing one of his cars at the Indianapolis Motor Speedway. On his third lap, Tony turned one of the fastest laps ever recorded at Indy.

One time I asked Tony how he could race for five hundred miles at speeds up to 220 mph. "It's easy, Coach. Even you could drive one of these cars. They're engineered to stay stuck to the ground no matter how fast you're going." Well, I worried about what happened when they became unstuck. Tony had broken his hip in one bad crash.

When Tony came to Joe Gibbs Racing from open-wheel racing, he asked if he could still race the Indy 500. Twice, he raced at Indy and then flew to Charlotte to race the Coca-Cola 600 for us on the same day. Think of it—1,100 miles of high-speed, high-stress, physically demanding racing, all in one day.

Of course, we were concerned about Tony physically. In 1999, the first year he drove in both races, he wanted to eat the same junk food between races that he normally ate before a race. By the end of the second race that day, he was toast.

The next time Tony flew between races, we had a trainer on board who administered an IV and made sure Tony ate well and rested. After the second race, he jumped out of the car and joked, "Hey, are there any dirt tracks racing tonight?"

Tony certainly has skill and smarts. And one thing he has in abundance is courage.

Or consider Pro Bowl punt returner Mike Nelms, who played for me in Washington.

I've always admired special teams players—especially kick returners. Think about it: You're standing downfield looking up in the air as the ball takes its time coming to you. Meanwhile, ten guys intent on killing you are thundering down the field. For thirty, forty, or fifty yards, they're building up momentum and thinking about one thing—making a big hit! Mike prided himself on rarely calling for a fair catch.

Many times during our preparation for the draft, a scout would say, "This guy can return punts." We coaches would chuckle and say, "Yeah, right. I'll bet he can't return punts in the NFL." That takes real guts.

Tony and Mike are two good examples of courage from my life as a coach and team owner. In the game of life, I've found it takes courage to truly follow Jesus Christ.

Nothing in popular culture encourages us to make a commitment to Christ. Religion, especially Christianity, is often the target of ridicule. But the fact is, in the game of life, there are only two teams—a winning team and a losing team. Which team are you playing on? If you're like me, you want to make sure you're on the winning team that will end up in Heaven.

It's really pretty simple. Jesus says, "I am the way and the truth and the life. No one comes to the Father except through me."[1] There's not a lot to be confused about in that verse. On the other hand, the exclusivity of that verse offends a lot of people; so yes, it takes courage to commit to Christ. It takes courage to share your faith with others in a culture that is more likely to make fun of Christians than to acknowledge all of the good that Christianity has done for mankind throughout the centuries.

God made the salvation message so simple that even a child can understand it.

Our son Coy was ten years old when he came to Pat and me and told us he wanted to give his life to Christ. I called our pastor and told him Coy wanted to talk to him about it. The pastor met us for breakfast at a little restaurant, and before we went in to eat, Coy and I joined him in his car in the parking lot. Coy sat in the front seat with the pastor, and I sat in the back.

"So, Coy," the pastor said, "You want to give your life to Christ?"

Coy said, "Yes, sir, and I want to be baptized, too."

The pastor asked him a series of questions and prayed with him, and then we went in for breakfast. The next week, Coy went forward in church to make his commitment publicly and was baptized.

A week later, as we drove past the restaurant where we'd had breakfast, Coy said, "Yep, that's where I met the Lord—in the parking lot!"

It's never too early to commit your life to Jesus Christ; and as long as you have breath, it's never too late, either. I told you my dad had a drinking problem. He was a tough guy who had spent his life in law enforcement and wasn't afraid to fight. He wasn't afraid of anything. Everybody liked my dad when he was sober, but he could be a handful when he'd had too much to drink.

Late in his life, I tried to share my faith with him and make sure he knew that salvation was a free gift that had nothing to do with how good or bad a person was. "But I've done too much stuff," he'd say, entirely missing the point. He just couldn't grasp that salvation was free, not something you qualified for or earned.

He and my mother wound up living out their retirement years in Sun City, California, and he used to tell me that the only exciting thing around there was watching the ambulances come to pick up the old people. He joked, "I guess that's the way I'm going to go—getting run over by an ambulance."

I also learned from my mother that a local minister used to visit my dad and sit and talk with him about his relationship with Christ.

In the middle of one football season, I got a call from my mother telling me that Dad had had a stroke and was in the hospital. I flew all night to get there, wishing the whole way that I'd been more forceful when I'd talked to him about Christ. Well, I was going to make sure this time.

But by the time I got to him and stood at the foot of his bed, he was in a coma, and he never came out of it. I sat at his funeral desperately wanting assurance that he had become a believer and had gone to Heaven. Sitting there with that question on my mind was torture.

The first pastor to speak at the funeral service pulled a piece of paper from his pocket and said, "I want to read to you what J. C. Gibbs wrote in our register when he first came to church here. He wrote, 'I gave my life to Christ and asked Him to be my Lord and personal Savior,' and he recorded the date." Then the pastor said, "I want to give this to Joe Gibbs," and he handed me the sheet.

What a gift!

Of course, I wish Dad had been able to enjoy life as a Christian, rather than waiting until the last minute. But my point is that it's never too late. People ask if that's fair, if it's right for God to let people into Heaven after they've lived for themselves for years.

Well, no, it's not fair, but there's nothing fair about grace, either. If God were fair, we'd all go to Hell. The deciding factor isn't a life of good works; we've already established that. It's a matter of sincere belief and trust in Christ. The thief on the cross, the one Jesus promised would be with Him that very day in paradise, didn't have time to change his ways or get baptized or do any good works. He believed and trusted, and that was enough.

But don't wait until the last minute, because you never know when that might be. You need to be ready for your chance, so be sure you are on the right team. Don't ever think it's too late—or too early, either.

Chuck Colson is a man with a lot of personal courage. In fact, I'll never forget his invitation to me, just after the Redskins had won Super Bowl XXII, to go with him to the Lorton Prison in northern Virginia to visit prisoners.

Now, Lorton used to be where they housed the toughest of the tough. These guys were hard-core criminals. But as the coach of the Super Bowl champions, I need not have worried. I received a great welcome at Lorton, and the prisoners were hooting and hollering.

As Chuck and I toured the prison, with a group from Prison Fellowship, we soon found ourselves with the prisoners on death row. Chuck immediately began talking with three hardened inmates. From there, we were escorted to the AIDS ward. Chuck went in and spoke to every patient, taking the time to hold their hands and pray with them. That was back before AIDS was really understood—what caused it or how it was transmitted. I have to tell you the truth—I was hanging back. What Chuck did that day took a level of courage that few people have. I invite you now to consider what he has to say about getting yourself on the right team.

Early in his career, from 1969 to 1973, Chuck Colson was special counsel to President Richard M. Nixon, and his office was next to the Oval Office. In 1974, Chuck served prison time for obstruction of justice related to the Watergate scandal. After his release, he founded Prison Fellowship Ministries, an organization with fifty thousand volunteers reaching out to prisoners and their families in nearly ninety countries. His daily radio broadcast, Breakpoint, is heard on more than one thousand stations daily. In 1993, he received the prestigious Templeton Prize for Progress in Religion, and he donated the $1 million prize to Prison Fellowship. Chuck has written many books, including Born Again, *the story of his life and conversion to Christ. When I coached football, I always wanted the tough guys on my team. I've got a feeling I could count on Chuck to throw a few blocks and make some tackles as we play the game of life.*

How Do I Get on God's Winning Team?

CHARLES COLSON

For two years, the agony of an Atlanta prison had spilled out of its rock walls into grisly headlines. Organized crime reached through the gates; death struck swiftly and often.

Over a period of sixteen months, extending into 1977, inmates brutally murdered ten of their own. One was burned to death in his sleep; others were savagely slashed or beaten. Rape was commonplace. The prison officials tried to clamp down, but the terror continued; two thousand inmates lived in fear for their lives in an old steel-and-concrete complex designed for twelve hundred.

In the midst of the carnage, Jack Hanberry was named warden. Hanberry had been chaplain at the penitentiary a few years before and had earned the respect of both inmates and staff. But now the current flock of inmates put him to the test. As a macabre welcoming gift, they carried out two killings, a string of assaults, and the setting of twenty-four fires in the cellblocks during Hanberry's first two months on the job.

I myself had once done time in prison, and I had later founded an organization called Prison Fellowship. I called Hanberry to offer our help. The warden quickly accepted and scheduled an in-prison seminar, including a speech by me, for the following month.

I had no idea what to expect from the inmates; we had been to the prison before and had found only a few strong believers in Christ. The chaplain's core group consisted of only eight men.

Tension built as the date approached. The summer of 1977 was especially hot, and a fierce sun baked the buildings day after day. The cellblocks, ventilated only by old fans, were like furnaces. Most prison riots, I knew, erupted during such dog days.

The day I arrived to speak, walking through those penitentiary gates felt like walking through the gates of Hell. I was astonished—and more than a little uneasy—to learn that Warden Hanberry had decided to throw open the meeting to the entire prison population.

As I walked through the maze of gates into the main corridor, I faced hundreds of curious eyes. Chaplain Charlie Riggs escorted me to his office, where I enjoyed a joyous reunion with several of his core group: handsome Sunshine, a man in his early thirties; Carl, a smiling man who'd spent forty years behind bars; square-jawed Cal, who had once been a gospel singer and showed three missing teeth; and Don, who was studying for the ministry by correspondence course and was four years into a forty-year sentence for kidnapping.

Cal stepped forward. "Look, Chuck, things are bad. The men are really tense. Some dudes are expecting trouble here tonight."

I tried to act calmer than my stomach felt. "We'll be okay. This is the Lord's night."

Cal frowned. "There's another thing. You can't talk about Jesus. The men won't take it. No religion, okay?"

Sunshine chimed in, "Trouble is, the men think you're out to con them. The warden's been saying good things about you, but the men are suspicious. But they'll show up. Maybe a thousand."

A thousand in one room? Anything could set them off!

Now I was really scared, doubting whether we should have come at all.

"You could talk about prison reform," Don said.

Carl nodded. "That would be good. Everybody's for that."

Chaplain Riggs agreed.

"I came here to tell these men what Christ can do for them," I said.

"Some other time," Carl said softly.

When it was finally time for the meeting, we made our way into the stifling, crowded hall where a thousand inmates had gathered. As I moved to the microphone, I abruptly took off my suit jacket and threw it on the floor. Every face I saw, even inmates I knew to be friendly, appeared stern.

Lord, if I've ever needed Your help, it's now.

"I know what many of you are thinking," I said. "What is Chuck Colson doing here? What's his game? Is he here to make money? There's got to be an angle, right?"

Heads nodded all over the hall.

"And look at these nice people from town," I said, pointing out our Prison Fellowship volunteers. "Why are they here? Just so they can go back to their nice churches in the nice part of town and tell the nice people they've done something good?"

There were even more nods now. I didn't know where the words were coming from, because this wasn't remotely what I had planned to say. I never looked at my hastily scribbled notes on prison reform.

"Well, let me tell you why we're all here. It's because we have committed our lives to Jesus Christ, and this is where He calls us to be."

Down front, I saw Cal's horrified look. I knew he was afraid those very words would set off the crowd. But this was no time for caution. If I was sure of anything this night, it was that I would talk about Jesus Christ—come what may.

We Are All Losers

Despite the withering heat, I felt a strength rising in me. I talked about my own prison experience, about my decision to go into prison work full-time, and about the amazing love that Jesus has for those of us who have fallen.

"Jesus Christ came into this world for the poor, the sick, the hungry, the homeless, the imprisoned," I told the men. "He is the prophet of the loser. And all of us assembled here are losers. I am a loser just like every one of you. The miracle is that God's message is specifically for those of us who have failed."

I had just told nearly a thousand angry, overheated convicts that they were losers. They sat staring, fixed on every word. What was going to happen next?

From the White House to the Big House

I knew better than most how quickly violence could erupt in a sweltering prison filled with angry men. Just a few years before, I had finished my own term at Alabama's Maxwell Prison, serving seven months of a three-year sentence for Watergate-related crimes. I had gone from a handsome office in the White House, where I carried out the orders of President Richard M. Nixon, to a stinking prison where I spent my days washing socks. Talk about becoming a loser! I'd let down my president, my country, and my family.

And now I was an ex-con, visiting prisons from coast to coast. How had I managed to go from being a feared White House aide, who dined with world leaders on a gleaming presidential yacht, to a prison evangelist who shared meals with drug dealers and murderers?

I certainly hadn't planned it that way. Growing up in Boston during the Great Depression, I had big dreams—and they didn't involve helping those in need. After graduating from Brown University on a full naval ROTC scholarship, I was commissioned as a lieutenant in the Marine Corps. To my great disappointment, hostilities ended in Korea before I could get there. (Amazing how brash I was.)

After the Marines, I attended night law school at George Washington University, graduating at the top of my class. During those years, I served full-time as administrative assistant to a Republican senator from Massachusetts. I was hooked on politics. After managing the senator's reelection campaign in 1960, when I was twenty-eight years old, I joined forces with a brilliant young lawyer I'd met in my political travels. We opened a Boston and Washington law practice, worked hard, and became extremely successful.

Riding High

By the time I was thirty-eight, I was, by most standards, on top of the world. I had become special counsel to President Nixon and a close confidant of his. The grandson of immigrants, I had clawed my way out of the Depression era to occupy an office right next to the president's. During my four years of service to Mr. Nixon, I was known as the White House hatchet man, feared by even the most powerful politicos. I had a wonderful wife and three great kids—everything any man could want.

Or so I thought.

In 1972, I helped manage President Nixon's historic reelection land-slide, then decided it was time to go back to my law practice. I had done my service for my country and had reached the pinnacle of power. Yet despite all this, I felt a curious deadness in my life, an emptiness I had no idea how to fill.

I recall one day in particular, sitting in my office looking over the beauti-fully manicured lawns of the White House to the Washington Monument in the distance. *Shouldn't I feel joy and excitement?* I thought. *Is this all there is to life? What can I do to top this? What is my purpose, anyway?*

Soon after that, I found myself mired in the Watergate scandal—the crimes associated with the break-in at Democratic Party headquarters during the 1972 presidential campaign. Almost every day, I'd see my name in front-page headlines. It was as if I were public enemy number one. My world was collapsing. The deadness I felt after the election was now joined by fear.

A Life Transformed

My life changed forever on a hot, sultry summer evening—August 12, 1973—when I visited a good friend, Tom Phillips, who was then the president of Raytheon. His company was one of my law practice clients. I'd noticed he seemed so at peace, not the way I'd known him before. He'd become a Christian, whatever that meant. I was determined to find out what had happened in his life.

I had gone to church occasionally and thought of myself as a Christian, the same way I thought of myself as an American. I believed in God, but as for what it really meant to know Jesus Christ, which Tom Phillips said he did, I hadn't a clue.

That night as we sat on his porch sipping iced tea, Tom told me that my mistake was that I had put my whole trust in life in politics and worldly success—things that were empty and meaningless. He read to me from a little book by C. S. Lewis titled *Mere Christianity*. He read a full chapter on how a proud man walks through life looking down on other people and never seeing anything immeasurably superior to himself; namely, God.

The author, a great Oxford scholar and Christian apologist, had no idea when he had written those words forty years earlier that they were aimed right at my heart. Oh, sure, I'd been to religious services at the White House, and I knew all the formalities. But until that night, I never understood who

I really was. I sat squirming, more from Lewis's words than from the heat. I realized I'd been driven all my life by pride, trying to prove I was better than anyone else.

Tom, too, had been a huge success. He told me that before he turned forty he was president of one of the largest companies in America. But he, too, had felt the same deadness I had. One night while in New York on business, he had attended a Billy Graham meeting and heard the good news that Jesus Christ had died for his sins and that he could be set free. He said that that night he had accepted Christ and found peace and significance.

If that sounds strange and foreign to you, you can imagine how it sounded to me. Tom had believed in Jesus and surrendered himself to Him, receiving God's gift of salvation. I was stunned. I couldn't imagine personally surrendering to anything or anyone. Tom wanted to pray with me, but I couldn't. I was too proud. I told him I'd read his book and tucked *Mere Christianity* under my arm. I headed to the driveway, but just as I got behind the wheel of my car, I had a strong urge to go back and pray with Tom after all. But still I couldn't.

I sat there watching the house lights go out as he and his wife retired for the evening. I started to pull out of the driveway but got only about a hundred feet before I had to pull over. This former White House hatchet man, ex-Marine captain, and tough guy was crying too hard to drive.

I sat there a long time, deeply aware and ashamed of my own sin and desperate to know God. I didn't know the right words to pray. I simply called out to Him, asking Him to take me, to come into my life.

Is There a God?

I had never been one to break down in tears, or show it if I did. And yet the next morning, I felt a tremendous peace—a sense of relief. In the days that followed, during a vacation on the Maine seacoast, I began to explore intellectually what had happened to me emotionally in Tom's driveway. I knew I had surrendered myself to something—or Someone—that night. But I had to be sure it wasn't just an emotional experience. My legal training insisted that I marshal the facts, pro and con, for the very existence of the biblical God. I wrote at the top of a legal pad: "Is there a God?" I plunged into *Mere Christianity,* the book Tom Phillips had given me.

Does Evil Exist?

As a lawyer, I couldn't help but be impressed by C. S. Lewis's arguments about moral law. The very fact that it exists, *despite* humanity's best attempts to defeat it, proves that man has not been the one responsible for moral teaching. Its long existence shows some other will behind it. Again, God.

But the next question was this: "If God is good, why does He allow evil to exist?" Maybe you've asked this question yourself. It's one that has held back many would-be followers down through the centuries. Again, my legal training provided a useful parallel. In the beginning, God created humans to live in perfect harmony with His will—actually, to live in paradise. He called us, in fact, to be His agents, to take dominion over this beautiful earth.

That's an exciting thought. In law, serving as an agent means you're being commissioned to act on behalf of someone else. So God is asking us to do His will and to be used by Him. What an exciting prospect!

At the same time, being a loving God, He doesn't force us to do it. He gave us a free will. Anyone who has a free will can defy those limits—or, as we say in the law, violate our role as agent. That happens all the time; thousands of lawsuits prove it. In the same way, humans are often tempted to disobey God.

The Bible tells us that's exactly what happened to Adam and Eve in the Garden of Eden. They listened to Satan's temptation instead of obeying God. This same pattern appears all through human history. Down through the years, man's abuse of God's authority, and his cruelty toward his fellow men, has resulted in endless human grief.

As C. S. Lewis puts it, "The moment you have a self at all, there is a possibility of putting yourself first—wanting to be the centre—wanting to be God."[2] How devastatingly I now saw that in my own life. It's exactly what I had done. I had allowed myself to think I was doing good for my country and for my family, but the truth was I was just trying to prove to myself and to the world how smart and good I was.

Is Jesus God—or a Raving Lunatic?

I went on reading, underlining, and making notes in Lewis's book and on a yellow legal pad: there is a God, there isn't a God; Christ is who He says He is, He isn't, and so on. It became crystal clear to me that there is a loving, infinite God. The evidence was powerful. But I was still perplexed by Tom's statement that he had *accepted Christ*, that he had actually given his life to Him.

Lots of people believe in God. Lots of people also think He can be worshipped in any way one wants. So what's so different about Jesus Christ?

As I studied Lewis's arguments, I realized that I had to make a choice about who Jesus really is. The Bible tells us that Jesus Himself claimed to be one with God.[3] In other words, He is God. It doesn't say He's *a* god, part of God, merely sent by God, or related to God. *He is God.* This is the essence of Christianity, and it is the central theme of Lewis's book.

Lewis puts it so bluntly you can't slough it off: For Christ to have talked as He did, lived as He did, died as He did, He was either God or a raving lunatic. People like to say that Jesus was just a great teacher and a good man. But He claimed to be God! Regardless of how great a teacher one is, or how good a man, wouldn't you think he was crazy if he claimed to be God?

This was my choice. There were no fine shadings, no gradations, no compromises. I'd always thought about Jesus, born in the manger, as being the child of God perhaps, and a great moral teacher who walked the sands of the Holy Land some two thousand years ago. But Lewis's reasoning would no longer allow me to accept this. Jesus wasn't just a babe in a manger, nor could He be just a great moral teacher. A man's claim to be God—if he wasn't—would disqualify him as a moral teacher. He would be, as Lewis said, a raving lunatic.

So there was the stark question: Was Jesus Christ a lunatic—or is He God?

If He is who He claimed to be, He is nothing less than God in the flesh. And because God became man, He gave us the chance to know Him. To personally know Him.

On that sunny morning in Maine, it was hard for me to grasp the vast extent of this point: that Christ is the living God who promises us a day-to-day living relationship with Him. But Lewis would not let me squirm off the hook. His words—both exciting and disturbing—pounded at me.

The Ultimate Question

I knew I could no longer sidestep the central question before me—the central question for every human being. Saying "maybe" or "I need more time" would be kidding myself. Did I believe what Jesus said in John 14:6, that He is the way, the truth, and the life and that no one can come to the Father except through Him? If I did, by faith or as a result of reason or both, then I had to accept.

My search during that vacation week returned me to where I had been when I asked God to "take me" in that moment of surrender in front of Tom Phillips's home. What I had studied so intently that week opened the door a little wider into a new world in which I had already taken my first, halting steps. As I sat alone staring at the sea, words I had not been certain I could understand or say fell naturally from my lips. "Lord Jesus, I believe You. I accept You. Please come into my life. I commit it to You."

With those few words that day came not only a depth of feeling in my heart; there also came strength and serenity, a wonderful new assurance about life, a fresh perception of myself and the world around me. I was coming alive to things I'd never seen before, as if God were filling the void I'd known for so many months, filling it to the brim with a whole new kind of awareness.

A Career of Serving God

My newfound faith kept me sane when I returned to Washington to find myself entangled in Watergate, the biggest political upheaval in American history. Special prosecutors, grand juries, congressional investigations, and headlines, day in and day out, accused me of all manner of dreadful deeds. Some were true; most were false.

In Washington, I was welcomed by a small prayer group of men who had learned of my commitment from Tom Phillips. These were men in politics, both Democrats and Republicans, along with Doug Coe, a wonderful Christian worker and part of what's called the Fellowship. They taught me and counseled me week after week, prayed with me, and sustained me. They really kept me alive during a very tough period of my life.

It was all a private matter until the day I accompanied my new brothers to a prayer breakfast in the White House staff dining room. At the press briefing later that morning, Dan Rather of CBS News asked the president's deputy press secretary what I had been doing back at the White House when I had left to return to my law practice and was now a targeted Watergate figure. The deputy press secretary peered out over his glasses and hesitantly said, "He was at a prayer breakfast."

There was pandemonium in the pressroom, reporters slamming their notebooks on their laps, laughing, and gasping in disbelief. Chuck Colson a Jesus freak? Impossible. It became the networks' lead story that day and a headline story for weeks. In fact, it seemed to be the number one story of Watergate: that the unlikeliest of persons had become a Christian. The *Boston Globe* editorialized that if I could become a Christian, there had to be hope for just about anybody.

Over the next several months, I got bags full of mail in my law office. "Now that you're a Christian," half of them said, "you can defend our wonderful president." The other half said, "Now that you're a Christian, you can tell the world what a horrible man Richard Nixon is."

I soon realized that my Christianity was going to be on trial even more than my Watergate misdeeds. After a long session of prayer with my fellowship group and consultation with my wife and children, I walked into the prosecutor's office and offered to plead guilty. Though I couldn't plead guilty to what I'd been charged with, because it wasn't true, I confessed to an offense I hadn't been charged with but of which I was actually guilty. And so, after fourteen months of investigations, testifying under oath forty-four times and never once being charged with perjury, I pleaded guilty at the Federal District Courthouse and was sentenced to one to three years in prison.

My conviction made headlines worldwide. One of the closest men to the president of the United States was about to go to prison. Oddly enough, I'd never felt freer in my life.

The toughest part about prison was not being strip-searched, thrown a pair of underpants with five numbers stenciled on them (so you knew you were the sixth person to wear them), or being thrust into a dormitory crowded with drug dealers, murderers, embezzlers, and car thieves. I had been in the Marines; I had lived in every kind of environment; I could handle prison.

What I couldn't handle was the despair of the men around me. Prison wasn't doing anything to rehabilitate them. These men were only being embittered and learning how to commit new crimes when they got out. They had no hope. Many never received mail from home. Most didn't see their children. Many would "do time," as it is called, by lying on their bunks, staring into the emptiness, their souls corroding, their bodies wasting away.

I grew to care deeply for those men, to anguish for them. And I told God daily that I would do something to help them.

One night, in the dayroom, where inmates gathered before lights out, some were watching television, others playing cards. I happened to be writing a letter to my wife, Patty, when a tall African-American inmate stood and yelled over the din, "Hey, Colson!" The room instantly went silent— a reflection of the prison's deep racial tensions. "What are you going to do for us when you get out of here?"

"I'll never forget you guys," I said. "I'll do something. I don't know what, but I will."

The inmate slammed his cards to the ground and said, "Oh, bull! Big shots like you come to prison, you leave here, and then forget little guys like us."

But I wouldn't ever forget the men I'd come to know and love in prison. In fact, our prayer fellowship in there was the liveliest, most meaningful I'd experienced. Six of us—two dope peddlers, a car thief, a bootlegger, a bank embezzler, and a former special counsel to the president of the United States—were on our knees praying each night, joyous in our faith.

That time in prison taught me the greatest lesson of my life, the great paradox in the truth of what Jesus meant when He said, "Whoever wants to save his life will lose it, but whoever loses his life for me will find it".[4] When I got to the top, achieving wealth and power, I found it all empty and meaningless. But there on a prison floor, kneeling with my fellow convicts, I found a fulfillment I'd never known before.

When I was released from prison in 1975, I had many lucrative job offers. Patty wanted more than anything to live a quiet life, out of the headlines—to simply spend time with our family and friends. But God would not let me find peace. One day it became clear that He was calling me into the prisons. So, with Patty's agreement, we started Prison Fellowship. Our goal was to go into prisons, tell inmates about Christ, help start discipleship groups, and restore inmates to their families, letting the world see God's transforming power in the lives of the most unlikely people.

Along with two Christian friends we rented a small office, using royalties from my first book, *Born Again,* to get started. We began by taking inmates out of prison and bringing them to Washington for two weeks of discipleship training. Night after night, we took these men to local churches, where they would tell others what had happened to them.

Prison Fellowship grew rapidly, and we were soon teaching seminars in prisons. This began to spread across the country. Thus it was that I found myself on that hot August night just a few short years after my conversion, on a stage in a roasting Atlanta prison, preaching to the toughest crowd imaginable—and calling them losers.

"Yes," I said, "*losers*. But Jesus came into the world for men such as us—for all of us who have failed in life.

"Jesus rode into Jerusalem on a donkey," I told them. "He did this so people would know He came from the dirt and the mud, that He had been with weak and ordinary people and those who hurt and suffered.

"The message of Jesus Christ is for the imprisoned—for your families, some of whom aren't making it on welfare. Christ reached out for you who are in prison, because He came to take those chains off, to take you out of bondage. He can make you the freest person in the entire world, right here in this lousy place."

Some of the men still appeared hateful, but I began to see hope in the eyes of others.

"Jesus, the Savior, the Messiah, the Jesus Christ I follow, is the one who comes to help the downtrodden and the oppressed and to release them and set them free. This is the Jesus Christ to whom I have committed my life. This is the Jesus Christ to whom I have offered up my dream and said, 'Lord, I want to help these men because I have lived among them. I came to know them, I love them. There is injustice in our society, but we can change it. Yes, God, we can change it. I give my life for it.'"

What happened next can only be explained as an extraordinary outpouring from God. Men not only stood throughout the auditorium, but they also climbed on their chairs, clapping and shouting. There were tears in the eyes of many, where before there had been only contempt and distrust.

When I urged the men to pray and receive Christ, they flooded to the front. For more than an hour, I stood in one corner of that auditorium praying with some, counseling others, and simply holding out a friendly hand to many.

An African-American man, tall and lean with ugly scars on his neck and arms, tried to speak to me, but he couldn't. He leaned his head on my shoulder and cried like a baby.

Another inmate—a tough-looking white man—told me, "My whole

thirty-nine years were a waste, twenty of them in joints like this. But those were only a preparation for this night. For the first time in my life, I know someone loves me. It's Jesus. God bless you."

Then there was Joe the Butcher, whose nickname had nothing to do with a meat market. Putting his beefy hands on my shoulders, he announced, "Mr. Colson, I'm gonna do something I ain't never done before. I'm gonna apologize. But wait a minute. I want my friends to be in on this."

Joe turned and shouted, "Pete, Charlie, Frank, come here!" No one argued with Joe. "Over here, Fink. Yeah, you too; get over here." Soon, there were more than a dozen in a half circle around us. "Okay, now," Joe said, pointing his finger into my chest. "Mr. Colson, I thought you was a phony. I told these guys that. Told 'em not to listen. Well, I was wrong. You are our friend, and so is Jesus."

Then the Butcher fell to his knees and prayed for Jesus to come into his life. He asked forgiveness for his sins, thankfully not listing them all—we'd have been there all night. Many of Joe's buddies followed him. The angels in Heaven must have sung an especially joyous chorus that night. How many men encountered the living Christ that night? We didn't count, but a year later, nearly four hundred prisoners were participating in chapel programs.

Talking and praying with these men—many in tears for the first time in their adult lives—I felt overwhelming love. I realized that these men were my brothers; God loved them as much as He loved me. I didn't want to leave; I wanted to be with them. I had grown up with no siblings, but these men were my brothers, and I truly loved them.

I told Chaplain Riggs and his core group that I didn't want to leave. They said, "No, dear brother—go. Go, because we need you out there. Go, and God bless you."

Later that night, I lay in a Motel 6 just off the highway, so excited about the incredible way God worked that I couldn't sleep. Little did I know how God would use that night, nor all He had in store for me.

Joining God's Team

Looking back, I can now see clearly the two great lessons from my life. The first was the paradox I discovered in prison: If you really want to find your life, you have to lose it for Christ's sake. After years of success and power, clawing my way to the top, I ended up empty and desperate. But when I surrendered my life to Christ, I found it in prison, real peace and joy—and purpose.

The second great lesson is also a paradox. God didn't choose to use me when I was at the top. He used me when I was broken and at the bottom.

In prison, it wasn't the physical environment that bothered me so much, or even the danger to my life. What bothered me was my despair over what I could do with my life. I'd been an idealist since I was a kid during World War II, when I had helped to raise money to buy a jeep for the Army by selling all my model airplanes.

After college, I went into the Marines to serve, to make this a better country. And my deepest passion in politics was to do something significant to change the lives of people, to make our country a better and stronger place. But here I was in prison, disgraced. I was convinced I would never have a chance to do great things again. Sure, I could make a living; I had plenty of job offers. But never again, I thought, would I have a chance to really affect how people lived.

What I didn't understand was that nothing is beyond the power of God. In fact, God chose me precisely when I was weakest and most broken. Why? Because then my own pride was out of the way and I could never glory in anything I did in the future. And I haven't. God has used my life for His much greater purpose—to spread prison ministries around the world, far beyond anything I could ever dream of. Indeed, he uses the weak and broken to shame the wise and mighty.

So no matter your circumstance in life, whether you're successful and powerful, as I was, or poor and powerless, you need to be broken inside. You need to surrender yourself and give up your life. If you *are* powerless and desperately broken, this may be the greatest opportunity for you to get off a losing team and onto a winning one. The great paradox is that God will use your weakness, not your strength.

How can you get on God's team? You need to acknowledge that you can't do it yourself, that you have broken God's holy laws. That's what I realized while sitting in my automobile in my friend's driveway. As we read in the New Testament, "All have sinned and fall short of the glory of God".[5] For all of us, the punishment for breaking God's laws is eternal separation from Him: "The wages of sin is death".[6]

But God loves us and does not want to be eternally separated from us.

Two thousand years ago, He sent His Son, Jesus Christ, to take the punishment for the sins of all humanity. In 1 Corinthians 15:3-6, we read that Christ died an excruciating death on the cross for our sins. Yet God raised His Son from death three days later. Jesus then appeared to His closest followers, and then to more than five hundred others.

So we must accept the great gift of Christ's sacrifice. When we do, God will forgive our sins and we will receive His guidance for our lives (through prayer, reading the Bible, and regularly gathering with others to worship God). And one day, we'll dwell with Him in Heaven.

As I told the inmates in that hot Atlanta prison more than three decades ago, Jesus Christ came into this world to free those imprisoned by sin. He came for losers in need of a Savior.

This former Marine captain and powerful White House aide thought he didn't need God; the convict washing socks in a prison laundry knew how wrong he was. I have now followed Jesus and served Him for thirty-six years. If I didn't know for a fact that Christ had died for my sins, I couldn't live with myself. I'd have suffocated in the stench of my sinful nature. Every single day, I thank God for saving me—for putting me on His team for life.

My prayer is that you, too, will allow God to break you out of the hold sin has on your life—and accept the gift of His Son, Jesus Christ. Without Christ you, too, are in prison, whether you realize it or not. Once you join God's team, you may find as I did that your life will go in a totally new and unexpected direction.

How much significance has God given to the wreck of my life—to the life He broke and rebuilt in His image? More than I ever could have imagined. And He will do the same for you—if you let Him.

God chose the foolish things of the world to shame the wise; God chose the weak things of the world to shame the strong. He chose the lowly things of this world and the despised things—and the things that are not—to nullify the things that are, so that no one may boast before him.[7]

JOE'S TWO-MINUTE DRILL
Salvation: How Do I Get on God's Winning Team?

In the game of life, there are only two teams: a winning team and a losing team. You are either on God's team and will inherit eternal life in Heaven, or you are going to be on the losing team. The good news is that God wants you on His team! Let me recap several truths about salvation that Chuck points out for us:

- ✓ We all have failed God and fall short of what He expects from us.
- ✓ Living life by any plan other than God's plan leaves us empty and asking, *"Is this all there is to life?"*
- ✓ Jesus came into this world to save those who know they fall short of God's expectations. He came so that we can become players on God's team.
- ✓ Jesus was and is who He claimed to be—God. He was also a man.
- ✓ In order to get on God's team, we need to accept Christ—admit we need Him, confess our sins, and ask Him to come and live in us. This process is so simple even a child can understand it.
- ✓ God *will* forgive you—no matter what you have done.
- ✓ Jesus will change your life. He will give you significance and renewed purpose.

CHAPTER EIGHT

Relationships

It's no accident that I chose one of my closest friends to contribute the chapter on relationships. I met Don Meredith after we won our first Super Bowl and after I had made a huge investment in an Oklahoma real estate venture that went sour—a deal that my wife had opposed from the beginning.

By the time I'd met Don and found him to be a humble, wise, soft-spoken brother in Christ, I needed his help in ways I never would have dreamed. I had gotten so deep into the real estate deal that, when it began to unravel, it nearly sent me into bankruptcy. At the same time, I was gearing up for the next football season, and the Redskins had a Super Bowl title to defend. I had hoped the big investment would pay for itself and I wouldn't have to manage it. I certainly didn't have time.

I asked Don if he would go to Oklahoma and see what could be done. It's one thing to ask a friend for a few dollars or a day or two of his time. I didn't realize I was asking my new friend to spend more than two months away from home, trying to unravel a colossal mess.

Had it not been for Don's kindness and the Lord's leading, I never would have survived the long process of extricating myself from that financial trap. And even as it was, I sustained a huge loss.

That real estate fiasco taught me the value of true friendship as embodied in a man like Don Meredith. The Bible says, "A friend loves at all times, and a brother is born for adversity."[1]

I also learned the hard way to trust my wife's intuition and to listen to her.

Pat's a discerning person, and when she makes up her mind, she's tough. So I had to laugh when, just a short while after the Oklahoma deal was settled, a friend of ours approached us with an oil deal he thought would make us some money. I knew there was no way that Pat Gibbs was going to let us get involved in that one.

After my friend told me how the oil deal would work, I had a great idea: Let's punt this one to Pat. "From here on out," I said, "we're making our financial decisions together."

So he came over to the house and shared the details. We would try to win an oil lease by participating in a lottery. The whole time he was explaining it, I was laughing to myself, anticipating Pat's response. As soon as he finished, Pat looked at me and said, "I think we need to do this."

"What?" I said. "This is crazy." I was pretty leery after the Oklahoma debacle.

The long and short of it was that I deferred to Pat and we did the deal. Can you believe it? Just a few months later, we hit the lottery and got our investment back plus a great return. From then on I said, "She's the one on finances!"

Not long ago, Pat and I were disagreeing about some trivial thing, and I grumbled something to my son J.D. about it. He gave me a look and said, "Dad, she has sacrificed her entire life for you." He was right. Think about her life with me—waiting for hours outside of football locker rooms and being dragged to racetracks all over the country.

Can you imagine Pat having to sit outside the locker room after I made that bad call in the Buffalo game? She has been there through all the ups and downs, helping me get it right when I'm off and helping me to keep a long view of life.

When you talk about relationships, friendships and marriage naturally come to mind. But another topic that inevitably comes up is sex.

Our culture today is sex crazed. You almost can't sit down in front of the TV without having to cover your kids' eyes and ears. A single sporting event might have beer commercials with strong sexual messages; aftershave commercials showing a guy with a half-dressed girl; and—more recently— repeated commercials for erectile dysfunction drugs, with disclaimers that make every member of the family blush.

I love to laugh and enjoy a funny show or movie as much as the next guy.

But today, in sitcoms, it's a foregone conclusion that the guy and the girl—or sometimes even the guy and the guy—will wind up sleeping together. Though a lot of people I know don't support those kinds of values, Hollywood knows that sex sells.

And forget about watching the news with kids around. Who knows what sordid stories they'll dredge up and how much you'll end up having to explain.

Here's my point: Our culture has degraded sex, which God intended to be an incredible gift for the ultimate relationship—marriage. Instead, sex has become a crude punch line, or more than we need to hear in a lurid news story. Rarely, if ever, do we discuss the problems that come from following sexual lust to its conclusion—such as broken marriages, sexually transmitted diseases, out-of-wedlock births, and abortion.

I've always admired Hall of Fame quarterback Roger Staubach of the Dallas Cowboys—as much for his character off the field as his play on it. Roger was once asked about his views on sex. He said, "I like sex as much as the next guy does. But I like it with one woman—my wife."

How often do you hear an answer like that?

I happened to be in a church service one time when an attractive young lady stood and told her life story. She had been sexually involved with a great race car driver named Tim Richmond. (A lot of people think the character of Cole Trickle in the movie *Days of Thunder* was loosely based on Tim.) He was a phenom—a natural-born racer—and many thought he could have been one of the best that NASCAR had ever seen.

The thing was, Tim Richmond died of AIDS in 1989.

By his own admission, he had lived a wild life of sex, drugs, and rock and roll. He was the ultimate party guy. Those who knew Tim said he was always pushing the limits, racing—and living—on the edge.

Now, a few years later, here was a woman telling us that she had slept with Tim Richmond *one time,* and now she had AIDS, contracted from him. She was a committed Christian, with her hope in Christ, and had since married, but her point was that it takes just one misstep, one night, to change a whole life.

Ever see that in a TV show?

Or how about the harm an extramarital affair can do to the people involved?

In the NASCAR world, there's a lot of travel, with many days and nights away from home. This can lead people to a lot of temptation. Once, we had to address an extramarital affair that one of our valued employees—a leader—was having. We warned him, but eventually we had to let him go when it became clear the adultery hadn't stopped. I've said that, as a head coach, you have to look out for your people. The families of our racing team need to know that we keep high standards so they can have peace at home when we are on the road.

This incident caused a lot of difficulty for our race team, not to mention the devastating consequences as it played out with the man's family.

In the Bible, God has detailed the right game plan for building worthwhile relationships that last. When Jesus was asked which of the laws was most important, He said, "'Love the Lord your God with all your heart and with all your soul and with all your mind and with all your strength. . . . Love your neighbor as yourself.' There is no commandment greater than these."[2]

This is one of many instances in the Bible where we see that God has created us to be in relationship with Him first and others second. Many are tempted to sit on the sidelines and avoid relationships, but that is clearly not God's plan.

When we follow God's game plan for relationships—as Don Meredith will explain—we find that our relationships work out better and are more satisfying. Tell me, what could be better than a lasting, valued friendship—and sex—with a faithful and loving spouse?

Don Meredith is a guy who takes ideas and makes them a reality. He was a founder of Campus Crusade's FamilyLife Ministry, which has taught Christian marriage principles to millions. Many of those principles were developed and taught by Don. His book Two Becoming One *has been widely used in marriage seminars. Don was also instrumental in starting the Fellowship Bible Churches in Dallas, Little Rock, and other cities. In D.C., when I was coaching the Redskins, he helped me start a home for at-risk boys and girls, called Youth for Tomorrow. Christian Family Life is Don's nonprofit organization dedicated to teaching Christian marriage concepts to couples. CFL has also developed small-group materials on marriage, for churches. Don helped me start Joe Gibbs Racing, and his son and my boys work together there. I sometimes introduce Don as Pat's and my full-time marriage counselor because of all the guidance he has given us over the years.*

What Does God Say about Marriage and Sex?

DON MEREDITH

Today, it seems you have a better chance of winning the lottery than seeing your marriage succeed. For every marriage that begins with all the hopes and dreams of making it last, only about half actually do. Okay, so those are way better odds than the lottery, but it's likely you or someone you know will experience the bitter pain of a broken marriage.

No coach creates a game plan hoping to win 50 percent of the time. That's not likely to get you into the playoffs in any sport.

Does it have to be this way? Why are so many couples simply playing at marriage, hoping for—and sometimes actively looking for—greener pastures?

Maybe the problem is that too many of us have been following the wrong game plan for our relationships. Perhaps we've bought into society's notion that the ideal couple is Mr. Stud and Ms. Body—some combination of sports idol, movie star, supermodel, and blonde country-western singer.

The Hollywood model is focused on looks, material success, and sex appeal, but the odds are that today's hot couples won't even still be together a year from now.

Yet we're led to believe that if we can just tap into that glamorous game plan, we're guaranteed a marital Super Bowl ring. The problem is that the glamour game doesn't last long, and when the score is tallied, those kinds of relationships rarely succeed, let alone portray the real thing called marriage.

The Right Game Plan

If you've read this far in Coach Gibbs's *Game Plan for Life*, I'm going to assume you're open to the possibility that God has a plan for your life. I can tell you firsthand that He also has a plan for your marriage that produces long-term success. I intend to show you that God Himself is involved in every marriage that is committed to Him. Yes, God designed marriage, and He alone can make it work.

I confess that when Sally and I married in 1967, we had not yet discovered God's plan for our marriage. Like most other couples, we had no specific goals or objectives for our marriage, and we did not depend on God to help our relationship thrive. We suffered as a result, became lost in the weeds of hurtful behavior toward one another, and remained independent from God and His purposes. If you believe in real forces of evil (as I do), you'll understand when I say we were exactly where Satan hoped we would stay—on the road to that day when we would just give up and get divorced.

Instead, we turned to God and His Word and made an amazing discovery. There is only one right game plan for marriage: God's.

My Football Bride

You may think from what I have said that Sally and I weren't even Christians back then. But when we married, at age twenty-seven, we both had a strong faith in God. We assumed marriage would be easier for us than for others. It didn't take long to learn that we were naive and overconfident. To be honest, we struggled from the very day of our wedding.

The ceremony was scheduled at four o'clock on a Saturday afternoon in the early fall. I was running ahead of schedule, so I flipped on the television to catch the first University of Texas football game of the season. Before I knew it, it was 3:45, and I wasn't completely ready for the ceremony. Frustrated that I had to leave the game before halftime, I rushed off to the wedding.

After the ceremony, which was in Boulder, Colorado, we left for Vail, where we had reservations at a lovely hotel. As soon as we pulled out of the church parking lot, I switched on the radio, trying to catch the end of the Longhorns' game. After all, this was to be their year, and I just had to know the score!

No luck. The mountains limited our radio reception, so I decided to stop short of Vail and find another motel, because I didn't want to miss the ten o'clock news and the Texas score. When I suggested stopping early, Sally naturally thought I was eager for the honeymoon night. And, of course, I was. But the football score was what was *really* important!

As soon as we checked in, I clicked on the television and learned the big news: *Texas had lost.* I still remember trying to regain my composure as Sally entered the room. I didn't set out to frustrate my bride, but I couldn't hide my disappointment. My selfish interest in football and Sally's desire to relate to her new husband hardly mixed well, and when the Dallas Cowboys (my favorite NFL team at the time—sorry, Joe; you know I've since converted) lost the next day, to me the honeymoon was over.

By the time we headed home, Sally was one disappointed bride. She sat in silence in the car, and sensitive ol' Don just figured she didn't have anything to say. But from her perspective, the honeymoon (and perhaps even the marriage) was a disaster. She was quickly learning where she fit on my list of priorities, and already seeds of conflict were beginning to germinate. Oh, I meant well; I didn't want to hurt her. But I did!

Meaning Well and Falling Short

In spite of our good intentions, we began to find it hard to live together. My football fanaticism caused Sally to let me know how she felt, and I remember soon thinking that I couldn't let things continue the way they were going. I was amazed at how my feelings of love for Sally could change so quickly when I was hurt. A marriage in conflict can be intensely painful. Rejection, insults, insecurities, and lost devotion ravage one's emotions.

As our relationship worsened, our tendency to focus on performance increased. We began noticing every failure and flaw in each other. (Sound familiar?) Rather than focusing on God and His promises, we focused on each other's weaknesses.

Thankfully, however, we didn't give up. We realized our situation would soon become desperate, so we ran to the only source of help we knew—the Bible. There we discovered some key insights that helped us form the basis of a great marriage that has lasted the test of more than forty years.

Our pain led us to discover God's plan for marriage. As soon as we began to gain insights, our marriage enjoyed incredible changes. We knew we needed to share these principles with others, and just four years after our rocky beginning we launched an organization called Christian Family Life. Then, in 1976, we were asked by the staff of Campus Crusade for Christ to help launch FamilyLife, along with Dennis and Barbara Rainey and others. Today, through Christian Family Life and FamilyLife, thousands of couples have seen their marriages change for the better.

God's game plan for marriage begins by understanding why He designed marriage in the first place. So, to get an idea of what the objectives of the marriage game are, we need to go back to the beginning: Genesis 1 and 2.

God's Purposes for Marriage

When Sally and I took the time to really study the Bible, we learned that God not only created the institution of marriage, but He also has three important purposes He wants every marriage to accomplish. Just like every NFL player knows that the ultimate goal is to win a Super Bowl ring, and every NASCAR driver wants to lead his team to a Cup Series championship, we know that our marriages will succeed when they fulfill God's goals.

Purpose #1: Reflect

The first reason God created marriage was for a man and a woman to reflect His image together as a couple. "God said, 'Let us make man in our image, in our likeness, and let them rule over the fish of the sea and the birds of the air, over the livestock, over all the earth, and over all the creatures that move along the ground.' So God created man in his own image, in the image of God he created him; male and female he created them."[3]

It should be clear from the above context that *man* means *people,* because, plainly, God created *man* as male and female.

Notice that God uses the word *image* three times and the word *likeness* once to emphasize that He wants mankind to *reflect His image.* It's also clear, from the plural pronouns used for God (*us* and *our*), that God intended mankind to reflect the oneness of the Trinity: the Father, Son, and Holy Spirit. Not to get too theological, but each person of the Trinity is unique in function, yet one in nature and purpose.

Likewise, a husband and wife are unique in function, yet represent one purpose. Genesis 1:27 mentions that "male and female he created them." Even though God made Adam and Eve to reflect His image individually, He also created them to reflect His *unity* or *oneness* in a profound and mysterious way.[4]

Married couples best reflect God's image by *becoming one.* In creating Adam and Eve as the parents of all humanity, God desired for them to model oneness to all couples who would follow. When couples reflect oneness— the oneness of the triune God—God is truly glorified.

On the other hand, when strife replaces unity in marriage, a couple misses their greatest opportunity to reflect a loving God and experience how wonderful He intends for marriage to be. To me, that means that divorce is not an option for Sally and me. I would be incomplete without her, and we would lose our ability to fully reflect God's image.

Purpose #2: Reproduce

Genesis 1:28 says, "God blessed them and said to them, 'Be fruitful and increase in number; fill the earth.'" So God also designed marriage to produce children, whom God regards as a *blessing* second only to the marriage relationship itself.

With nearly seven billion people on the earth, you might think this purpose for marriage has been met. But look closer and you'll see that God's plan is not only for marriages to reflect His image and produce children, but also to produce disciples. In this way, God makes marriage a strategic element in the fulfillment of the Great Commission spoken by Jesus in Matthew 28:19-20: "Therefore go and make disciples of all nations, baptizing them in the name of the Father and of the Son and of the Holy Spirit, and teaching them to obey everything I have commanded you. And surely I am with you always, to the very end of the age."

In the same way that we nurture our children at home, we are to nurture and train disciples of Jesus to further God's Kingdom on earth.

Purpose #3: Rule

God's third purpose for marriage is also found in Genesis 1:28: to subdue the earth and rule over every living creature. God intended for Adam and Eve to have dominion over the earth and its creatures—in other words, to rule. Believe it or not, this still applies to our marriages today. God makes it clear throughout Scripture that married couples are to rule with Him over everything He has created, including property, children, income and assets, as well as social and political influences. All earthly resources are to be used to bring honor to God, and marriage is to be a fundamental building block of civilization.

God's charge to "subdue and rule" the earth includes not only the physical domain but the spiritual realm as well. Throughout the Old and New Testaments, men are told to "be strong and courageous"[5], "put on the full armor of God," and "take [their] stand against the devil's schemes."[6]

Maybe until now you've been unaware of God's three purposes for marriage, and now you're feeling overwhelmed, wondering, *How can I possibly carry out these purposes for my marriage when I can't even get through one day without fighting with or insulting my wife?* Great question. Knowing these purposes is the first step. Understanding and applying "oneness" to your marriage is the key to fulfilling them.

Oneness: A Crucial Concept

While Genesis 1 shows how married couples best fulfill God's purposes for creation by reflecting, reproducing, and ruling, Genesis 2 teaches us how to experience the *oneness* that allows us to fulfill these purposes. Oneness is a God-given state of unity based on His promises. Oneness enables us to live together in true harmony and fruitfulness, despite our personal limitations and sin. Though the word may sound foreign to you at first, let me explain it, because it has proved to be one of the most powerful tools Sally and I received from God to make our marriage succeed.

Oneness is revealed in Genesis 1:26-28, where we see that God viewed the first couple—Adam and Eve—as one. He referred to the couple as "them" ("let them rule" and "God blessed them"). In Genesis 2, we find four clear steps toward reaching oneness.

Step 1: God creates a need

God created in each of us a deep-rooted need for a spouse. This becomes clear in Genesis 2:18. At the time of Creation, Adam was different from you and me. First, he was without sin (a really big difference!). Second, he lived in a perfect environment—before the Fall. Adam could actually experience God with at least two of his five senses (sight and hearing). Scripture suggests that Adam walked and talked with God.[7] Everything seemed just right for Adam.

However, for the first time in all that had He created, God observed that something was "not good." "The LORD God said, 'It is not good for the man to be alone. I will make a helper suitable for him.'"[8] The word *suitable* here means "to complete or to correspond to." By calling attention to Adam's being alone, God emphasized clearly that humanity was not yet complete.

Step 2: God reveals our need

After creating in Adam a need for a suitable helper, how did God show Adam his need? "Now the LORD God had formed out of the ground all the beasts of the field and all the birds of the air. He brought them to the man to see what he would name them; and whatever the man called each living creature, that was its name. So the man gave names to all the livestock, the birds of the air and all the beasts of the field. But for Adam no suitable helper was found."[9]

As Adam began naming the animals, it became clear to him that not one corresponded with him. Surely he noticed that there were two distinct kinds of every animal, yet there was no one for Adam to talk to, no one to eat with, and no one to complete him as a companion. Through this experience, Adam learned of his need for a partner. I believe God showed Adam his need so he would trust God for the fulfillment of it.

Step 3: God provides

Genesis 2:21-22 records that "the LORD God caused the man to fall into a deep sleep; and while he was sleeping, he took one of the man's ribs and closed up the place with flesh. Then the LORD God made a woman from the rib he had taken out of the man, and he brought her to the man." Clearly, Adam had nothing to do with the provision of Eve. It was all God's doing.

The most strategic statement in the passage seems odd at first. God "brought her to the man." Why not create Eve right next to Adam? Why did God take Adam's rib, go somewhere else to form her, and then *bring* her to Adam? I believe it was because God wanted Adam to know that it was He who had created Eve, and also He who would present her as His greatest gift.

If you want a thriving marriage, view your wife as *the perfect provision for you* from your heavenly Father who loves you. Understanding this leads to the fourth and final step to reaching oneness.

Step 4: We receive

Once we see that God has provided for our need, we must *receive* His provision. Your wife is your perfect provision from God. There is no greener pasture or better soul mate for you. Your heavenly Father has provided the perfect person for you to live life with, so receive her as such.

Notice how Adam embraced God's provision: "This is now bone of my bones and flesh of my flesh; she shall be called 'woman,' for she was taken out of man."[10] The English text does not fully communicate Adam's excitement. The idea here is, "Great! Fantastic! Thank You, Lord! I'll take her!" Adam's acceptance of Eve was based on his trust in God, not on Adam's ability to inspect Eve. God had created Adam, created his need, and showed him his need. And God then met his need in Eve.

It's one thing to glean from Scripture that there are three purposes for your marriage and four steps to reaching oneness, but now what? You might be thinking, *If she is the perfect wife for me, why do we have so much conflict? And how can we overcome this?* These questions lead to one of the most important concepts of Christian marriage: learning to love one another through the eyes of faith—or, as Sally and I have come to call it, having a "faith relationship."

Freedom to Stop Trying to Change Your Wife

Even if God has given you just the person to meet your needs, it does not mean that she is perfect. In fact, no one is perfect. "For all have all sinned and fall short of the glory of God."[11] Under the pressure of married life, our imperfections become painfully obvious, leading to conflict and disappointment.

The natural response of couples throughout the ages has been to try to change the other person.

- "If he would only finish that project . . ."
- "If she would only stop trying to change me all the time . . ."
- "If he would just listen for once . . ."
- "If she would just be stricter with the kids . . ."

Yet nowhere in the Bible are we told to change other people. Change starts with *ourselves,* through the power of God. This lesson has become crystal clear to me through my own marriage, and through hundreds of counseling sessions with others whose marriages have been in tough places.

Years ago, I viewed Sally's weaknesses as a limitation to me, with little hope of ever changing them. Sally saw my problems the same way. The notion of God meeting our needs *through* our mutual weaknesses made no sense. Yet Scripture seemed to tell us that we were the perfect provision for the other. I began praying for the faith to stop seeing Sally's weaknesses as a limitation, and instead to see how those same weaknesses could somehow become a blessing to me. When I took my eyes off of Sally's performance and looked to God to help me be a better husband, Sally asked God to help her be a better wife. The results were remarkable.

As I began to see Sally through the eyes of faith, I immediately experienced a new freedom and hope in my marriage. I gave up trying to change her and accepted her by faith as a gift from God. As time passed, our marriage became great.

What changed?

God certainly didn't.

But as my faith in Him grew stronger, my perception of the value of His gift to me changed dramatically for the better. The attributes in Sally I would have changed in the beginning have become the very things I love most about her now.

When Sally and I first married, I quickly realized she was not goal-oriented. I couldn't understand that. I had always been a goal setter. I tried to get her to establish personal goals, but that didn't work. After asking God to change me to look at her (perceived) weaknesses differently, I finally realized that I loved her flexibility. Imagine two type A personalities setting daily goals. That could have been a disaster! Instead, we complemented each other. She was free to help me achieve my goals by giving advice and encouragement. What I had seen as a weakness was actually one of her strengths.

Consider these five truths when considering your wife's weaknesses:

1. God will meet your relational needs in spite of your wife's weaknesses.
2. God's only agent for changing your wife is unconditional love.
3. God can actually use your wife's weaknesses as a tool to perfect *your* character.
4. Your wife's weaknesses are an opportunity for you to be needed in her life.
5. What you view as a weakness in your wife today may become a great blessing tomorrow.

If you are judging your wife instead of believing God, she is certainly living under the burden of performance. Ask God to forgive you. In faith, accept your wife just as she is and thank God for meeting your needs through this special person. Trust me, if you move from a performance-based relationship toward a faith-based relationship, not only will you improve your marriage, but you'll also stand as a witness, to everyone who knows you and your wife, of the power of God to give everyday people the grace to love unconditionally, even as Christ loves His church.

Leaving and Cleaving

Genesis 2 concludes by revealing a formula for marital oneness: "Therefore shall a man leave his father and his mother, and shall cleave unto his wife: and they shall be one flesh. And they were both naked, the man and his wife, and were not shamed."[12] Here in principle is God's game plan for marriage.

The word *leave* here means to "abandon" or "break dependence upon." Though you should never dishonor your parents, getting married means breaking your dependence on them. In fact, this principle includes severing any strings to a former lifestyle: past relationships, sports, finances, and so on. Countless couples get off to a rocky start because they are unwilling to assume total responsibility for their new household. Your marriage relationship should be placed ahead of all other relationships, including those with your parents, siblings, and friends.

The word *cleave* here means to "stick like glue." This same imagery was used in biblical days to describe melting metals together to form a stronger alloy. Faith in God is required to cleave. Our part is to leave, and God's part is to cleave us together. To the extent that we trust God for the health of our marriages, we will find the faith to "stick like glue."

In the New Testament, Jesus Christ reinforces the application of this principle to all marriages when He says, "Have you not read that He who made them at the beginning *'made them male and female,'* and said, *'For this reason a man shall leave his father and mother and be joined to his wife, and the two shall become one flesh'*? So then, they are no longer two but one flesh. Therefore what God has joined together, let not man separate."[13]

The Gift of Sexual Intimacy

Cleaving also includes a unique attribute of marriage: physical intimacy. Though there are many misguided views on human sexuality today, God's Word does not shy away from describing marital intimacy as one of His greatest gifts to humanity.[14] One passage in particular—1 Corinthians 6:18–7:5—describes God's blueprint for a loving and joyous marital sex life. Here God lays out two basic principles: *body ownership* and *body stewardship*. In short, we men are to save our bodies for our wives and focus on meeting their needs in sexual intimacy.

Body ownership

Our bodies are God's property. Believers in Jesus Christ are commanded to "flee from sexual immorality."[15]. That means avoiding adultery, strip clubs, Internet pornography, and all other forms of sexual immorality.

God is not just being a cosmic killjoy. The Bible gives four reasons[16] for this command:

1. The immoral person sins against his own body (implying the potential for both sexually transmitted diseases as well as sexual addictions);
2. The believer's body is the temple of the Holy Spirit (the dwelling place of God);

3. Therefore, the believer is not his own (implying that he belongs to God); and

4. The reason the believer's body belongs to God is that he has been bought with a price—the crucifixion of Christ.

The believer is then commanded to "glorify God in your body."[17] How do you do this? By fleeing sexual gratification outside of marriage and by finding (and bestowing) it inside of marriage—what we call "body stewardship."[18]

Body stewardship

Once Sally and I were married, God made me the steward of her body, and vice versa. I was not free to meet my own sexual needs at my wife's expense. God empowers us to meet each other's sexual needs—not our own selfish needs.

Interestingly, we are instructed not to deprive our wives of sexual intimacy, "except by mutual consent and for a time, so that you may devote yourselves to prayer. Then come together again so that Satan will not tempt you because of your lack of self-control."[19]

Oneness is essential to a successful marriage, but sin always works to erode it. Oneness can be recaptured only through faith in God and by applying His principles to your marriage. Every person has the need to be loved unconditionally. However, that will happen here on earth only if you *choose* to love your wife by faith.

If you were formerly divorced, or not a Christian when you married, or you just aren't sure you married the right person, the principle of oneness still applies. Scripture tells us that God hates divorce, and He desires that you remain married.* But God also forgives failures when they are confessed to Him.[20] He gives us a new beginning and tells us not to look back.

Every Couple Has Hope in God's Game Plan for Marriage

Sally and I have now been married more than four decades, and we have ten grandchildren. We have had the privilege of seeing how God's game

---

*Don't mistake me for saying that a person must remain in a dangerous environment. If you are in an unhealthy, abusive relationship, it is essential that you seek counsel from your pastor, priest, or marriage counselor. And though divorce should only be a last resort, no one should ever tell you to risk your life or your children's lives in an abusive or violent relationship.

plan can turn a marriage around. We couldn't have had a rockier start and couldn't be happier now. Do we occasionally hurt and disappoint each other? Absolutely. We are still mere sinners saved by grace. Yet we've learned over the years to give our hurts and disappointments to God and to focus on His promises for our marriage. In short, we've learned that to unleash the full power of a strong Christian marriage we need to do the following:

- Make a decision to move our hope for marital success from our own personal strategy to God's.
- Rely on the source of our Christian wisdom for our marriage: the Bible, the playbook with the winning strategy.
- Understand the three purposes for marriage and accept them by faith.
- Embrace and act out the four steps to spiritual oneness.
- See our spouse's weaknesses as a blessing and stop inspecting his or her performance. Instead, love unconditionally.
- Leave, cleave, and become one with each other in our marriage.
- Have healthy sexual relations leading to biblical oneness.

Most important, we learned that God cared enough for our marriage to give us the Bible as a playbook to reach victory. God is unchanging: "Jesus Christ is the same yesterday and today and forever."[21]

Yes, God designed marriage; and yes, He can make it work!

JOE'S TWO-MINUTE DRILL
Relationships: What Does God Say about Marriage and Sex?

The Bible is the best source for help and insight for having a successful and fruitful marriage. Marriage was God's idea, and only He can really tell us how it should work. Let me recap several truths about relationships that Don points out to us:

- ✓ The world's game plan for marriage focuses on looks, material success, and sex appeal. Marriages built on these rarely succeed. God designed marriage, and His game plan produces long-term success.
- ✓ The Bible lists three purposes for marriage: to reflect the oneness of the Trinity; to reproduce children who also share faith in God; to honor God in how they care for the things (physical and spiritual) God has entrusted to them.
- ✓ These purposes are fulfilled only as a couple experiences oneness with each another—living in unity despite individual imperfections.
- ✓ Your wife is the perfect provision from God for you—there is no better mate; trust God's plan.
- ✓ Love your wife unconditionally; stop focusing on her imperfections and trying to change her. Ask God to give you the faith to see your wife's weaknesses as a blessing to you.
- ✓ Sexual intimacy is a gift from God. Enjoy it in your marriage.

CHAPTER NINE

Finances

$\mathbf{A}$s so often happens, the deepest waters I've tried to swim through in my life taught me the best lessons I've ever learned.

I don't know if it was because of my upbringing—we didn't have a lot of money, but I barely knew it because my mother somehow managed to make it work—or if I just had stars in my eyes and started coveting all the nice things that everybody else seemed to have, but along with my new job with the Redskins and the early success, I started really hungering to set myself up financially.

I admit it. I wanted to be comfortable, even rich. Problem was, the financial world is hardly where I belong. If I learned nothing else from the mess in Oklahoma—besides what a friend Don Meredith was and that I should always listen to my wife, especially in the area of finances—it's that a man has to play to his strengths. I'm a team builder, a coach, an owner. I'm not a financial genius.

Coaching is a high-pressure game. No matter how good you are, it's a business of "What have you done for me lately?" You can have winning seasons, make the playoffs—even win the Super Bowl, but the only security that buys you is a little more time.

Still, I was dumb enough to think I could find financial security through my own investment "strategies."

I listened to pitches, heard schemes that sounded good, believed "guarantees" and "no-brainers" and "can't-misses." Even after we won Super Bowl XXII, I was still feeling pressure to find financial security, and I was looking in the wrong places. In the oil boom years of the 1980s, Oklahoma turned out to be an exceptionally wrong place for my particular lack of investment savvy.

The deal was pretty simple. A friend of mine from college was building homes and apartment complexes in Norman, Oklahoma. He would build them, and I would pay the closing costs—a few thousand dollars per property. Then he'd lease them until we sold them at a profit. The fees from renting the properties would more than cover our expenses.

This was my kind of deal. I was excited about getting in on the oil and gas boom in Oklahoma. More jobs meant more people needing homes, right? With these two commodities driving the local economy, there was no way we could lose. Also, this venture would require very little of my time or attention. I could concentrate on coaching while my money grew in Oklahoma.

My liability was limited, too. Of course it was! One of the partners told me, "Joe, don't worry. Before you lose a dime, we'll lose everything we own."

Guess what? They did!

For a couple of years, we could hardly keep up with the demand for more building. Such a deal! It was working. But as I said, with oil and gas driving the economy, we couldn't lose. Unless oil and gas quit driving the economy. When the boom busted, the savings and loan debacle quickly followed, much of which involved Oklahoma real estate.

The local economy died.

At first, I was oblivious. I was focused on football and pursuing another Super Bowl championship.

Then I started getting late notices on my payments. I had agreed to become part of a simple partnership, which meant that when the partnership signed for something, I was on the hook for it. Had I followed one of the basic principles in God's game plan for finances—"Do not be among those who give pledges, among those who become sureties for debts"[1]—I would have avoided this personal disaster. But I had been blinded by the possibilities. I was playing the game but ignoring God's financial playbook.

Here I was, trying to coach a professional football team—one of the most time-intensive jobs a man can have—and all of a sudden I had to worry about this land deal. The fact was, I didn't have a spare moment for it, and that's when Don Meredith's friendship really came into play. When the season was finally over and I could join him in Oklahoma, I found a mess I couldn't believe. I was soon losing far more money each month than I was making.

Don had discovered that the partnership was millions of dollars in debt. The interest payments alone were more than $35,000 a month, on top of all the mortgages. More disturbing, after assembling a team of accountants and lawyers to help, he learned that the partnership had borrowed money and, through a maze of holdings, diverted it to pay off other debts.

Pat had tried to talk me out of this investment, but I had pressed her into agreeing. When I finally started to get the true picture—that I was in so far over my head that I couldn't see a way out—I had to make the toughest phone call of my life. I had to tell Pat that not only had she been right, but that I had been a fool and now we were going to be broke, probably even bankrupt.

To her credit, Pat was wonderful about it. She could tell over the phone that the whole mess was tearing me up. "Joe," she said, "Come on home. You've done all you can do. If we need to file for bankruptcy, that's what we'll do." I told her I was determined to fulfill all my obligations and not hide behind bankruptcy, but she said she could even endure that rather than watch me kill myself trying to pay everything back.

The frustrating thing was that it wasn't as if I hadn't received warnings prior to this.

Early in my career as an assistant coach with the St. Louis Cardinals, I really got into racquetball. In fact, some say I became obsessed with it—competing in thirty-five-and-older competitions and winning a number of them. Well, racquetball was a growing sport at the time, and I knew there would be a demand for more courts across the country. A friend in construction suggested we build and manage a racquetball club. Maybe this would lead to a bigger opportunity.

I was to be a minority shareholder with a 10 percent interest. Pat didn't think it was a good use of our savings and really didn't want us to get involved. As I sometimes used to do, I badgered her into doing it, and her resistance finally caved in. We built the court and I won racquetball's National Seniors Championship that year. Our little business took off, and soon we built a second club.

Then, as quickly as the racquetball craze had taken off, it crash-landed.

Our business slowed to a halt. A few of the partners ran out of money. My ten percent share was now making me responsible for 50 percent of the losses! Finally, my partner and I gave up—but not before we had each lost more than $200,000. That was a staggering amount in the late 1970s, even for an assistant coach in the NFL.

Then, a little later, I was looking for ways to capitalize on my reputation as the head coach of a prestigious NFL franchise. Someone told me about the endless possibilities of home nursing care. Well, as you can probably guess, this was a business I knew absolutely nothing about. You can also probably guess how it turned out.

Once again, I put a lot of money into the deal. Once again, we lost a lot of money. I was still looking in the wrong place for my financial security and relying on my less-than-perfect instincts to discern a good deal.

As I look back on these two business ventures, it's clear the Lord was trying to warn me; but I refused to listen.

Back at the hotel in Oklahoma, I remember getting down on my knees and praying, and the tears were rolling. This was it. We were going to lose our home, our cars, everything we had. I'd be humiliated publicly and would embarrass the Redskins organization. I had completely let Pat and the boys down.

I was like George Bailey in *It's a Wonderful Life,* when his uncle misplaces a large deposit. He winds up standing on a bridge in the snow at the end of his wits. He prays, and God sends him a guardian angel. In my case, I learned the most important truth about financial security.

"I admit I've been a fool," I prayed. "I've never felt more stupid in my life. I'll go through with the bankruptcy if I need to. I would like to work this out, but You know I don't have the resources to do it. Only You can straighten this out. Please show me what to do, and I'll do it."

From that point forward, I determined to do my best to understand and live by biblical financial principles. I would individually contact all the creditors of the partnership, admit my mistakes, and see if there were creative ways to work out some sort of payments.

At this point, I received peace in my heart and a renewed sense of God's mercy.

Nine different banks were involved. I owed one of them a $1.2 million note on some apartment complexes. There was also a $70,000 loan and seventeen unsold lots. I met the banker, told him I didn't have the money, and asked if there were some way we could work out a payment plan. He asked to study the documents and for us to return the next day.

When we sat down the next day he said, "You turn over your properties to the bank, free and clear. You give us $95,000, and we'll put that money in a maturing note that pays us dividends for seven years. Does that sound manageable?"

"That's it?"

"That's it," he said. "Do we have a deal?"

The bank was letting us off the hook for a fraction of the value of the note.

Don and I left quickly, before the banker could change his mind.

In the end, because of many miraculous turns of events and generous strangers—including bankers and Christian businessmen who worked creatively with us to plan a long-term, though hardly easy, payoff plan—we avoided filing for bankruptcy. It took more than five years and an awful lot of scrimping and saving and eating crow, but eventually we worked our way out. It was hard and humiliating, knowing I was responsible for putting my family through this mess for so many years, but all I could do was face it and accept the tough lessons.

Today, Pat and I try to live with minimal debt, as does Joe Gibbs Racing. If you ever make it to Charlotte to see the race shop, you'll see what a miracle it is. We've got some pretty sophisticated machinery that costs a heck of a lot, not to mention our four hundred thousand square feet of facilities and hundreds of employees.

Maybe you can relate to my failures with money. Do you have too much credit card debt? Do you wonder what a long-term strategy might be for preserving your savings in a bleak economy so you can put your kids through school or retire with dignity?

Maybe you're facing the prospect of trying to avoid bankruptcy, as I did.

As I write this, the stock market has taken a drastic turn for the worse. A lot of people in different walks of life have seen a quarter—even a third—of their savings simply disappear. Others are just hoping to keep their jobs, or have already lost them. In NASCAR, some teams have lost sponsors because corporations have cut back on marketing dollars. The NFL announced recently it was laying off some staff.

Our survey revealed that finances are the number one concern of men today. They want guidance here. And this is a great area where the Bible can still be applicable to daily life more than two thousand years after it was written.

I'm an optimist, and I believe that although we are going through tough times, America will work its way out of them by learning some important lessons: spend less than you earn, save for the future, and avoid get-rich-quick schemes.

What you may not know is that many key financial principles come from the Bible. Did you know that the Bible speaks to the issue of money more than two thousand times? That's more than it discusses any other subject.

These are not financial shortcuts or "name it and claim it" principles. They are sound values based on an understanding that God is the ultimate owner of everything. They involve discipline and sometimes sacrifice. But they will pay off if you wholeheartedly apply them to your life. Like Pat and I did, you will experience financial benefits as well as spiritual ones.

Ron Blue founded a CPA firm in 1970 that has grown into one of the fifty largest in the United States. In 1979, he founded a biblically based financial planning firm that has grown to manage more than $4 billion in assets for more than five thousand clients, with a staff of more than 175 people in fourteen regional offices. Ron retired from financial planning in 2003 in order to lead Kingdom Advisors, an international effort to equip and motivate Christian financial professionals. He is the author of sixteen books on personal finance, including the best-seller Master Your Money *(now in its thirtieth printing). I have followed the principles he learned from the Bible. They work! Ron, why couldn't I have met you earlier in life—it would have saved me a lot of misery.*

How Do I Master My Money?
RON BLUE

"Vacation, all I ever wanted . . ."

Maybe you don't remember that lyric from The Go-Go's and their 1982 hit song, but I'm guessing that you, like most people, want to provide a fun vacation for your family.

Okay, maybe in a tight economy, a vacation is the last thing on your mind. Maybe you're wondering how you're going to put food on the table next week while still paying your rent or mortgage. Well, stay with me, because I'll get to those issues shortly. But let me begin by telling you what vacations looked like for my family during two very different stages of our lives. I think it will be instructive.

When my three daughters were young, I was riding a wave of success based on hard work. Every summer, Judy and I rented a little house at Lake of the Ozarks in Missouri, took our boat, and enjoyed a week off as a family. The girls learned to water-ski. We relaxed on the dock. Judy and I reconnected.

Several years later, we enjoyed a fabulous summer vacation with all five of our children at a family ranch in Colorado. The kids rode horses. Judy and I walked and talked. We took in great entertainment each night. We all left reenergized.

Our lake and mountain vacations might seem similar, but very different life patterns allowed me to take my family on those trips.

By the time I was thirty-two years old—this was during the lake vacation years—I had worked on Wall Street for the world's largest accounting firm. Judy and I had followed our dreams as we lived in New York, San Francisco, Dallas, and Indianapolis. I had started my own CPA firm and purchased two small banks. I had two country club memberships and a beautiful family. I have to tell you, I was proud of my success. Having grown up in the Midwest, I put my values to work to make me a leader in my field and in my city.

My success was built on an effective pattern I had learned. With consistent hard work, attention to client needs, expertise in my field, talented employees, and social networking, I could almost guarantee financial security. I felt good about where I was headed.

Then my wife became very ill and almost died.

Through that experience, Judy became a believer in Jesus Christ, and she began to share her faith with me. But having endured a legalistic form of Christianity as a child, I was extremely resistant to her newfound faith. I was not about to revert to those kinds of demands on my life.

God lovingly pursued me for about two years, until I finally chose to surrender my life to Him. That point of yielding changed my marriage, my relationship with family members, my friendships, and the way I spent my spare time. It even helped in my understanding of the financial services field. In fact, of all the changes my faith in Jesus Christ has brought to my life over the past forty years, the subtle differences in my understanding of money are the ones I find the most fascinating and compelling.

Our family vacations illustrate this. Those early lake trips were a product of my success habits. I had worked hard to earn money to take my family on such trips, and I don't mind telling you that I reveled in my ability to provide.

Our later ranch trips were provided for in a radically different way. One winter evening, I stood at a crossroads of faith, realizing that my yearly giving pledge to a certain ministry would have to come out of our family vacation budget—it was the only discretionary income available. As I prayed and read my Bible, God impressed upon me to keep my pledge by faith—even though I knew it would cost us our summer trip.

Within days of committing to fulfill our pledge, Judy and I were floored by God's provision of a trip to a ranch in Colorado—all expenses paid. All I had to do was share some of my financial planning teaching with the staff at the ranch.

See the difference? To go to the lake, I worked hard, planned carefully, and controlled each step of the process. To go to the ranch, I worked hard, planned carefully, and surrendered our finances to God. I obeyed, and He provided.

God's economy is so much more flexible, abundant, rich, and freeing than our own. God's program for success is amazingly timeless and refreshingly simple.

When I began to move vocationally in the direction of Christian financial advising, my goal was to see what the Bible had to say about money management. Based on what God had done in my life, I wanted to add a biblical perspective to what I already knew about money. Over time, I realized that the Bible is not just one more weapon in an arsenal of financial information. Rather, biblical principles lay the foundation for all wise financial decisions. Any wisdom I had ever gained about money had its root in biblical truth.

I believe that wise financial thinking and decision making are attainable for everyone—yes, even during this time of what appears to be a horrible economic disaster.

We've been experiencing tremendous volatility in the stock market recently, and this is not the first time. A little more than twenty years ago, the stock market declined 22 percent in one day, and 36 percent from its high point in just a few months. So these are not new times in terms of stock market volatility, but they appear to be because we're experiencing something that feels different and thus threatening.

If there's one thing I know for sure, it's that the greatest barrier to faith is fear. And economic volatility naturally brings fear. The best way I know to overcome the fear is to go to the Bible and determine God's thinking about our current circumstances. Is He surprised by what's been happening? Hardly.

I tell people the same thing whether the markets are going up or down, whether they're in crisis or doing really well. There are really only five fundamental money management principles, and each one is rooted in God's Word:

1. *Live within your income.* Do you have a budget? Are you spending less than you earn?
2. *Avoid debt, or use debt wisely.* Are you avoiding the debt trap?
3. *Save.* Are you saving a portion of your income? Do you have emergency funds?
4. *Set long-term goals.* Are you organizing your financial life around a set of priorities?
5. *Understand that God owns it all.* That means we're just stewards, managers, or trustees of God's resources. Ultimately, even if we lost everything, it would still be okay because it's His.

Now, I'm not suggesting you or I are going to lose it all. As a matter of fact, I think that people who follow the five fundamental principles are in the best position to take advantage of bad economic times. I want to tell you why it's important to reduce your spending, live within your income, get rid of debt, maintain your savings, and set some priorities.

This should be not a time of fear, but rather a time of faith. I was asked recently on a radio show what key economic indicator I look at to determine where the economy is headed. I said I look at my checkbook, because it's the only thing I ultimately have control over. Inflation, deflation, stock market booms and busts, trade balances—I have no control over those; but I do control how I spend my money.

My encouragement to you is this: If you adhere to some fairly clear guidelines, you can achieve financial success. If you can learn to trust biblical wisdom with your finances, you can transcend economies, family circumstances, and life stages. Through forty years of working with people and their money, I have heard thousands of stories—from bankruptcies to billion-dollar gains. Amazingly, the very same truths apply to the most destitute and the most affluent in our world. God's words on finances can become a solid foundation for anyone who seeks wisdom in decision making. Be assured that all my advice as a longtime professional in this area now has its roots in biblical wisdom. The principles in Scripture are timeless, so your decisions can be made confidently and safely.

What Is Stewardship?

If you were to ask fifty people, "What are your financial goals?" the most common answers would probably include getting out of debt, saving enough for retirement, or becoming financially independent.

I've helped many people identify their goals and implement plans to reach those goals. My personal financial goal is to be a wise steward of the resources with which I've been entrusted. A steward is simply a manager or a trustee—someone to whom resources have been entrusted for wise use. The concept of stewardship appears often throughout the Bible. Stewardship is more than just giving a certain percentage of our income to the church or other ministries. The biblical concept is that God owns everything and we are temporary managers of what He has allowed us to have.

If you agree that all we have is from God's hand, you'll quickly grasp my definition of stewardship:

> *Biblical stewardship* is the use of God-given gifts and resources (time, talent, treasure, truth, relationships) for the accomplishment of God-given goals.

God cares about stewardship, and He knows the challenges we have with money. In fact, the Bible mentions money and property more than twenty-three hundred times. One example is a word picture that Jesus provides of what the Kingdom of God is like—and that also tells us what a good and wise steward is like. In Matthew 25:14-30, a property owner goes on an extended trip after entrusting each of his servants with a sum of money. Two of the servants invest what they've been given and double their money. The third servant buries his portion and manages only to preserve his original stake. Upon his return, the owner commends the two servants who doubled their assets, but he is angry with the third servant, who did nothing with what he had been given.

The above definition of biblical stewardship also defines *success*. As God's steward, I want to use whatever He has given me to advance His objectives, trying to accomplish what's He's asked me to do by making wise use of His resources. I want to someday hear Him say, "Well done, good and faithful servant!"[2]

Biblical wisdom is always relevant, always right, and will never change.

God Owns It All

If it's true that God owns it all, then He has the right to whatever He wants, whenever He wants it. It's all His. Owners have *rights;* stewards have only *responsibilities.* As stewards of God's resources, we may receive some benefits while meeting our responsibilities; but as the owner, God retains possession. It's like the property where I now live. I manage my backyard for now, but that land was here long before I came into the world, and it will be here long after I'm gone.

The second implication of God's ownership of everything is that not only is our *giving* a spiritual decision, but *every spending choice is a spiritual decision.* In the parable from Matthew 25, notice how much leeway the master gives the stewards. He doesn't set limits or state restrictions. To me, that means that even buying a car, taking a vacation, buying food, paying off debt, paying taxes, and so on are all spiritual decisions. God owns all that we have, and we're responsible to use His resources wisely.

Wise stewardship is an indicator of spiritual health. Your checkbook reveals all that you really believe about stewardship. Here are the key characteristics of a good steward:

- Proportionate giving
- Controlled, debt-free lifestyle

- Taxes paid with integrity and even thanksgiving
- Financial goals set as a family
- Accountability

Money Is Part of Our Growth Process

I believe that God uses money and material possessions in our lives as a *tool,* a *test,* and a *testimony* (an example to others). The apostle Paul seems to have mastered this growth process:

> I am not saying this because I am in need, for I have learned to be content whatever the circumstances. I know what it is to be in need, and I know what it is to have plenty. I have learned the secret of being content in any and every situation, whether well fed or hungry, whether living in plenty or in want.[3]

Money and material possessions are effective tools that God uses to help us grow. Money is not only a tool; it is also a test:

> If you have not been trustworthy in handling worldly wealth, who will trust you with true riches? And if you have not been trustworthy with someone else's property, who will give you property of your own?[4]

Our attitude toward wealth becomes an example to others, our way of testifying to the world how we feel about God. What kind of an attitude do we display when God withholds a desire? Do we verbally give Him the credit when He sends financial blessing—or (just as important) prevents our undoing?

Has God worked a financial miracle for you? Don't discount it as coincidence. Don't forget it years down the road when you enjoy more affluence.

It's also important to understand what money is not:

- Money is not a measure of our self-worth.[5]
- Money is not a reward for godly living.[6]
- Money is not a guarantee of contentment.[7]
- Money should never define us.[8]

Faith Requires Action

The lazy and wicked servant in Jesus' story knew he had his owner's money. But simply *knowing* that God owns it all isn't enough. The servant knew better, but he did nothing. Many of us *know* what we ought to do, but we disobey or delay, often out of fear. I have learned that faith and fear cannot coexist.

Four Principles of Financial Success

Beyond the big-picture definitions of stewardship and the purposes of money, I believe there are financial steps that work in any region, in any economy, in the past and in the Internet age, in any political administration, and in any interest-rate environment. I'm convinced that all people can improve their financial position by doing four things:

1. Spending less than they earn
2. Minimizing their use of debt
3. Maintaining emergency savings
4. Thinking long-term

I've spoken of these simple financial principles to U.S. Congressmen and to football stadiums full of men. These principles are so simple that they may easily be overlooked, yet they have stood the test of time. After all, they were developed thousands of years ago and outlined in the Bible.

I've had professional clients, such as doctors and engineers, who at first think these four steps are too simplistic. They want to make financial success as challenging and sophisticated as other aspects of their professions. But simple or not, you can't go wrong if you follow these steps. What kind of financial trouble would you ever get in if you spent less than you earned, minimized debt, kept savings available and liquid, and thought about the long term?

Five Buckets

Perhaps thinking about managing your money is overwhelming. You're bombarded by information from the Internet, advertising, water-cooler talk, and pitches by financial service companies. Let me simplify things for you. There are really only five uses of money. If you can picture each of these uses as a bucket you're trying to fill, maybe that will make it easier. In the short term, your income will flow into one of these five buckets:

1. Giving
2. Taxes
3. Saving or investing
4. Debt repayment
5. Living expenses/Lifestyle choices

THE ONLY 5 SHORT-TERM USES OF MONEY
5 BUCKETS TO BE FILLED

INCOME

GIVING　　TAXES　　INVEST/SAVE　　DEBT　　LIVING EXPENSES

How much of your money should go into each bucket? I can't give you exact amounts, but though the Bible doesn't directly command a certain percentage, it gives us many principles and guidelines about each of these five areas.

First, we're instructed to *give:*

> Honor the Lord from your wealth, and from the first of all your produce.[9]

> On the first day of every week each one of you is to put aside and save, as he may prosper, so that no collections be made when I come.[10]

Second, we're instructed to *pay taxes:*

> Render to all what is due them: tax to whom tax is due; custom to whom custom; fear to whom fear; honor to whom honor.[11]

> Render to Caesar the things that are Caesar's; and to God the
> things that are God's.[12]

Third, we're instructed to *save:*

> Go to the ant, you sluggard; consider its ways and be wise! It has
> no commander, no overseer or ruler, yet it stores its provisions in
> summer and gathers its food at harvest.[13]

Fourth, we're instructed to *pay our debts* (not doing so makes you no
better than the wicked):

> The wicked borrows and does not pay back, but the righteous is
> gracious and gives.[14]

Fifth, we're to provide for our *family's needs* (this is the lifestyle bucket):

> If anyone does not provide for his own, and especially for those
> of his household, he has denied the faith and is worse than
> an unbeliever.[15]

From our talents, skills, and opportunities, God provides our income. But
we have great freedom. Along with that freedom comes responsibility. We're
responsible to prioritize the use of our income and other resources to obey
God's commands to give, pay taxes, repay debt, and provide for our family's
needs. The balance left is the amount available to be set aside for the future
or to fund the lifestyle we believe God would have us live, based on the full
counsel of Scripture.

For most people, however, their lifestyle becomes their top priority.
They let their giving fall to fourth or fifth place. The reasoning typically goes
like this: "I'd like to give, but by the time I pay my taxes, repay my debts, and
provide for my family, there's just not enough left over."

Because our lifestyles are funded with after-tax dollars, it takes more
income than many people realize to finance the typical American household. To have $30,000 to spend, you must earn $42,857 if you're in a 30
percent combined tax rate (federal, state, and local). I don't believe the
Bible expects you to live at a poverty level. But neither does it expect you

to live in luxury. You can prayerfully determine an appropriate lifestyle for your family and control spending from the lifestyle bucket by taking the following steps:

- Estimate your living expenses.
- Record your actual spending.
- Refine your spending, based on biblical priorities.
- Control your spending.
- Evaluate your results, and revise, revise, revise.

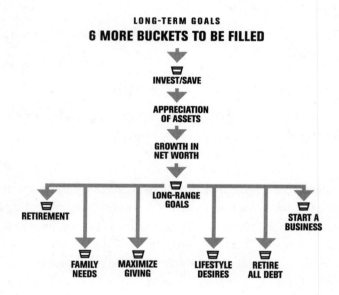

Simplifying the Long Term

We've looked at the five short-term uses of money. When there is a surplus, or margin, your net worth grows. Talking about surpluses and margins in the present economy may sound ridiculous, but with careful planning and following the biblical principles, you can actually see this happen. And as your net worth grows, you can use the accumulated assets to meet your long-term goals.

Though everyone's goals are unique, most tend to fall under one of the following categories:

- Financial independence
- Debt elimination
- Starting a business
- Family needs (college education, dependent care)
- Lifestyle choices (travel, cars, boats, vacation homes, eating out)
- Maximized giving

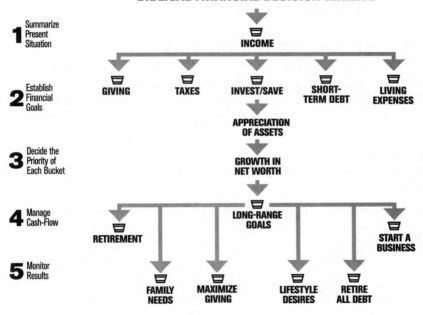

BIBLICAL FINANCIAL DECISION MAKING

The Biblical Financial Decision Making chart illustrates three important implications:

1. *There are no independent financial decisions.* If you decide to spend in one area, naturally you cannot use that same money in other areas. If you decide to spend on lifestyle desires, you no longer have that money available for paying off debt, investing for college, or any other short-term or long-term goals.
2. *The farther out you plan, the more likely you are to make a good financial decision now.*

3. *Financial decisions have lifetime implications.* You may have heard it said that when a football team passes the ball, three things can happen (completion, incompletion, or interception) and two of them are bad. Well, of the five things you can choose to do with your money, three involve spending it and two involve keeping it and seeing it grow. You don't need me to tell you that once you spend it, it's gone forever. I counsel my clients that *decisions determine destiny.* Once you decide to either save or spend, you have set your financial destiny.

Wise Financial Decision Making

You can put off financial planning, but you still make financial decisions every day. The previous diagram is all about financial decisions, not planning. The late Peter Drucker, a distinguished management consultant, once said, "A decision is a judgment. It is a choice between alternatives. It is rarely a choice between right and wrong. It is at best a choice between 'almost right' and 'probably wrong.'"[16]

Many things get in the way of making wise money decisions: time pressure, too many options, no process or a poor process, asking or answering the wrong questions, or basing your choices on your emotions.

When was the last time you had ten minutes alone to really think about a decision? Try a media fast. Turn off the radio, TV, iPod, cell phone, and Internet. Schedule a slot between soccer practice, Wal-Mart, and piano lessons.

Include God in your decision making. Seek His will, not just your own. See decision making as a team sport, with you on God's team. That may seem foreign to you, but be alert for His guidance as you read Scripture, pray, and respond to His promptings. And listen to counselors. Often, God will put just the right person in your path.

Key Questions When Making a Financial Decision

What do you think God would have you do? Some alternatives will have black-and-white moral implications from biblical commands. Obviously, God would never have you cheat. Other, more neutral decisions, such as which college to attend or which career moves to make, involve alternatives that may not be black and white. If you ask only, *What should I do?* you're limited to your own alternatives. You want to determine what God would have you do.

- What is the best use of this money?
- How does this decision align with your priorities?
- Are you and your spouse unified about this?
- Will you regret this decision years from now?
- What's the best outcome from this decision? What's the worst? How likely are these outcomes?

5 Biblical Tests for Decision Making

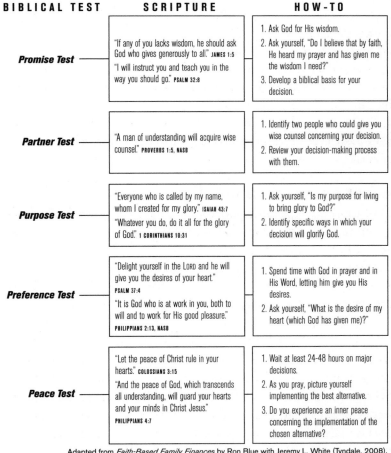

BIBLICAL TEST	SCRIPTURE	HOW-TO
Promise Test	"If any of you lacks wisdom, he should ask God who gives generously to all." JAMES 1:5 "I will instruct you and teach you in the way you should go." PSALM 32:8	1. Ask God for His wisdom. 2. Ask yourself, "Do I believe that by faith, He heard my prayer and has given me the wisdom I need?" 3. Develop a biblical basis for your decision.
Partner Test	"A man of understanding will acquire wise counsel." PROVERBS 1:5, NASB	1. Identify two people who could give you wise counsel concerning your decision. 2. Review your decision-making process with them.
Purpose Test	"Everyone who is called by my name, whom I created for my glory." ISAIAH 43:7 "Whatever you do, do it all for the glory of God." 1 CORINTHIANS 10:31	1. Ask yourself, "Is my purpose for living to bring glory to God?" 2. Identify specific ways in which your decision will glorify God.
Preference Test	"Delight yourself in the LORD and he will give you the desires of your heart." PSALM 37:4 "It is God who is at work in you, both to will and to work for His good pleasure." PHILIPPIANS 2:13, NASB	1. Spend time with God in prayer and in His Word, letting him give you His desires. 2. Ask yourself, "What is the desire of my heart (which God has given me)?"
Peace Test	"Let the peace of Christ rule in your hearts." COLOSSIANS 3:15 "And the peace of God, which transcends all understanding, will guard your hearts and your minds in Christ Jesus." PHILIPPIANS 4:7	1. Wait at least 24-48 hours on major decisions. 2. As you pray, picture yourself implementing the best alternative. 3. Do you experience an inner peace concerning the implementation of the chosen alternative?

Adapted from *Faith-Based Family Finances* by Ron Blue with Jeremy L. White (Tyndale, 2008).

Contentment

King Solomon is known as the wisest man who ever lived. He wrote, "He who loves money will not be satisfied with money, nor he who loves abundance with its income. This too is vanity."[17]

Contentment has nothing to do with money. True contentment comes when money and financial decisions do not dominate our thoughts.

Here's a common misconception: *If only I had more money, I would be financially free.* Money may come from a pay raise, a profitable investment, or a business success. The truth is that no amount of money is ever enough to provide contentment. Just the opposite may be the case. Think of Howard Hughes, Michael Jackson, or Ebenezer Scrooge.

Our culture encourages us to spend all we make. It says, "We need to stimulate the economy!"

Our culture says, "You deserve a break."

We need to realize that we're in a battle with a culture that attaches self-worth to net worth; a culture that wants us to believe that we're winning the game because of what we own.

The late American sage Will Rogers said, "Too many people spend money they haven't earned, to buy things they don't want, to impress people they don't like."

How Much Is Enough?

If you seriously consider this question and allow God to reveal the answer, you will be able to bring your spending into alignment with God's priorities for your life.

Consider two related questions:

1. Will I ever have enough?
2. Will it continue to be enough?

All of us, rich or poor, ask ourselves these questions more frequently than we might realize.

These questions are important because we live in an uncertain world, full of terrorism, health threats, inflation, real estate downturns, stock market crises, soaring interest rates, skyrocketing medical costs . . . and the list goes on.

In training financial counselors at Kingdom Advisors, I refer to the process of determining how much is enough as "knowing your finish lines." Two good reasons for determining how much is enough are to give hope and to avoid hoarding. Answering that question with a dollar amount will give you hope of achieving the goal you have set. And then accumulating "enough" will enable you to avoid the temptation to hoard more than you need.

I don't mean to imply, however, that there is a definite answer, in terms of dollars, to the question of how much is enough. The exact amount depends on the needs and goals of the individual answering the question. And of course there are two ways to get enough: *accumulate more* or *desire less.*

Your definition of *enough* may change as circumstances change (marriage, divorce, illness, death, additional children, children leaving the nest, retirement, changes in income or net worth, and changes in your goals).

I believe that God can be trusted to provide the income we need in order to obey His commands for the use of our money. My challenge to you is that you reprioritize the way you use your money in line with the Scriptures and see how amazingly God will work in your finances.

JOE'S TWO-MINUTE DRILL
Finances: How Do I Master My Money?

Without a doubt, if we do not learn to master our money, it will master us (as it did me!). However, as Ron Blue shows us in this chapter, successful financial management is possible, but it comes only by doing things God's way—according to His game plan. Let me recap the truths about our finances that Ron points out for us:

- ✓ Wise financial decisions have their foundation in the principles of Scripture.
- ✓ The Bible mentions money and property more than 2,300 times.
- ✓ There are five fundamentals for successful money management: Spend less than you earn; avoid or minimize the use of debt; make sure you save; set long-term goals to prioritize your spending; understand that God owns it all and we are only stewards or managers.
- ✓ Financial success is achieved when we manage wisely the money God gives us to further His objectives and try to accomplish what He's asked us to do with it.
- ✓ There are five uses of money (i.e., spending): giving, taxes, debt repayment, saving/investing, and lifestyle choices. How we choose to spend is a great responsibility. Prioritize according to God's principles.
- ✓ Seek God when making financial decisions. And do not be afraid to seek godly financial counsel.
- ✓ Remember: net worth is *not* a measure of self-worth, and *no* amount of money is ever enough in itself to provide contentment.

CHAPTER TEN

Vocation

As you can tell from my story, I was driven for much of my career. In the early days, I wanted to be a head coach so badly I could taste it. My dream was to be a head coach in the NFL, but I applied for top college jobs too. After spending four seasons under Don Coryell at St. Louis as the running backs coach, I thought that moving on to the Tampa Bay Buccaneers for the 1978 season to be John McKay's offensive coordinator was just the right move. But as I told you, John was used to calling his own plays. By the end of the year, he had reinserted himself as the one calling the plays and the season became a nightmare for me. I was frustrated, and we had an awful year. After having told myself at the beginning of the season, "This is it, God's plan, what He has been preparing me for," I had now hit a new low. I couldn't hold my hand out in front of me without it shaking like a leaf. Here I was in my late thirties, and I thought my dream was gone. No one would want to make a head coach out of an offensive coordinator whose team wasn't a winner.

At the end of the season, I agonized over whether to stay in Tampa or try to find another team. Meanwhile, Don Coryell had left the Cardinals and had been hired as head coach of the San Diego Chargers. When I heard that, I prayed, "Lord, don't have him call me unless You want me to leave Tampa Bay."

Sure enough, the next morning, Coryell called. But he wasn't offering the offensive coordinator's job. If I went to San Diego, I would be an assistant coach again, a demotion. I was torn. I loved coaching under Coryell, but I wanted to stay on track for a head coaching job. But if I stayed in Tampa as the offensive coordinator, there was no guarantee things would work out any better.

While I was waiting for my turn to talk with Coach McKay about the future, three assistants of his who had been with him forever came out of their postseason meetings with him only to report they had been let go. I got a sinking feeling. Maybe this was my time to get fired too. At least I had the offer from Coryell. I wouldn't be out of work, but I'd sure be taking a step back. And though it happens a lot, no coach wants a firing on his résumé.

When I finally got into John's office, he said, "Hey, I want you to stay." He added that he wanted to keep calling the plays, but said, "I want you here."

I told him I'd think about it, and we agreed to meet the next morning. And boy, did I think about it! I couldn't think of anything else. Should I stay in a bad situation and hope it turned around so I'd look like an offensive coordinator worth taking a chance on as a head coach? Or take the demotion and work for Don Coryell again, hoping for a break? I talked it over with Pat, wrote out all the pros and cons, prayed over it, and stayed up all night.

In the morning, while I was getting ready to go, I told Pat, "I still have no idea what to do."

She suggested I go to the meeting with no agenda. "Just let him do the talking. You say nothing until you're ready."

Pat really does have great wisdom! On the drive in, I resolved to wait—in absolute silence, if necessary, even if it went on for fifteen minutes. I wouldn't say a thing, not one word, until I had heard John out and had a real solid feeling about how I should respond.

When I got to the meeting, Coach McKay had a yellow pad in front of him, and he went down a long list of things he wanted to talk about, reiterating that he wanted to call the plays but that he wanted me to stay, and on and on. The longer he talked, the more certain I became that it was time for me to move on.

I told him his ideas were good and sound and that I appreciated the opportunity he'd given me, and added, "But I've made up my mind, and I want to leave."

John was great about it. Though he tried to talk me into staying, we parted as friends. I believed I had made the right decision, but I was still in turmoil. Should I go with Coryell to San Diego, taking the demotion? I couldn't relax, couldn't sit still. My mind was all over the place, and the more I talked with Pat about it, the more restless I became. I decided I needed to talk to my spiritual father, George Tharel.

I flew into Fort Smith, Arkansas, to connect to a flight to Fayetteville; but when I got to Fort Smith, it was snowing hard and the next flight was canceled. I pleaded with God to let me get to Fayetteville, knowing I was doing the right thing in trying to see George. Then I overheard a couple of guys talking about renting a car.

I said, "You going to Fayetteville?"

They looked at me warily. "Yeah."

"I'm going with you."

No suggesting, no asking, I just announced it and climbed into the back seat of their rental. It quickly became clear they had never driven in snow before. We took off down the freeway, and within a mile and a half I could tell we'd never make it. It was hilly and slippery and the car was all over the road.

Well, these guys thought I was crazy anyway, so when I insisted they pull over, they were more than happy to let me out. Now I was on the wrong side of the highway and had to lug my bags over the median. My glasses were all fogged up, I was freezing, and worst of all, I was defeated.

What was going on? All I was trying to do was get to my spiritual father, and God wasn't going to let me do that? I hitched a ride back to the airport and checked in for a flight back to Tampa. As I sat down to wait and thaw out a little, what did I notice on a table right near where I was sitting? A Bible. Strange.

Curious, I flipped it open to the first chapter of James, which I'd been studying recently because it deals with making decisions. All of a sudden, I felt a nudge on my shoulder, and a guy said, "I claimed that chapter in my life about six months ago."

What? I couldn't believe it. With everything that had already happened that day, I found a Bible where one shouldn't be, and I turned to a specific passage—and then a stranger comes along and says he recently claimed that very same passage for himself? This was too bizarre. All I could manage was, "Really?" and then he told me his whole story.

He was a pharmacist, and he had moved to his dream job in another state only to discover that he had to pass a huge pharmaceutical test once he arrived. He had been out of school for a long time, and there was no way he'd be able to pass such a test.

He told me he had been in a real quandary, wondering why he had left his home state and a good job, chasing a dream, only to see it come crashing down. He said he had studied that first chapter of James and finally came to the end of himself. "I told the Lord, 'I'm done. I'm turning this all over to You. You know what I want to do in life, but I can't do this. I'm going to have to trust You.' And would you believe it? I went in and breezed that hard test, and now I'm loving the best job in the world."

I was speechless. Some would call this a coincidence, but I knew better. I hardly had time to even respond. My plane was boarding, and I never saw that guy again. But one thing I know for sure: Whether he was an angel or just someone I needed to run into right then, God put him there specifically for me.

When I got on the plane, I prayed, "Lord, I get it. That message was for me. I'm done with this. You know I want to be a head coach, but I want what You want. I'm turning my career totally over to You, and I'm not going to worry about it anymore. I'm going to have peace about this and relax."

And I did. I took the Chargers job and we moved to San Diego. Two weeks after I got there, the offensive coordinator left to take a head job somewhere else. Don Coryell asked me to take over the coordinator's spot, and the next two years were unbelievable. Our quarterback was Dan Fouts, a great passer, and he went on to set all kinds of offensive records over the next two seasons. That made me look good, and after that I was offered the job as head coach of the Redskins.

God had taken me to the lowest point in my coaching career to impress upon me that I should focus on being the best coach I could be and let Him control my future.

Oddly enough, that's how we had to handle the racing team as well. I was busy coaching the Redskins when J.D. graduated from college in the early 1990s. He told Pat and me that he had seen the coaching lifestyle up close and he didn't want a life that would take him away from home that much. What he really wanted was to get into some form of racing. Well, Coy loved that idea too. When the boys were little, they'd had motorbikes and jet skis, and I'd taken them to car races every chance I got. Also, when Pat and I were high school sweethearts in the 1950s, I had driven all different kinds of hot rods and had gotten involved in drag racing. So getting into racing sounded like a fine idea to me.

I had long since learned to consult Pat on such decisions, so I hit her with the idea of starting a race team. Her first question was whether I was planning to drive. When I assured her I was not, she agreed we could take a shot at it.

We had no idea what we were doing. We had nothing. No cars, no drivers, no money. Just an idea. I called Rick Hendrick, a successful NASCAR team owner, and he suggested that his general manager, Jimmy Johnson, could help us put together a proposal that we could take to a few companies that had the potential to help sponsor the operation. I figured we had time to visit four or five such companies before I had to start the football season.

I knew it would take a grade-A miracle, but by then at least I had learned to leave such things in God's hands. It wouldn't help for me to fret over it. I started making calls. I had heard good things about Norm Miller, owner of Interstate Batteries, and after getting a few turndowns elsewhere, I decided to call him. But before I did, I went to a race and saw the Interstate Batteries decal on the back of a car. I was certain we were too late. He was already a sponsor.

Well, I called him anyway, and we immediately hit it off. We must have talked for about forty-five minutes. He invited me and my boys down to show him the proposal, so we flew to Dallas. I told him straight-up what we wanted—to start a race team and have a major sponsor. I teased him about the fact that he was a Cowboys fan while I was the Redskins' coach.

I felt it was a good meeting, but he made no promises. When we hadn't heard from him for a couple of days, I assumed it wasn't going to happen. I called Norm and said, "Maybe you'd consider just being an associate sponsor," which would require a whole lot less of an investment.

Norm said, "No, we've been thinking about doing this." I realized, *This is actually going to happen!* Pat and I put a lot of our own money into the team, too, but of course we couldn't have done it without Interstate Batteries.

Once again, I turned to Don Meredith for help. I asked him to go down to Charlotte to help start the race team, with just sixteen people, while I spent most of my time with the Redskins. The only time I could devote to Joe Gibbs Racing was the occasional Thursday night dinner after my weekly TV show. I'd meet with Don, and he'd fill me in on how things were going. I'll never forget the time he and I were having a nice dinner and he said, "We've got a little hiccup in the budget."

A little hiccup? "Really? What?"

"We're about four hundred thousand over budget."

Here we go again, I thought. *Pat's going to kill me!*

We weathered it through and survived, but our new race team had just started learning the ropes that first year, and we didn't win a thing. The second year started with the Daytona 500, and we were all there—Pat, Coy, and J.D. (who was on the pit crew). And of course Norm Miller was there. We had a good car, and veteran Dale Jarrett was our driver. I was hoping for a great day.

I wanted things to work out for Norm, and certainly for us, but after that first year without a win, I had to wonder if we belonged there. Starting that way reminded me of my first year with the Redskins when we lost our first five games. The press was calling for my head; the fans wondered where this no-name had come from and whether he could succeed at all. The owner of the Redskins, Jack Kent Cooke, gave me a public vote of confidence (which is usually what happens just before a coach is fired). Can you believe we finished that year 8–8 and went on to win the Super Bowl the next season?

I could only hope we'd be as successful in NASCAR. There I stood in the infield for the first big race of the season, having finally retired from coaching (a decision that would also allow me to watch Coy play football his last two years at Stanford). I wasn't dreaming of NASCAR championships. I just wanted us to start our second season well.

The year before, we had run up front early at Daytona but wound up wrecking; so, though I enjoyed it when Dale was among the early leaders, that earlier disappointment was still in the back of my mind. But as the race wore on, we were among the leaders all day. You can't imagine how exciting it was!

Close to the end, our car was among the top three, and I was starting to allow myself to hope. With about three laps to go, Dale dove down on the inside of the front-runner, Dale Earnhardt, and pulled into the lead. With two laps to go, he was still leading, and I was as crazy as the rest of the team—wishing, hoping, and praying he could pull it off.

We were jumping and craning our necks and trying to follow the action, when finally the leaders came barreling off the corner around the last turn, and there was our green Interstate Batteries car out in front! Jarrett roared across the finish line, and we all started crying and hugging, and the kids were wrestling in the infield. We didn't even know where the winner's circle was, but you can bet we found it.

An awful lot has happened in our lives since then. We have 440 employees at Joe Gibbs Racing, and J.D. now runs the day-to-day opera-tions for the NASCAR team. Coy is following his dream by starting a motocross team for us. I went back to coach the Redskins for four seasons, after being away from the game for twelve years, and I've now come back to focus fully on NASCAR again. So far, Joe Gibbs Racing has won three NASCAR Cup championships.

I'm excited about this chapter about vocation because my own career journey is an example of someone making a decision to quit performing for man's approval and start performing for an audience of one. That decision finally led me to a peaceful and fulfilling career, and that's what Os Guinness talks about here.

If the name Os Guinness sounds familiar, it may be because he's the great-great-grandson of Arthur Guinness, the Dublin brewer. Os's parents were medical missionaries to China during World War II. He studied at the University of London and earned his doctorate of philosophy in the social sciences from Oriel College, Oxford. Os was a freelance reporter with the BBC before coming to the United States in 1984. He has been a guest scholar and visiting fellow at the Brookings Institution, and for many years was a senior fellow at the Trinity Forum. Os has written and edited more than twenty-five books, including his latest, The Case for Civility: And Why Our Future Depends On It. *As we were doing research on who would be the right person to handle the subject of vocation, a number of our contributors recommended Os. He has impressed me as a true gentleman and a great scholar. He is also a Redskins fan and lives in Washington, D.C. He was there for both of my coaching stints. Can you imagine how many times someone as smart as Os has second-guessed my football calls?*

How Do I Build a Successful Life and Career?

OS GUINNESS

So many voices. So many claims. So many offers. So many surefire formulas for winning and success. Promises, promises, promises.

That's the world we live in today. Our problem is not one of choice; our problem is how to make the *right* choice—the one that will lead us into the ultimate game plan for life. Or, to put it another way, how can we find our own unique purpose in life? After all, we have only one life to live. Are we making the most of it, or are we missing out? What does it mean to make the most of life, especially if how we live this life will affect the life to come?

What is a winning game plan for life itself?

When the former British prime minister Winston Churchill was in his nineties, he said, "It has been a grand journey—well worth making once."

What made it a grand journey for him? Perhaps it was his power, wielded over armies and nations in World War II; the success of his heroic and history-changing struggle against Adolf Hitler; his worldwide fame as a statesman, orator, author, and Nobel Prize winner. Or maybe it was his long, privileged life, his friendships, and his marriage to a strong, beautiful, and adoring wife.

What would be *your* criteria for a good life? What would make it a grand journey for you? Our lives are very different from Churchill's and from each other's. Would your criteria for a good life measure only what you have done or are doing, or would it include your family and friendships, too? Have you made a good game plan for your life? Are you living up to it and realizing your dreams, or would you admit you are settling for something less?

Let's face it—most of us live most of our lives working forty-plus hours a week. But is that all there is to life? Jesus himself said, "I have come that they may have life, and have it to the full."[1] He means that our lives—and I believe, specifically, our jobs—are a calling from God.

The Unexamined Life Is Not Worth Living

What would you think of a coach who went into a game without a game plan; a business leader who launched a company without a business plan; or a general who launched a war without a strategic plan? You'd expect them to fail.

Yet it seems many people give no thought to planning for the most important venture of all—life itself. Have you considered what makes for a good life and how to make the most of it? The Greek philosopher Socrates said famously that "the unexamined life is not worth living." That may be the most quoted and least followed quotation from the classics, for most people never get out of the starting blocks in the race of the examined life. They don't really think about their lives; they just live without thinking.

How can this be? Doesn't everyone want to make the most of life? I know I do, and I believe you do too—otherwise you wouldn't be reading this book.

One reason people live unexamined lives is because of what Blaise Pascal, a seventeenth-century French scientist, called "diversion." We are reluctant, even afraid, to admit that we all, without exception, will die. We surround ourselves with entertaining distractions so we don't have to think about death. We tranquilize ourselves with the trivial. Has any generation ever been able to divert itself so happily for so long and with so many fascinating toys as ours? With our BlackBerries, iPhones, iPods, and TiVos, we can lose ourselves in virtual reality and be entertained and distracted forever—"amusing ourselves to death," as best-selling author Neil Postman puts it.

Another thing we do rather than examine our lives is called "bargaining." We don't want to think about life, or especially death, so we negotiate with the future. "Later on," we say. We tell ourselves there will be time to think about serious issues after we are out of school; after we have made it to the top and made a name for ourselves; after our families have grown up; after we have secured a nest egg for our retirement; and so on. But eventually we run out of *later,* and there is no more *after.* We have traded all our tomorrows for an endless series of todays. But finally there is an end, and death draws the celebrated bottom line across our life's account in thick black ink.

Who do we think we're kidding? It's impossible to avoid reality, to slow time, and to deny death forever. As the Greek warrior Achilles says brutally in the *Iliad,* "Come friend, you too must die. Why moan about it so?"[2]

We can get so caught up in the race of life that we forget where we are going and what it's all about. We go to school, try to get a good job, buy a home, start a family, enjoy vacations, and look forward to retirement. But what then? Is that all there is?

Most of the things we do are worthwhile in themselves, but what do they all add up to? Do they fit into a larger purpose? Jesus told a story about a farmer who was always expanding his little empire with bigger and better barns; until one day time ran out and God said: "You fool! This very night your life will be demanded from you. Then who will get what you have prepared for yourself?"[3]

Jesus Himself said, "What good will it be for you to gain the whole world, yet forfeit your soul?"[4]

The Russian novelist Leo Tolstoy told the story of a peasant who worked furiously to acquire more and more land—all for good and worthy reasons—until he finally dropped dead in the process. Tolstoy called the story "How much land does a man need?" and he answered his own question at the end: "Six feet from his head to his heels."

So what does it mean to lead an examined life, a good life, and to make the most of the one life we each get? Do you have a game plan that inspires you to see your life as purposeful?

Who Are We? Why Are We Here?

It's not easy to make sense of life. We are born into a world that doesn't explain itself, and life doesn't seem to come with a user's manual. Jewish philosopher Abraham Heschel writes, "I want to know how to answer the one question that seems to encompass everything I face: What am I here for?"[5]

Unpack that profound question, and you'll see it includes three closely connected things that we all long for: a deep sense of identity, a clear sense of purpose, and the pleasure and satisfaction of our purpose fulfilled.

That's why we all have to have a game plan. Too many of us make life decisions without considering God's plan for our lives. We have a grand shopping mall of ideas and ways of life from which to choose, so the challenge in leading an examined life is to choose wisely.

Three main options are available to us today, and when you really examine them you will see that there are huge differences between them. Think them through carefully.

Option #1: Forget it and forget yourself

The first option comes from the Eastern family of faiths, which includes Hinduism, Buddhism, and the New Age movement. Their answer to how to find individual identity, purpose, and fulfillment is to, in essence, *forget it, and forget yourself.* From an Eastern perspective, your goal should not be freedom *to be an individual,* but freedom *from* individuality. To me, that eliminates any purpose for our individual lives.

For many people today, beliefs such as reincarnation are "cool" ideas, but only for those who have not thought them through. You'll do yourself a favor to think a belief through to its very end—to its logical, or illogical, conclusion. The Eastern view, the goal of freedom *from* individuality, requires that we deny who we really are. Does that sound like a plan for finding a life of identity, purpose, and fulfillment? Why work? Why pursue a career? Why strive for excellence? In the end, forgetting yourself will hardly lead to personal fulfillment.

Option #2: Do it yourself

The second option comes from the secularist family of faiths, which includes atheism and agnosticism. As those see things, we are born—or thrown into—a world in which everything comes from chance and is moving toward extinction. So, if you want meaning in life, there is no point in looking for it. It is up to you to create it for yourself. To paraphrase the Frank Sinatra song, we're to do it "*our* way."

While some are drawn to the Eastern view, others are invigorated by the secularists' do-it-yourself mantra. It complements our sense of independence and self-reliance. But what happens when the strong impose their will on the weak? In a survival-of-the-fittest world, the victory goes to the strong. And in the end we will all be extinct anyway, so what's the point?

Option #3: Become who you were meant to be

The third option comes from the Bible, the foundation for the Christian faith. Here the question of our human identity, purpose, and fulfillment begins with our being addressed as persons created in the image of God. Right from the start, we are acknowledged as unique individuals with inalienable dignity. The Bible also says we are each called by God, so that we can fulfill our unique potential when we answer that call.

No doubt you can imagine the ramifications of this biblical answer to the questions of your identity, purpose, and fulfillment. There is nothing like it in any other religion or worldview. Not surprisingly, it has unleashed the highest view of human dignity and the greatest sense of human purpose and fulfillment in all of history.

Our calling is closely related to Creation, in that what God's Creation meant for the universe, His calling means for our lives. God's word was dynamic in the Creation. God said, "Let there be," and the result was the very universe itself. In the same way, God's word is dynamic in His call to us. "Follow me," He says, and our response can trigger an explosion into being that defines, inspires, and completes our lives and gives us a lifelong source of identity, purpose, and fulfillment.

Master Theme #1: Becoming What God Wants Us To Be

Here is the first master theme of our life's purpose: God has created and called us to become who we were meant to be. In answering that call from the great personal and infinite God, we can go further, rise higher, and bring into play parts of ourselves that no one else would ever believe we have or are capable of exercising—except the one who knows us intimately and has personally called us. In stark contrast to atheists and agnostics, followers of Jesus should never see our ultimate game plan for life as our own design, but as God's great plan for us.

What do I mean, then, when I use the word *calling*?

When God, through Jesus, says, "Follow me," everything we are, everything we have, and everything we do is infused with dynamic direction because it is done as a response to His summons. No wonder this *calling* can be seen as the ultimate game plan. Jesus' invitation for us to follow Him represents two words that have changed the world and should revolutionize our lives.

A mere sentence describing our calling can be dry, but of course the dynamic reality of our calling is anything but dry. The idea of a calling from the God of the universe needs to be felt and seen to be appreciated. People just like you and me have found their identity, purpose, and fulfillment in following the call of Jesus and have made this the driving inspiration for their careers.

I urge you to follow the call of Jesus because I believe it will transform your sense of identity and purpose by allowing you to become all He wants you to be. God calls us to be the people He created us to be and to use the gifts He has given us.

Have you ever thought about the natural talents God has given you? I have observed that Joe Gibbs is happiest when he's coaching football or building a racing team. Sitting at a desk from nine to five was clearly not his calling. We are never happier than when we are expressing and exercising the gifts God has instilled within us.

Knowing your gifts is a key part of your identity and self-awareness. God normally calls us along the lines of the way He has gifted us; but the purpose of this giftedness is stewardship and service to Him, not selfishness.

I must immediately caution you that giftedness alone should not be how you determine your calling. Giftedness must line up alongside factors such as family heritage, your own life opportunities, God's guidance, and your willingness to do whatever God leads you to do.

Understanding your giftedness is a central way to discern your calling, but that reverses the way most people think today. In today's world, you are what you do. We are defined by our jobs and our work. When we meet someone new, it isn't long before one or the other will ask, "What do you do?" From then on, we are identified as a teacher, a truck driver, an athlete, a lawyer, a computer scientist, or whatever. Because our work provides our livelihood and occupies the bulk of our waking hours, we tend to think that our jobs define us.

Answering God's calling reverses that thinking. Instead of saying, "You are what you do," God says, "Do and be what I've called you to do and be."

When Art Monk, the celebrated Washington Redskins wide receiver, was inducted into the Pro Football Hall of Fame, he stated flatly that he was defined by something other than football: "The one thing I want to make very clear is that my identity and my security is found in the Lord. . . . What defines me is the Word of God, and it's the Word of God that will continue to shape and mold me into the person that I know He's called me to be."[6]

For Joe Gibbs, coaching meant becoming what God wanted him to be. For Art Monk, a football player was what God wanted him to be. For my father-in-law, a builder of cars and a pilot of airplanes was what God wanted him to be. For me, a speaker and writer is what God wants me to be. For followers of Jesus, it is His call to us as His created beings that transforms our giftedness into a lifelong discovery of identity, purpose, and fulfillment.

We live in an imperfect world that the Bible describes as "fallen" because it has been marred by sin. As a result, sadly, not everyone can even find a job; and if they do, it might not fit their giftedness. Regardless, it's important that we clarify our calling before we try to choose a career and that we recognize our giftedness as we evaluate our calling.

Saying, "I'm doing what God has called me to do" must never become an excuse for selfishness, or a blank check for self-indulgence. Our calling is never an excuse for "doing our own thing." Our goal should be to become like Christ, for His glory and for the benefit of others. If that means we make sacrifices and suffer, those sacrifices will be worthwhile. We should be able to find meaning even in suffering if it is part of our calling by God.

What are your gifts and talents? Are you a natural leader or more of a team member? Are you a thinker or more of a doer? Are you more skilled with your hands or as a speaker? Are you gifted at getting things organized and done, or do you shine in relationships and hospitality?

Are you tempted to spend your gifts only on yourself? Or for the glory of God do you want to link your best abilities to your neighbor's needs? Listen to Jesus of Nazareth. Answer His call, and you will discover your true identity and your purpose in life.

Master Theme #2: Everyone, Everywhere, in Everything

Consider this second master theme. Your calling can transform your life by challenging you to integrate your faith with everything you do. Such faith transforms us because it becomes a matter of *everyone, everywhere, in everything.*

What am I saying?

Perhaps you saw the film *Amazing Grace,* the story of how William Wilberforce fought to abolish both the slave trade and then slavery itself throughout the British Empire. Wilber, as his friends called him, was the greatest social reformer of all time and was described at the end of his life as the "George Washington of humanity."

Most extraordinary is that he almost missed it all.

At the age of twenty-six, Wilberforce experienced what he called his "great change." He turned from a life of wealth and careless self-indulgence to put his faith in Christ, and immediately presumed that he should quit politics and become a minister. Fortunately, a minister—John Newton, a former slave trader himself and writer of the song "Amazing Grace"—persuaded Wilberforce to stay right where he was and to ask God what He wanted him to do. Two years later, Wilberforce wrote in his journal, "God Almighty has set before me two great objects: the suppression of the Slave Trade and Reformation of Manners." He chose to stay in politics, which he had come to see as his calling.

What gave Wilberforce the idea that it might be better for him to be a minister than a politician? Sadly, a strand of false teaching going back centuries sees the "spiritual" as higher than the "secular," regards ministers and missionaries as more important than lay people, and therefore values "full-time Christian work" above secular jobs.

Martin Luther and his fellow reformers attacked this notion head-on during the Reformation. If a farmer in the field and his wife in the house were doing their work by faith and as a calling, their work was just as high and holy as the work of the preacher in the pulpit. William Tyndale wrote that if our desire is to please God, then pouring water, washing dishes, cobbling shoes, and preaching the Word "is all one."

"God and the angels smile," Luther said, "when a man changes a diaper." In other words, when life is lived as a response to the calling of Jesus, there is no spiritual versus secular, no higher versus lower, no full-time versus part-time, and no superiority of the clergy over the laity. It is all a matter of different gifts and callings. In short, vocation is everyone, everywhere, in everything, doing the bidding of God.

Jesus called His followers to be "salt and light" in the world, challenging us to engagement with the world around us. Living out our faith is not meant to be restricted to our homes and churches. Rather, following the call of Jesus should transform the whole of our lives. It should shape how we make a business deal as much as how we pray. It should be seen in how we treat a client as clearly as in how we share our faith. It should be reflected in our bank statements and not simply our prayer journals. It has everything to do with the worlds of business, law, science, politics, education, engineering, and the media. Again, it's a matter of everyone, everywhere, in everything following God's call.

Integrating faith with the whole of life is the secret of how the Christian faith has been so dynamic in shaping history and changing cultures. It is also why the Christian faith becomes so spineless, ineffectual, and—let's be blunt—unappealing to others when we don't "walk the talk" and live our faith wherever we go. There's a word for saying one thing and doing another: *hypocrisy.*

Accept the challenge that will tie together every aspect of your life; that will stretch your energy, your enterprise, and your emotions to the maximum. Listen to Jesus of Nazareth. Answer His call. Live your life as a response to His summons.

Master Theme #3: The Audience of One

This is a third master theme: answering God's call transforms our lives, because it means living before *an audience of one.*

Think of the audiences in your life. It is common to think of our aims, ambitions, achievements, and assessments; but people rarely speak of audiences. Yet only madmen and supreme egotists do things purely for themselves. Most of us, whether or not we are aware of it, do things with an eye to the response of some audience. The question is not *whether* we have an audience, but *which* audience we have.

Our modern world has shifted enormously from one in which people take their cues from internal things, such as conscience and character, to one in which we are swayed by peer pressure, opinion polls, and the siren song of advertisers.

God's calling makes a decisive difference here. Yes, we have many audiences. Football players and race car drivers require spectators; writers require readers; doctors require patients; and politicians require citizens who will listen to them and elect them. All such audiences are natural and legitimate; but for followers of Jesus, they are hardly the final audience. In the end, we live before an audience of one. What God sees and what God thinks are ultimately what matters.

Living before the audience of one is practical and decisive. What counts as success? That we make a fortune? That we become famous? That we rise to extraordinary power over people? Such may be impressive in the eyes of our generation; but for the person following the call of Jesus, they are irrelevant. All that matters is whether God says, "Well done" in the end. Only the verdict of the audience of one counts.

Another reason the audience of one is important today is that—due to our mobility and technology—more people are anonymous than ever before. Naturally, this affects the way we behave. What we call morality can be described partly as "accountability through visibility." People do what is right because they are seen. The real moral test is what we do *when no one sees us.*

Many people use anonymity to get away with whatever they can. In their minds, what no one sees is fair game. But answering God's calling makes all the difference, because we realize we can never again really be anonymous. For the follower of Jesus, no one sees but God. Sometimes this brings assurance, as in the old gospel hymn "His Eye Is on the Sparrow." Sometimes it means accountability, because we perform for that audience of one.

The Ultimate Why

Our world is abuzz with talk of purpose and fulfillment. Never have so many books and seminars offered such simple steps and such easy answers that promise to fulfill us in five minutes or less. We're taught to develop "mission statements" and target "measurable outcomes," to assess the "opportunity costs" and to "maximize" every waking moment. Though some of this can be good, much of this talk is empty and deceptive and can leave us spinning our wheels.

However, answering the call of our Creator is the ultimate "why" for living and the greatest game plan in life. Down this road lies the surest path to identity, purpose, and fulfillment. Follow Jesus and you will see all of life as a grand enterprise transformed by His call. God's call will lead you into your deepest fulfillment.

Those of us already in the game can tell you what Jesus told His first followers: Come and see. Answer His call and you will never regret the life that will be yours. God's great game plan for your life will be better than your wildest dreams.

JOE'S TWO-MINUTE DRILL

Vocation: How Do I Build a Successful Life and Career?

Nothing in life can be as frustrating as wondering what it is we were put on this earth to do. Only by following God's game plan can we figure out our vocation—the one that God would have us pursue to find ultimate satisfaction in life. Let me recap several truths about our vocation that Os points out for us:

- ✓ It is important to examine the way you live life. Stop and reflect. What is your plan? The unexamined life is not worth living.
- ✓ Only God's game plan for your life will give you a sense of identity, purpose, and satisfaction (making the most of your life).
- ✓ You are created in the image of God, and He assigned to you a unique calling—which includes your work. This call is your ultimate game plan. Only after discovering it can you become who God means you to be.
- ✓ A central way to discern your calling is by understanding how God has uniquely gifted you. Let God use you where you are gifted.
- ✓ Your occupation is only one part of your calling. God has also gifted you in other areas. He desires your faith to transform everything that you do and everyone you meet.
- ✓ Having a successful career begins with understanding that we live and work ultimately to please God, our audience of one.

CHAPTER ELEVEN
Health

For most of my life, I considered myself healthy as a horse. The joke was, Eat like a horse, work like a horse, look like a horse.

I've always struggled a bit with my weight, but I was a driven man, so I was going, going, going all the time. I worked out a lot, including running on a treadmill, so I didn't worry too much about my health. A lot of men, I think, have no idea how stress affects them. Sure, during an NFL season, a coach and his staff will spend several nights a week working until well after midnight. But we enjoy that. It's a challenge, it's fun, and it's necessary.

Shortcut the planning process and you'll get beat by teams whose coaches are outworking you.

When the Washington coaches and I would gather at all hours of the night at Redskins Park, we knew it was time to start wrapping things up and get to bed when the garbage truck would rumble through at 3:00 a.m. Well, by then we had also been gorging on sweets. I've been told that I would sit there watching films and commenting, all the while idly opening a half-pound chocolate bar and eating the whole thing myself.

Toward the end of the 1991–1992 season, the last year of my first tenure with the Redskins, I started getting tremors in the night. One day, after my treadmill workout, I was trembling from the knees down and wondering what was going on.

Every eighteen months, I go to the Mayo Clinic for a complete physical;

so after that season I scheduled my appointment right away. After they put me through every test imaginable, I was told I had a lot of prediabetic symptoms, but that if I lost a certain amount of weight, it should take care of itself.

Eventually I developed full-blown diabetes, and I'm convinced it's because I pushed myself too hard and ignored the warning signs. I've also been able to prove that stress is a major contributing factor. When I went back to Washington in 2004 to start my second go-round with the Redskins, I was measuring my blood sugar and treating myself daily. I could have my breakfast, take my insulin, get a perfect blood sugar reading of 110, and then go coach a game. With no intake during the game except water, my blood sugar afterward would at times be as high as 500. No food, no sugar. Just stress.

The bottom line for me was this: Though some factors were out of my control, my bad habits had led to my getting diabetes.

Yet as devastating as physical health problems can be, mental health problems can be just as damaging.

Early in my tenure with Washington, I was in my office at Redskins Park when all of a sudden there was a commotion down the hall where the financial people were. We ran down there to see what was going on and found one of our key defensive players chasing the chief finance guy around his desk. The player wanted a check from the finance guy right then and there—forget payday.

It turned out that this player had a bipolar disorder and was off his meds. Any other time, he seemed the most squared-away guy in the room—great to work with, tough player, good teammate. Off his meds, though, it was truly Dr. Jekyll and Mr. Hyde.

Another time, he went missing for a few days. We finally found him in the woods near his home. He'd been living out of his car for some time. Imagine how hard that condition was for his family to deal with. We had to deal with it only some of the time. His family had to be on edge 24/7.

In all fairness, he usually kept on his medication and fit in like everyone else on the team. But it was an eye-opener to see someone change so drastically those couple of times. Until I saw it firsthand, I hadn't given much thought to mental health problems.

Our health expert, Dr. Walt Larimore, believes that four areas comprise our overall health. By now you can name two of them: physical and mental health. But Walt adds two more— relational and spiritual health—that I think really help to complete our individual health picture.

To illustrate the importance of good relationships, let me tell you about one of my friends. As I've mentioned, the sponsorship by Interstate Batteries was vital to the start of Joe Gibbs Racing. That company got on board with us when we had a vision for racing and not a lot more. It was a great experience to win the Daytona 500 in our second year, but it was at our very first Cup Series race—our first Daytona 500—that I got a glimpse into the personality of Norm Miller, the owner of Interstate Batteries and a great friend to this day.

Dale Jarrett had led for a good part of the race. Our #18 car was one of the fastest in the field. We were beginning to think we might have a great finish, maybe even win.

Well, Norm and I were in the infield admiring how well our car was doing. We were excited and the anticipation was building. What we didn't know was that there had been a terrible crash on the backstretch of the track behind us—a huge wreck involving a lot of cars.

Sure enough, coming around the track at almost 200 mph, Dale didn't have a chance to avoid the pileup. Our great car was soon a mass of twisted metal. Dale was fine, but we couldn't finish the race.

As Norm and I walked to the garage where the car was being towed, there were TV cameras all over the place. Now, Norm is the consummate salesman—that's why he's been so successful with Interstate. "Hey," he said, "this isn't half bad. Next time we're not running well, we just need to wreck. This is great publicity!"

Well, I was glad that our primary sponsor was happy; but no, I wasn't planning to keep on wrecking $200,000 cars.

But that's Norm—ever the optimist. Norm and Ann have become dear friends to Pat and me, and we often vacation together. Our two companies have a special relationship, too. Over the years, Interstate has gone the extra mile for Joe Gibbs Racing, and we've done the same for them.

I know I can talk through anything on my mind and heart with Norm, so he's a positive factor in my relational health.

When it comes to spiritual health, you know I wasn't healthy that way until we moved to Arkansas. That's where I met George Tharel, and where, at age thirty-two, I recommitted myself to following Christ. Ever since then,

I've been on a road of spiritual growth—not always without pain, but ultimately rewarding.

Our research for *Game Plan for Life* indicated that the topic of health was one of the top three of importance to men. I really wanted to make sure we got the right guy to share with you, and we found him in Walt Larimore. Until I met Walt, I hadn't looked at my health through the four key areas he outlines: physical, mental/emotional, relational, and spiritual.

Dr. Walt Larimore earned his medical degree at Louisiana State University and completed his family medicine residency at Duke University. He practiced medicine for more than twenty years before becoming vice president and family physician in residence at Focus on the Family. Walt has appeared on countless radio and television shows, including hosting more than 850 live daily episodes of the national cable TV show Ask the Family Doctor. *One expert said that Walt had "more actual on-air TV experience than any physician in the history of television." Dr. Larimore has published eighteen books and more than six hundred articles. He is now a full-time author, educator, and journalist. Anyone who has hosted 850 live daily TV shows has my respect. After my first coaching stint with the Skins, I signed on to do TV analyst work for NBC, and I couldn't make one hundred pregame shows before being fired.*

How Do I Achieve True Health?
WALT LARIMORE, M.D.

What does it mean to be healthy? Is it being not too fat? Just feeling good?

Do you, like most men I talk to, believe that if people don't feel sick, then they're healthy? If so, you're in the vast majority.

But God's game plan for health, found in the Bible, teaches something completely different.

A young man in a men's group I teach—let's call him Terry—seemed to be in great health and hadn't seen the need for even a physical checkup in more than a decade. His wife had asked him to get one a number of times, but he kept putting it off. (Can you can relate?) Then the results of a routine insurance exam blindsided him: he had high blood pressure, high cholesterol, high blood sugar, and traces of blood in his stool.

His doctor immediately prescribed a diet and medications for hypertension and diabetes. Two weeks later, a colonoscopy led to surgery for colon cancer that had already spread to his liver.

Three months later, Terry was dead—from diseases that could have been prevented, or at least easily controlled, had he only committed earlier to understand what it meant to be truly healthy.

Terry was doomed by what we physicians call one of the silent killers. He had no symptoms. He felt good. He believed he was healthy.

Another friend, Cameron, completed several Ironman triathlons. (To complete even one is an amazing physical accomplishment.) Cameron was in great condition—disease free—yet he suffered from severe depression. The problem was that he focused so completely on his physical health that he essentially had no friends and no social life. His wife and kids left him, and his business collapsed.

Was Cameron healthy? He was a world-class triathlete, but emotionally and relationally he was a couch potato.

For a time, I provided medical care for prisoners in a county jail. Many had healthy bodies, but many described the sick pleasure they felt while raping, robbing, or murdering. I was convinced that some would coldly commit more heinous crimes if they ever got out. These men had disease-free bodies, but no one would call them healthy.

My medical training initially led me to emphasize the physical side of health, particularly the treatment of trauma and illness. I considered patients healthy if they were free from disease and injury. But the more I learned about God's game plan for health, as described in the Bible, and the more experience I gained, the more I saw that having a well-functioning body is not all-important. In fact, that isn't even the main factor in being healthy.

God's game plan calls us beyond just physical health to what I call being *highly healthy*. The Bible has some clues about what this means.

I'm not a trained theologian, but as a student of the Bible for more than thirty-five years, I'm convinced that this ancient book of wisdom contains timeless principles of health that are supported by the most modern scientific research. So, let's take a look.

God's Definition of Health

The concepts of *health* and *healing* permeate the Bible from start to finish. True health is viewed as *completeness* and *wholeness*—two words that appear hundreds of times in its pages. In fact, our modern word *health* is derived from an Old English word that means "whole" or "holy." God's design for true health—for being highly healthy—is intended to include those things that make us *whole*. Obviously, that means much more than just physical well-being.

The Bible talks about preventing and healing physical and emotional disease. Some Old Testament laws demonstrate God's concern for the physical health of His people. The Israelites were commanded not to eat foods that we now know likely carried diseases. The Old Testament also has commands for quarantining people with infectious diseases,[1] similar to the ways we modern doctors prevent the spread of infection. Throughout the Gospels, we see Jesus (and later His disciples) healing people of physical maladies. But God's plan for our being highly healthy is much broader and deeper than this.

We find a clue in the parable of the Good Samaritan, the story of a man caring for an injured stranger. First, he cared for his obvious physical needs, pouring oil and wine on the man's wounds and bandaging him. But he also took the man to a safe place where he could rest and recover, even covering the cost of this care.[2]

In *The Bible and Healing,* John Wilkinson, a British physician who was both a medical missionary and a biblical scholar, describes God's game plan for health this way: "Human wholeness or health is the main topic of the Bible. . . . It is only when human beings are whole, and their relationships right, that they can be described as truly healthy."[3]

The World Health Organization's definition of health conforms to a biblical definition: "Health is a state of complete physical, mental, social, and spiritual well-being, and not merely the absence of disease or infirmity."[4]

A physician friend of mine writes, "The Bible teaches that true health involves our entire beings—the physical, mental, and spiritual elements must all be functioning as God designed them. . . . The physical may actually be the most unimportant of the three, because with good mental and spiritual health we can still be content, even though our bodies may be unhealthy."[5]

Physical health last on the list? In God's design for true health, the promise of blessing and wholeness is based primarily on really knowing God, which I believe comes by believing in His Son, Jesus Christ, and through reading the Bible "Faith comes from hearing, that is, hearing the Good News about Christ."[6]

The Hebrew word *shalom,* often defined as *peace,* does not mean just the absence of conflict. The root meaning of *shalom* is *wholeness, completeness,* and *general well-being*—it carries a strong emphasis on relational well-being, especially our relationship with God.

The Bible teaches that true *shalom* comes only from God: "The LORD gives his people strength. The LORD blesses them with peace [*shalom*]."[7]

In other words, you and I cannot be highly healthy physically, emotionally, and relationally, unless we are also growing spiritually.

The Old Testament also teaches that living one's life according to God's design produces *tsedeq,* which means *righteousness,* or "being in a right relationship with God," leading to a long (eternal) and healthy (whole) life.

The Bible teaches that *eternal life* is not just "pie in the sky when we die by and by." It's not even just a long or never-ending life. Jesus defined *eternal life* when praying to His Father: "This is eternal life: that they may know you, the only true God, and Jesus Christ, whom you have sent."[8]

He also taught us, "'You must love the LORD your God with all your heart, all your soul, and all your mind.' This is the first and greatest commandment. A second is equally important: 'Love your neighbor as yourself.'"[9]

True health (or wholeness) is based on trusting and obeying God and His principles. This part of the game plan is not easy, because it requires humility. The Bible says, "Don't be impressed with your own wisdom. Instead, fear the LORD and turn away from evil. Then you will have healing for your body and strength for your bones."[10]

The Four Wheels of Health

From my perspective, the Bible's holistic view of health is most easily seen in Luke 2:52, where the writer (a physician) describes the preteen Jesus: "So Jesus grew in wisdom and stature and in favor with God and all the people."[11]

Jesus grew in stature (physical health), wisdom (emotional/mental health), and in favor with God (spiritual health) and others (relational health).

God's game plan for life, the Bible, focuses on pursuing physical health, emotional health, spiritual health, and healthy relationships with your family and others. I call these elements *The Four Wheels of Health,* the importance of which has been confirmed by thousands of scientific studies.

Simply put, if any one of our four wheels of health is wobbly or flat, our health—and our potential—will suffer. Life certainly won't run as smoothly, or as far, as it was intended.

Make no mistake—God is concerned about our physical bodies. Jesus Christ's healing miracles prove that. And the apostle Paul teaches that physical training has value, even referring to our bodies as "the temple of the Holy Spirit."[12]

Preachers tell us men that we need to be good stewards of our *time,* our *treasure* (the money God entrusts to us), and our *talents;* but He also wants us to be good stewards of our *temples.* So, we need to take care of our bodies—but God also designed three other wheels of health.

Mental health researchers tell us that our emotions are linked to our physical health. So does the Bible: "A cheerful heart is good medicine, but a broken spirit saps a person's strength."[13]

The apostle John wrote to you and me when he penned these words: "Dear friend, I hope all is well with you and that you are as healthy in body as I know you are strong in spirit."[14] John was not only wishing his friend good *physical* health, but also that his *mind, emotions,* and *relationships* would be healthy as well.

King David poignantly describes how guilt over wrongdoing affected his physical and spiritual health. After committing adultery and murder, David said, "When I refused to confess my sin, my body wasted away, and I groaned all day long. Day and night your hand of discipline was heavy on me. My strength evaporated like water in the summer heat."[15]

The Bible tells us that poor spiritual decisions can result in physical consequences. Referring to taking Communion, Paul writes, "If you eat the bread or drink the cup without honoring the body of Christ, you are eating and drinking God's judgment upon yourself. That is why many of you are weak and sick and some have even died."[16]

The Old Testament writers also use the word *rapha',* which describes the process of healing. The various derivatives of this word occur at least eighty-six times and tell us that God's activity as healer touches all four wheels of a man's health.

One doctor told me about a man in the prime of his adult life who became paralyzed from the neck down in an accident, yet who exudes hope and enthusiasm and maintains rich family and social relationships.

"The essence of true health," this doctor said, "is physical, emotional, social, and spiritual well-being. When these four dimensions are singing in harmony, you're healthy. That doesn't mean there's no room for a dissonant chord, but that the music of life is pleasant to the ear. My quadriplegic patient seems to me to be highly healthy, despite his sobering physical disability."[17]

What holds the four wheels together is spiritual health—that is, truly knowing God. How we can come to know God is explained in other chapters, including Joe Gibbs's own story of how he came to have faith in Christ. For now, let's examine each of the four wheels in more detail.

The physical wheel

Maximum physical health is achieved when your body—with all its chemicals, parts, and systems—is functioning as closely as possible to the way God designed it. As we learned from the tragic story of my friend Terry above, for a person to be as physically healthy as possible, disease must be prevented whenever possible, discovered as early as possible, and treated as effectively as possible.

When Joe Gibbs's NASCAR racing teams prepare for a race, they put the cars through a series of tests to check out all the systems in these expensive machines. Such tests are designed to either prevent problems before they happen, or find them early, when they are far less expensive to fix.

Though the cost to build the best race cars is well into six figures—not to mention the millions of dollars it takes annually to staff and support a team—your body is far more valuable than any automobile. Why wouldn't you want to treat it with just as much care and respect as Joe's mechanics and technicians lavish on his cars? To take care of your "temple" means seeing a doctor regularly—not only in an emergency or when your wife begs you or when you're forced to in order to buy an insurance policy.

When a disease or disorder proves incurable, physical health involves learning to cope and adapt. Can you see why the physical wheel may actually be the least important? With good emotional, relational, and spiritual health, a person can still be highly healthy, even though his or her body may not be "whole."

My daughter, Kate, was born with cerebral palsy. A significant portion of her brain died and dissolved before birth, leaving the left side of her body weakened and spastic. The brain damage slowed her physical development and led to many operations to straighten her limbs and her eyes.

Although Kate, now an adult, is not "normal" physically, and her condition is incurable, she has learned to cope and adapt physically. So, all things considered, her physical wheel is healthy and well-balanced. Even so, Kate's physical health is strongly dependent on her constant work to keep her emotional, relational, and spiritual wheels in balance as well. The responses we hear from people concerning her precious spirit tell me that she's healthy in those areas, too.

The emotional wheel

Emotional health refers to mental well-being. This is more than the absence of emotional distress. Being mentally healthy requires learning to cope with, and even embrace, the full spectrum of human emotions that face us every day.

My friend Ben is a model of emotional health. For years, I've watched him handle whatever life throws at him. Whether he is experiencing the jolt of loss, the joy of a dream realized, or the ordinary ups and downs of daily life, he wholeheartedly embraces the varied emotions associated with each. He doesn't pretend things are better than they are, nor does he treat the inevitable letdowns of human existence as catastrophes.

Ben is comfortable with his own emotions, neither running from nor chasing down the lows and highs along his journey. Now in his forties, Ben is one of the most authentic people I've ever known. His willingness to lean into and experience the rich scope of human emotion inspires me to do the same, even when it's uncomfortable.

Being mentally healthy requires healthy brain function. Charles, a former patient of mine, lives with a severe, inherited form of chemical depression. This dysfunction, if untreated, throws his physical, emotional, relational, and spiritual wheels out of balance.

At his worst, Charles loses his appetite, motivation, and concentration. But by taking a prescribed medication, eating right, exercising, and proactively balancing his other wheels, Charles has been able to dramatically decrease the impact that his depression would otherwise have on his mental and emotional health.

The relational wheel

We're socially healthy if we're succeeding in all our relationships—those with family, friends, neighbors, coworkers, everybody. Does that mean living without conflict? Absolutely not! We're talking about human beings, after all. But we can help prevent and even treat injured relationships— that's part of being highly healthy.

A pastor I know had a spiritual wheel that seemed intact, but he was a physical and emotional mess. As his doctor, I spent months trying to help him balance his physical and emotional wheels. But no matter what I did for him medically (every conceivable treatment), he always came to my office out of balance.

I finally realized that his real problem stemmed not from physical or emotional disease, but rather from a series of broken relationships— beginning with his own dad.

Only after he agreed to work on mending his relationships, with the help of a Christian psychologist and a support group, could the other parts of his life become balanced.

As his relational wheel came into balance, he began to experience a smoother ride, both physically and emotionally.

The spiritual wheel

What does it mean to be in a state of maximum well-being as we relate to our Creator? Obviously, for us to be spiritually healthy, any break in our relationship with God must be prevented or treated.

Your spiritual wheel must be seen as the most crucial one, because good physical, emotional, and relational health alone will not make you a highly healthy person. Spiritual well-being has to be a consistent priority.

What does this mean?

First, it means that we respond to the relationship God is initiating with us. If that is new to you, the very idea of a "relationship with God" may sound strange. But stay with me, because I believe, as does Joe Gibbs, that God loves you and me and wants to have a relationship with us. We believe this is possible through Jesus Christ, and we will do our best to make that clear and understandable.

Second, once your relationship with God is established, you'll want to understand His design for your physical, emotional, relational, and spiritual needs. The way to learn your Creator's personal instruction and direction for your life is by reading and studying the Bible.

What does a healthy spiritual wheel look like? Consider Mike. He was in my office almost weekly, and his list of complaints—both imaginary and real—was long. Mike was, in a word, neurotic.

Neurotic patients can be trying for a physician, because they simply choose not to get well. They seem to know it, and the physician knows it.

I assessed Mike's spiritual health, using what I call my G–O–D questionnaire, which is three simple questions:

1. Is *God,* spirituality, or religion of any importance to you?
2. Do you ever meet with *Others* in a faith community—church or synagogue?
3. Is there anything I can *Do* to help you in your faith journey?

When I asked Mike the G question: "Is God, spirituality, or religion of any importance to you?" he replied, "Nope."

Then the O question: "Do you ever meet with others in a faith community—church or synagogue?"

"Nooooooo way!"

By now I was hesitant to ask the D question, but I pressed on, whispering: "Mike, is there anything I can do to help you in your faith journey?"

"Are you nuts?" he said through gritted teeth.

Well, at least I knew where he stood.

I found myself frequently praying for Mike. Occasionally, I would suggest things I believed could change his spiritual health.

One day I told him, "I know you don't think much about prayer, but I really believe it's effective. I've been praying that we'd find some treatment that would help you feel better."

"Harrumph!"

I told him how my relationship with God affected my health, my marriage, my finances, my parenting, my doctoring—in short, my life. I quoted Bible verses I thought would answer questions he might have. I occasionally prescribed a book I thought would help. Over time, I saw minor breakthroughs.

Finally the day came when I shared with Mike how he could begin a personal friendship with God. He wasn't ready for that—not then—but he listened! I began to look forward to and pray about our visits together.

One morning, when I walked into the exam room, Mike leapt from his chair with a hearty laugh and enveloped me in a bear hug.

"Mike, what are you so happy about?"

"Doc, you'll never believe it, but your prayers have been answered! I've begun going to church because my neighbor wouldn't stop inviting me. I've learned some things about myself. I'm not saying I ever liked the way I was, but I never knew any other way. I don't know what happened, but something did, and I'm not the same man!" He looked me straight in the eye. "Doc, thanks for praying for me and caring for me—but most of all, thanks for caring *about* me."

Some might say that Mike was finally healed. I think he was—if not completely healed physically, he was at least transformed spiritually, relationally, and emotionally.

Clearly, all four health wheels are connected. If, like Mike, you want to be highly healthy, make sure all four of your health wheels are inflated to the right pressure and well-balanced. Pay special attention to your spiritual wheel.

In the New Testament, the apostle Paul instructs his young disciple Timothy about this very thing: "'Physical training [the physical health wheel] is good, but training for godliness [the spiritual health wheel] is much better, promising benefits in this life and in the life to come.' This is a trustworthy saying, and everyone should accept it."[18]

Can you see the value of learning to view your physical, emotional, and relational health as secondary to your spiritual health?

Though we're not promised a perfectly healthy physical life, the Bible does promise abundant life to those who have a vital relationship with God. An abundant life is one that will be full and meaningful—infused with purpose, contentment, and joy.[19]

Examining Your Four Health Wheels

One day, my wife, Barb, pointed out a nail in one of our car tires. All I could see was the head of the nail. No air was escaping, and we didn't have time to get it fixed, so I said, "Honey, I think we can keep going."

Barb looked skeptical. About twenty miles later, the tire blew. Worse yet, the spare was flat! How I wished I'd heeded her warning and taken the time to repair the tire before it went flat.

Your four health wheels have many miles to travel. To become a highly healthy person, you'll need to understand each wheel and take personal responsibility for your overall health.

I must warn you, though. You'll be tempted to abandon God's game plan for becoming highly healthy. It's hard work. It takes time. Some health care providers will promise simple, easy, and quick cures for everything that ails you. Beware.

Think about how complex your car is. It requires regular checkups and preventive maintenance. When it malfunctions, it often requires a professional's care.

Your body is hundreds of times more complex than any machine, and it requires even more special care. There is no cure-all.

Following God's game plan for being highly healthy may mean controlling your temper, eating better, exercising more, spending time in prayer, developing friendships, spending more time with your kids, or investing in your marriage. Becoming highly healthy requires a tough, honest assessment of your weaknesses, and then courage and a commitment to take action.

The Essential of Balance

Remember your first car? Mine was a two-tone 1958 Buick I bought for $100 after high school. I cared for that car, washing it, changing the oil, keeping it clean and lubricated. Plus, I learned basic tire care. As long as the tires were balanced and properly inflated, the car would roll smoothly. But if one tire was out of balance or improperly inflated, it affected the whole car.

In the same way, neglecting one or more of your wheels of health will result in problems.

Balance doesn't just happen. The first step in becoming highly healthy is diagnosing your unique areas of disease or imbalance.

Maybe you already know your health wheels are unbalanced. If so, welcome to the human race. Don't beat yourself up; just start working on your wheels. Encouragement, advice, and help are available. The fact that you've read this far tells me you truly want to know God's purpose and plan for your life, and that means there is great hope for you! You have begun the journey of discovering God's game plan for you and your family.

To help you on this journey, I have created an evaluation tool that allows you to examine your four health wheels. You can find it at www. DrWalt.com. Think of it as similar to one of the computerized tools that Joe Gibbs uses to gauge the performance of his race cars.

When it comes to God's game plan for your health, a little insight can make the difference between being out of the race and taking the checkered flag. Now it's up to you to get in the driver's seat.

JOE'S TWO-MINUTE DRILL
Health: How Do I Achieve True Health?

If you're at all like me, when you think of health you probably think only about the physical dimension. However, according to Walt Larimore, true health is much more than lack of physical disease or infirmity. Playing by God's game plan involves caring for every aspect of our being. Let me recap several truths about health that Walt points out for us:

- ✓ The Bible—both the Old and New Testaments—contains timeless principles of health that are supported by the most modern scientific research available.
- ✓ God's game plan for true health includes those things that make us whole beings—the physical, mental/emotional, relational, and spiritual. These four "wheels" are all connected, and if any wheel is wobbly or flat, your health and potential will suffer.

✓ The Bible says that our physical bodies are temples of God and should be cared for. See a doctor regularly.

✓ Maintaining emotional health requires learning to cope with and embrace the full spectrum of human emotions we face daily.

✓ Being relationally healthy means having success in all our relationships. However, it does *not* mean these relationships will be without conflict.

✓ Being spiritually healthy begins with having a relationship with God. Next, it involves beginning or continuing to read and study the Bible to learn God's game plan for your life.

✓ Regularly examine the status of each of your four wheels.

CHAPTER 12

Purpose

We could just as easily have titled this chapter "Living Life On Purpose," because that's the bottom line, isn't it? Don't you want to be proactive and live with passion, rather than sitting back and letting life happen to you? Maybe that's even why you're taking the time to read *Game Plan for Life.*

Many people ask me what makes one driver better than another. Here's the way I see it.

A lot of people want to drive race cars. Some kids are fortunate to get into a position where they can start working their way up through the racing ranks. Usually, it starts at go-kart races, where you'll often see parents supporting their kids. As in football and other competitive sports, as drivers progress up through the ranks, they get weeded out. Finally, there's a group that winds up getting to race the NASCAR Cup Series—only forty or fifty drivers at any one time.

Once a driver is racing at this level, he's reached the top. But even within this group, only a few gain the admiration of the other drivers. These guys are competitors and want to be the best of the best. Just as a good number of players finally make it into the NFL but only a handful make it to the Pro Bowl, a lot of drivers compete in the NASCAR Cup Series, but only a small number each year will end up in the Chase for the Championship.

Most drivers get better with practice and experience, but only a few are truly gifted. Take Kyle Busch, the driver of our #18 car sponsored by Mars

Candy (M&M's) and Interstate Batteries—he's got talent like few others. Recently, another team owner, who's been in NASCAR longer than I have, said, "Joe, I've got to tell you, Kyle Busch is the best I've ever seen."

It's true that Kyle is gifted. But I see a lot more than that in him.

Kyle is completely focused. He has built his life around racing, with few other distractions. He owns a number of late-model cars that he also races; so if he's not at a NASCAR race, he's racing one of them. His dad works on the late models with him. His girlfriend goes to the races. All Kyle wants to do every night is be in a race car, and he's arranged most of his life to do just that.

Kyle is very, very bright, as well. He knows his car and exactly what it needs to have the best shot at winning. Before a pit stop, he'll tell his crew chief, Steve Addington, "I need a pound of air in the right front and we need to come off of the spring in back." We can't put technology in the car during a race to tell us those things—that's a NASCAR rule—so Kyle, in effect, becomes the onboard computer. He takes in the data—the racing environment, the feel of the car, his position in the race—and offers Steve solutions that will make the #18 car more competitive.

Kyle is also like a test pilot when he's in his car. He's got the courage and confidence in his own abilities to push that technology to the very edge and get every ounce of speed he can from the car.

In NASCAR, if you are driving a car "loose," it is usually fast. But driving loose can be a challenge to the driver. A loose car feels as if the rear end is going to come out from underneath you.

When testing our Cup cars, we can put sensors on the car to let us know how many degrees a car is loose. We've seen Kyle go way beyond what the average driver could manage. During time trials at one race, I heard one of the top drivers ask another driver, "How can Kyle do that?" Pushing the envelope is just part of what makes him great.

Kyle's got the gifting, the brains, the courage, and the drive to compete in the top ranks of NASCAR. His purpose is to win every race.

His focus and determination remind me of Joe Theismann, the Redskins' quarterback during my first stint as head coach.

I'll always remember one particularly miserable game against our long-time rivals, the New York Giants. It was sleeting, and Joe had thrown three interceptions in the first half—in addition to being sacked hard a few times.

Right before halftime, we called a time-out, and Joe came over to the side-lines to talk about our strategy for our two-minute drive. He was literally spitting out blood and teeth. His two front teeth were gone.

If it had been me, I probably would have decided to sit out the second half. Not Joe Theismann.

In the fourth quarter, we were down by two points and the weather was getting worse. By this time, it had become a virtual sleet storm. Joe engineered a drive that took us down the field and put us in field goal range. Mark Moseley kicked the game-winning field goal into some of the worst weather we have ever played in (and in the process set an NFL record for consecutive field goals made).

When people quiz me about Joe Theismann and what a great player he was, I don't think of the Super Bowl plays he made. I reflect on that miserable day and his second-half play that proved how tough and deter-mined he was.

Joe's purpose was to lead the team to victory.

In professional sports, talent, focus, determination, and passion help create a sense of purpose. But when it comes to playing the game of life, we need another critical component as well.

Recently, the racing community attended the funeral of a beloved friend, Max Helton. Max had been a pastor before he founded Motor Racing Outreach, an organization that provides pastoral care to the teams and racing community at several hundred motorcycle, power boat, and NASCAR races each year. It was hard to see Max suffer from cancer and finally pass away, but I was struck by something unusual that happened at his funeral.

Max was widely known, and many people were interested in speaking at his service. It was a fitting tribute to Max, but it made for a long service. Toward the end, they introduced the chaplain of my son Coy's motocross team, a young man named Steve Hudson. Steve bounded onto the plat-form with energy, and when he began with, "Hey!" everybody sat up a little straighter.

What really got our attention was when he stood over Max's casket and said, "Every single one of us is going to end up right here some day. The question is, What are we going to do between now and then?"

This is where living a life of purpose comes into play.

The Bible tells us to store up treasures in Heaven. Is that what you're doing? That means doing things with God in mind—for the audience of one. So much of my life I've lived for myself, for my sense of achievement, and to gain riches, fame, or something else. But Matthew 6:19-21 plainly says, "Do not store up for yourselves treasures on earth, where moth and rust destroy, and where thieves break in and steal. But store up for yourselves treasures in heaven, where moth and rust do not destroy, and where thieves do not break in and steal. For where your treasure is, there your heart will be also."

Steve was saying that you need to live a life of purpose, and that includes having a view of the endgame. You've got to know where you're going in order to get there.

Don't be like I was, investing in real estate schemes just to try to get ahead; fretting over job opportunities rather than just giving my career up to God. It's all about priorities and pursuing life with purpose.

I've mentioned the value of trying to read the Bible every day. One of my favorite stories, when it comes to the issue of what we're doing with our lives, is the one where the disciples of Jesus had been fishing all night and had caught nothing.

Remember that? From the shore, Jesus tells them to cast their nets on the other side of the boat; and when they do, the nets are weighed down with fish.

Now think about that. These guys were full-time, lifetime fishermen with the best boat and the best equipment, and they knew that body of water. Do you really think they hadn't fished both sides of the boat that night? I bet they had!

What that story says to me is that no matter how good we are at what we do, or how well we think we can handle life on our own, if God's not in it, we're going to wind up with a big zero. If we put God first, then we've got a chance to fill the nets to the breaking point.

Do you have a passion and determination about your life? Are you focused on playing the full sixty minutes in the game of life? As a coach and race team owner, I've always emphasized a fast start to the season to instill confidence. Then I wanted the middle part of the season to set us up for a strong stretch run. Here, Tony Evans recommends the same strategy for life. I want to be consumed with storing up treasures in Heaven as I strive to finish well.

Tony Evans was the first African-American to earn a doctorate in theology from Dallas Theological Seminary. He has also received two honorary doctorates. He serves as senior pastor of Oak Cliff Bible Fellowship in Dallas, Texas, and is the founder and president of The Urban Alternative, a national organization that seeks to bring about spiritual renewal in the inner city. The Alternative with Tony Evans is broadcast daily over more than five hundred radio stations in the United States and in forty other countries. Tony has served as chaplain for both the Dallas Cowboys and the Dallas Mavericks. In 1989, he was named Father of the Year in Dallas. Author of nine books, Tony is a gifted speaker in great demand. If you've ever heard Tony speak, you know that no one is going to be falling asleep in that crowd. In this chapter, his energy comes through even in writing.

How Do I Get the Most Out of Life?

TONY EVANS

Seinfeld was one of the most popular TV sitcoms of the 1990s. At the height of the show's success, a class of drama students was asked to study it and explain why it was such a sensation. They concluded that what was missing from the program was what made it so immensely popular. *Seinfeld* was, self-admittedly, a show about nothing. Though it was often hilarious, it did not have an overarching plot; neither did it have any enduring substance or significance.

The characters were engaging, and the best punch lines were repeated around office watercoolers every week, but each episode drew record viewing audiences apparently because people seemed to enjoy meaningless programming.

Though *Seinfeld* may have been a harmless diversion, it strikes me that today, more than a decade since the series's final episode, the show mirrors what is happening in society. It affects all of us. Significance, meaning, and purpose are absent from too many lives, and our culture suffers from the crisis.

What does that have to do with you? Maybe you resonate with the man who said, "I was dying to finish high school so I could go to college. Then I was dying to finish college so I could start my career. Then I was dying to get married and start a family. Then I was dying for my kids to turn eighteen so they would leave. Then I was dying to retire. And now I'm just dying. I forgot to live."

Is that you? Do you find yourself wishing you were someone else? No? Can you say you've never worn a jersey with someone else's name and number on it? I meet men all the time who have no idea which way to go. They sleepwalk through decaffeinated lives and settle for existing rather than living life on purpose. Despite the occasional bright light of excitement— like watching their favorite team or driver win—things quickly fade to black as reality sets in.

In a world full of meaningless distractions, we can learn a valuable lesson about focus from one the greatest home run hitters of all time, Hank Aaron. In baseball, one of the goals of a good catcher is to distract the batter. Yogi Berra, the great New York Yankee Hall of Famer, taunted hitters every chance he got. In the 1958 World Series, against the Milwaukee Braves, Berra told Hank Aaron that the trademark on his bat was pointed the wrong way.

"Henry, you'd better turn the trademark around so you can read it. Otherwise you'll break your bat."

Aaron never took his eyes off of the pitcher. He knew better than to let what was going on around him deter him from the task at hand. When Berra kept telling him to "hit with the label up on the bat," Aaron finally said, "Yogi, I came up here to hit, not to read."[1]

When we know our reason for being, our purpose in life, we can keep from being distracted by what is going on around us.

Our Reason for Being

So what is our reason for being?

I'm a pastor, so indulge me as I show you three important truths that can be gleaned from one verse of Scripture. If you're a man who wishes to live a life of purpose, maybe you'll appreciate this.

Acts 13:36 says, "When David had served God's purpose in his own generation, he fell asleep; he was buried with his fathers and his body decayed."

This verse gives us three key perspectives that should mark each of our lives:

Truth #1: David served God's purpose

Clearly, there is a direct correlation between David's God-given purpose and his daily activities. He understood something that many of us today have missed. He acknowledged that his life was not his own and that his primary reason for existing was to serve the purpose of God. Do you ever find yourself trying to get God to serve *your* purpose rather than the other way around?

You've no doubt heard the slogan that goes, "The one who dies with the most toys wins." It may be meant in fun, but it represents the real goals and values of too many people. It has even inspired a counter-slogan: "The one who dies with the most toys is still dead."

If you identify with the message of the first slogan, you may be living to serve the wrong purpose, living to acquire more stuff, believing that what you possess will make you happy and fulfilled. But does the thrill of the new toy ever last? Does it ever really bring contentment? It never has for me. If you find that your priority is material gain, and your identity lies in your bank account, your spiritual life is probably on a back burner. Remember the story Jesus told about the man who, after he had built bigger and bigger storehouses for all his riches and was ready to retire, died that very night? Jesus said, "Watch out! Be on your guard against all kinds of greed; a man's life does not consist in the abundance of his possessions. . . . This is how it will be with anyone who stores up things for himself but is not rich toward God."[2]

Do you tend to find your life's meaning and purpose in your work, your position? I've seen men sacrifice their families for their careers, forgetting that no man on his deathbed ever wished he'd spent more time at the office.

Do you live for pleasure? Pornography addiction is epidemic in our country because men are, in essence, willing to settle for a two-minute thrill ride on a sexual roller-coaster at the expense of a lifetime of pure marital love.

David, however, understood that if a man is going to live a life that matters, he must focus on serving the purposes of God. Now, that's not some complicated theological idea. I believe God has a customized "reason for being" for every man, which He will reveal to us if we are willing to submit to Him.

You may have a TV in your kitchen—a small one, because watching TV is not the primary reason for being in the kitchen. You may glance at it while you're cooking or eating. But if there's a show you really want to focus on, you'll likely go into the family room or den, where you can relax and enjoy your program on a larger screen.

Have you relegated God to the kitchen of your life, occasionally glancing His way while focusing on other things? I think it's clear from Scripture that God does not want to be just another one of our activities. He wants to be front and center in our lives. What does that mean? That everything we do should serve His purposes. And what are His purposes? To bring glory to Himself and to draw all men to Him. The apostle Paul said, "Whether you eat or drink or whatever you do, do it all for the glory of God."[3]

I'm not saying that David was perfect. We know better. His experience with Bathsheba indicates that if he lived today, he would struggle with the same temptations we all do. However, Scripture eventually concludes that David was a man after God's own heart.[4] David understood his divine reason for being.

I don't know about you, but I'm deeply grateful that God can use imperfect people who yield themselves to His purpose. How freeing to know that if I give God my mistakes and flaws by confessing them and asking His forgiveness, I can still serve Him.

Now here's an illustration you may not expect from a preacher, but think about this: The appliances in your home do not determine their own purpose. They have been designed to meet a specific need. Refrigerators do not cook, stoves do not freeze, toasters do not open cans, and can openers do not make toast. For an appliance to have worth, it must perform the service that it was designed to perform.

You and I have been designed by the Creator with unique purposes. Whatever your purpose is, by finding it and living it out, you will bring God glory and draw others into His Kingdom.

If you are a believer in Jesus Christ, God wants you to act in such a way that attracts others to His way of life. Jesus said, "Let your light shine before men, that they may see your good deeds and praise your Father in heaven."[5]

As followers of Jesus, we need to become the tools He uses to bring His way of life to others.

On a public beach, sand is free. On the other hand, sand for a playground costs more than $25 a bag. That same sand, glued to a piece of paper and sold in a hardware store, may cost $5 a sheet. Sand (silicon) that is manufactured into computer chips is far more expensive. Sand is sand. All that's different is what the sand is used for. The more specific its purpose, the more valuable it becomes.

Without Jesus, and with no purpose, we are like free sand. When we come to faith and begin living for Him, we discover our true value.

A doctor who has surrendered his life to Jesus is more than a doctor; he becomes God's representative in the medical field, demonstrating what God looks like when He helps hurting people.

A lawyer who submits himself to Christ can reflect what God looks like when he tries cases.

A businessman can model what God is like when he cuts a deal.

A laborer, a mechanic, or a factory worker serves God by being a good employee, showing humility, and helping others.

David increased in value because he served the purposes of God. Because he was functioning according to God's design, his life had meaning, which laid the foundation for his reason for being.

Apart from living a life of purpose, we merely exist.

Truth #2: David influenced his generation

If there's one thing that hinders me from serving the purpose of God in my life—in a way that benefits others—it's selfishness. Everyone wants to *receive* a blessing, but not many want to *be* a blessing. What does it mean to be a blessing? It means affecting the lives of those around us for their good, which in turn brings honor to God.

Throughout the Bible, God blesses men. But if those men created a legacy, it was because of what they did with that blessing. For example, in Genesis, God tells Abraham that He will bless him, and that through him all the nations of the earth would be blessed.[6]

The story of Abraham tells me that God does not bless us simply so that we ourselves will be blessed. His blessing of us is to become a public benefit to others. A man living out his divine design will make a difference in the lives of others, starting with his own family. Sometimes that's the toughest chore, isn't it? The apostle Paul urges believers in Christ to consider others over themselves; but too often we're better at doing that away from home, aren't we?

David served the purposes of God, but just as important was the impact he made on others and the legacy he left. Through many of his psalms, generations of Christians have been blessed by David's life. If you're a Christian, you have benefited from someone's legacy—that of the person who led you to faith, if no one else's. Now it's your responsibility to pour that legacy of blessing into the lives of others by drawing them into God's Kingdom.

One of the great tragedies of the twentieth century was the sinking of the *Titanic* during its maiden voyage. More than fifteen hundred people lost their lives in the frigid waters of the North Atlantic. The greatest tragedy was that many of those people did not have to die. According to an article in the *New York Times,* at least three hundred people drowned because many of the lifeboats were sent off only half full.[7] Those who made it to safety were too self-absorbed to turn back and rescue others for fear of drowning themselves.

As Christian men, we need to resist the temptation to disappear into the safety of our "Jesus boats." Our culture is in desperate need of men of purpose to come to its rescue. We have to understand that serving the purposes of God includes rescuing a generation in crisis. Our every action can have an effect on others who need our direction and influence.

How do you discover your God-given purpose?

Look at it this way: Many major cities have what is called a stack interchange, or a mixmaster—an interchange where highways converge and intersect. In Dallas, where I live, it's the intersection of Interstate 35E and Interstate 30. I like to imagine God having a mixmaster—one that combines the "highways" of passion, abilities, personality, experience, and opportunity—to lead men to their purpose.

First, there's the highway of passion. God's purpose will always involve your passion. He will give you an internal fire for what He wants you to do. Jesus said that zeal for His Father's house consumed Him; Paul said his ministry was his ambition or passion; Jeremiah said his calling became like fire in his bones that he couldn't shake.[8]

God will give you a fire for what He wants you to do.

Second, there's the highway of abilities. God gives us talents or spiritual gifts that allow us to fulfill our passion. These abilities need developing or training to be fully maximized; but along with your passion will come the desire to hone your abilities.

Third, there's the highway of personality. You possess a unique soul— your personality—which is composed of your intellect, emotions, and will. Because whatever God calls you to will fit who you are, you will sense that you were made for it.

Fourth, there's the highway of experience. God uses life experiences to help shape us for our purpose—including the good, the bad, and the ugly. The family we grew up in, the education we received, the helpful people we have met, all these can be part of our preparation. The apostle Paul was uniquely prepared for his calling as the theologian for the church by his training as a Jewish leader, even while still an unbeliever. Once Paul was committed to Christ, God used him as the architect for the New Testament church and its theology.

God uses our bad experiences to shape us as well. Maybe a huge mistake taught you a lesson you might never have learned otherwise. Though God never authorizes sin, and sin carries consequences,[9] He still uses our failures to help fulfill His purpose for us.

It was Moses the murderer whom God used to lead Israel out of Egypt.

It was David the adulterer whom God used to write many of the psalms we lean on for faith and encouragement.

It was the same Peter who publicly denied Christ that God used to help found the early church.

The key is that these men repented of their sins, turned back to the Lord, and began to follow Him obediently. Some have referred to this path as God's "hitting a bull's-eye with a crooked arrow."

God also uses our ugly experiences—those negative experiences that were not our fault—to lead us to our purpose. Maybe a tragedy in your life has helped mold you into a compassionate counselor. Maybe you grew up fatherless, or were discriminated against racially, or were treated unfairly on the job. Those experiences, painful as they are, can shape you into a sensitive, caring man.

The story of Joseph is a classic illustration of how God can redeem the ugly events in our lives. Joseph was rejected by his jealous brothers and left for dead in a pit; he was sold as a slave, unjustly accused of rape, and forgotten in prison. But the Bible is clear that, each step of the way, "the LORD was with Joseph."[10] God used all the negative realities in his life to direct him to his destiny. Joseph would become the second in command in Egypt and be used by God not only to save the life of his family, but also to help fulfill God's purpose of founding a nation.[11]

So don't despair because life has been unfair. God knows how to take your good, your bad, and your ugly and use them for His purpose in your life.

Fifth, there's the highway of opportunity. God will open doors of opportunity for us to fulfill His purpose for our lives.[12] When you've committed yourself to living for Him, you'll be amazed at the people and situations He puts in your path.

When these five highways intersect, you will arrive at your destiny, your divine reason for being, where God gets the glory and we receive the good.[13]

Truth #3: David died

After David served the purposes of God and influenced his generation, he "fell asleep." (That's biblical language for dying.) In America, the average man lives to be seventy-five and the average woman eighty-one. With that in mind, we need to live each day with the goal of fulfilling our divinely ordained reason for being. We should weigh each action in light of the purpose for which we were created. Someone has said that Christians are not in the land of the living on our way to the land of the dying. We are in the land of the dying on our way to the land of the living.

My favorite game growing up was Monopoly. That was when I got to live large. I bought valuable real estate and would wheel and deal with wads of dough. The only things that mattered to me were Boardwalk and Park Place, the two most expensive properties on the board. If I was able to secure these two, my whole world changed. I became a real estate barracuda, the Donald Trump of the room, controlling the board and taking no prisoners.

But when the game was over, reality set in. I had to give the money back and close the box.

One day, each of us will be in the front of a church or a funeral parlor in a closed box. Game over! What we accumulated and left behind will not matter. All that will really matter is what we forwarded ahead. That's why living a life of purpose for God and His Kingdom matters.

In Acts 13:22, God writes King David's eulogy for him. It says, "[God] made David their king. He testified concerning him: 'I have found David son of Jesse a man after my own heart; he will do everything I want him to do.'"

God wants to write your eulogy as well. Despite all our activities, honors, and recognition, God desires our hearts. He wants men who will function according to His design and influence their generation for Him because they are committed, above anything else, to doing His will.

I long to be like Jesus, ready to leave this earth only after I have completed the work He has sent me here to do.[14]

A Life on Target

One day a man was driving past a barn when he had to stop and get out to look closer at something that stupefied him. On the side of the barn were painted twenty targets, each with a bullet hole right through the center of the bull's-eye. He didn't see another hole anywhere on the barn.

Just then, the farmer appeared and asked the man if he could help him.

"Yes. You can tell me who in the world did the shooting on the side of the barn."

"Oh, that was me."

"Twenty targets with twenty dead-center bull's-eye shots. You did that?"

"Every shot."

"Where did you ever learn to shoot like that?"

"Aw, it was easy. I shot first, and then I painted the targets around the holes."

Do you ever do that with your life? Do you do everything you can to give the impression that you're on target, when really all you've done is learn to paint well?

Too often we try to camouflage our emptiness with materialism and scrambling for success and significance. Some even try to fill their emptiness through religious activities such as church membership. We have learned how to look, talk, and act like Christians, but all these things are mere paint jobs to obscure the fact that we are tragically off target. We are missing the mark.

So, what will your life look like when it is full of purpose and on target? God has not left us to wonder. An entire psalm has been dedicated to profiling just such a man. Psalm 128 summarizes in six verses what I have just spent several pages trying to explain. Here is life as it was meant to be lived by Kingdom men.

> ¹*How blessed is everyone who fears the* LORD,
>   *Who walks in his ways.*
> ²*When you shall eat of the fruit of your hands,*
>   *You will be happy and it will be well with you.*
> ³*Your wife shall be like a fruitful vine*
>   *Within your house,*
>   *Your children like olive plants*
>   *Around your table.*
> ⁴*Behold, for thus shall the man be blessed*
>   *Who fears the* LORD.
> ⁵*The* LORD *bless you from Zion,*
>   *And may you see the prosperity of Jerusalem all the days of your life.*
> ⁶*Indeed, may you see your children's children.*
>   *Peace be upon Israel!*[15]

The psalm begins with a stirring challenge.

Blessed (or happy) is the person who fears the Lord. To *fear* God simply means to take Him seriously, holding Him in awe and reverence. It means God is not to be marginalized, discounted, or left on the sidelines. He must become the center of our lives.

So, the first thing the psalmist wants us to know is that if our lives are in line with God's Word, good things will happen, blessings will flow. But it all starts with you and me personally.

What happens when you fear God?

- He will take care of your fortune: "You shall eat of the fruit of your hands."
- He will take care of your feelings: "You will be happy."
- And He will take care of your future: "It will be well with you."

But we live in a culture that does not take God seriously. How can you know that you're not guilty of doing the same thing?

The psalmist answers that in verse 1. He says that we take God seriously when we walk in His ways—in other words, when we do what He wants done, and that becomes our goal and the pattern of our lives.

When you take God seriously in your personal life, the next place it shows up is in your family life. "Your wife shall be like a fruitful vine within your house, your children like olive plants around your table. Behold, for thus shall the man be blessed who fears the LORD."

Clearly this is a psalm for men, and God is saying to us, "Your family must be rooted in Me." The writer portrays the wife as a fruitful vine. As you study that, it becomes a beautiful word picture. There are three things you need to know about vines:

First, a vine clings. Now don't mistake that characteristic for a jealous wife who smothers you. Rather think of this comparison as a wife who takes hold and attaches herself to you in love, wrapping her "branches" around you for stability and security and support.

Second, a vine climbs. A healthy vine will spread out and take over a whole wall. When you as a husband provide the right atmosphere, your wife can flourish and grow, becoming a better woman than she ever was.

If you have a wife who seems to have stagnated spiritually or emotionally, it could be that you have not become the kind of a man she can cling to. She may not be getting enough spiritual nurturing. The wife of a Kingdom-focused man should be able to say, "When I cling to my husband, good things start growing out of my life that I didn't know were there."

Third, a vine produces fruit. A grapevine yields clusters of grapes. They start budding everywhere. If your wife becomes a clinging (in the best sense), climbing, and fruitful vine, your home life will become a delight instead of just a duty.

Before any of that can happen, a vine has to have the right atmosphere to grow in. Don't expect a summery wife if you bring home wintry weather every night. Don't expect a growing vineyard if you bring in snow and hail when you get home.

When it comes to children, the psalmist changes the imagery from a vine to olive plants. Notice that they are not trees yet, just plants that can take up to fifteen years to mature, provided they are nurtured. When nurtured properly, olive plants produce a multitude of benefits. Besides the fruit for eating, they also produce oil for cooking, medicine, massages, and many other profitable uses.

The psalmist is saying that men must provide a nurturing environment for their children if they're going to grow up to be olive trees. The beauty of an olive tree in biblical times was that, when it matured, it would produce olives for another forty years. That's the picture of productive children raised in a nurturing environment.

One of the great places to nurture your family is around the table (see verse 3 above). Mealtimes provide great teachable moments—but Dad has to be there with the kids if those moments are to be seized for God. The man who provides that kind of climate in the home will be blessed of the Lord (see verse 4).

In verse 5, we come to the third category of our lives that will benefit from our living out an agenda that honors God. Here the psalmist prays, "The Lord bless you from Zion."

Zion was the city of God, where families came to worship God in the Temple; so you may interpret *Zion* as your church. If you put God at the center of your life, you will lead your family to gather regularly with His people to learn the things of the Lord, and your home will be blessed.

Don't discount church, as so many do today. They say, "I'm spiritual and I love God, but church isn't for me." If you're serious about fulfilling the purpose God has given you, and if you're serious about passing on your faith to succeeding generations, I urge you to take seriously your role in the corporate body of Christ. The reason so many families fail is because men are neglecting to connect themselves and their families to the household of faith. Scripture calls this "forsaking the assembling of ourselves together" with other believers. [16]

Finally, the writer of Psalm 128 indicates that when a man has his personal, family, and church lives lined up with God's purpose, he will also have a powerful impact on society: "May you see the prosperity of Jerusalem all the days of your life. Indeed, may you see your children's children. Peace be upon Israel!"

Notice that last phrase. Peace is *shalom,* or well-being, in the community, which happens when individuals, families, and the church are right with God and right with each other through the purposeful leadership of godly Christian men. When we get everything lined up properly with God's purpose for our lives, we will see our communities prosper. Peace will take over. Our nation will recover its spiritual health.

Some of us won't get to see our children's children because there's violence and corruption in the world, rather than peace. The psalmist says, in essence, "If you want to fix the culture, start with your own spheres of influence."

How are we, as Christian men, going to influence the leaders of our society if we're not willing to commit our personal lives to Christ, to love and nurture our families, and to serve and strengthen the church of God?

We live in a world that has lost its morals and standards. Public schools are falling apart. Criminals dominate our neighborhoods. And sometimes we're just *having* church rather than *being* the church. That's not good enough.

When we break the huddle and go on offense, let's go out and let the world know who Jesus is. We have too many secret agent Christian men; too many covert operatives. Everybody else is coming out the closet; we might as well come out too.

Isn't it time for the people you work with to know where you stand? Will you live for Christ, by God's grace, even if you have to stand alone? The people in your neighborhood ought to know where you stand.

Our world needs to hear the truth about God from Christian men who know it.

Living out a Kingdom purpose starts with our walk with God, moves to our relationship with our families, and then goes on to our involvement in the church. Soon we'll see a difference in our cities, our states, and even our nation. That's Kingdom impact, and it starts with you and me.

Living a life of meaning by serving the purposes of God is challenging. We need to be consumed by the fact that one day our eyes will close, our hearts will stop, and we will stand before God to give an account of our lives.

If you never lose sight of the postseason, that perspective will empower you to live a winning life of purpose.

JOE'S TWO-MINUTE DRILL
Purpose: How Do I Get the Most Out of Life?

Can you imagine playing a football game without first spending time crafting a winning game plan? As crazy as it may sound, this is how many people live their lives. They lack direction and a defined purpose. As Tony Evans tells us, it is only as we study and implement God's game plan that we discover direction and purpose and get the most out of life. Let me recap several truths about purpose that Tony points out for us:

✓ The purposes of God are to bring Him glory in all we do and draw others to Him. Meaning in life can be found only by serving these purposes.

✓ God created each of us for a definite and unique purpose. We bring Him glory and draw others to Him when we discover and live out this purpose.

✓ Our God-given passions, abilities, personality, experiences, and opportunities help reveal our purpose to us. God also can use the good and bad experiences in our lives to help reveal our purpose.

✓ Make God the center of your life. Walk in His ways; do what He wants done.

✓ The results of making God the center of your life are living with purpose, fruitful relationships with family, and experiencing true community within your local church.

✓ When our personal, family, and church lives are aligned with God's purposes, we are positioned to have a great impact on the society around us.

CHAPTER 13

Heaven

What happens when the clock runs out in the game of life? In football, it's real clear. The scoreboard says it all: One team wins, the other loses. In the game of life, I've seen that it is not so clear for a lot of people—even for some professing Christians.

I've often told the story of our son Coy, when he was nine or ten, telling me he wasn't sure he was going to enjoy Heaven. The problem, he told me, is that there didn't seem to be any risk, any chance of losing. So, basically he was saying, What's the point? And won't it be boring?

I have to admit, I've had those same feelings. I was born to compete. If there's no sadness in Heaven, does that mean there will be no winning so that there will be no losing? People get the idea that Heaven is about sitting around on clouds and playing harps, but you won't find that in the Bible. My friend Randy Alcorn changed my entire outlook on eternity with his book *Heaven,* and I think this chapter will change yours, too. Frankly, I'm hoping for thousand-year football games and million-mile races.

The research we conducted as we were creating *Game Plan for Life* indicated that men want to know about Heaven and Hell. They want to know what happens when they die: Is there a Heaven and a Hell? Where is their soul going to go, if anywhere?

I believe we all want to know the answers to these questions because God has put eternity in our hearts. The Bible is clear: "He has made everything beautiful in its time. He has also set eternity in the hearts of men; yet they cannot fathom what God has done from beginning to end."[1]

Like I said, dogs don't sit around thinking about eternity. For all we know, they don't even think about dying; just surviving. Humans are different. We want to know when and how things started, and how we'll end up. It's in our spiritual DNA.

The Bible addresses these questions clearly. In it, we learn about ourselves, our Creator, and our future. The Bible contains the whole story of the human race from the beginning to the end. It describes Heaven and Hell.

Most of us have a picture of Hell in our minds. Artists and writers have created pictures of Hell for us throughout the centuries. Even if some people choose not to believe there is a real Hell, they have an idea of what it might be like.

Heaven, on the other hand, is a little different. For whatever reason, most of us don't really have this one down. If anything, we think what Coy thought: It's going to be nice but boring. That's one of the reasons I asked Randy to contribute to this project. He's taken the time to paint a clear picture of Heaven straight from Scripture.

As a Christian, I understand that I'll go to Heaven. But for most of my adult life, I just didn't think much about it.

But if you're in a game, there has to be something to strive for—something to win or lose. In football, it's putting the most points on the board. In racing, it's beating every other car to the finish line. In life, it's about where your soul will spend eternity.

The clock is ticking for both of us—me and you. Will your game end at twenty-four, like Sean Taylor; forty-two, like Payne Stewart; or forty-nine, like Dale Earnhardt? Maybe you and I will each live to a grand old age. But no matter how old we are when we die, life goes by quickly. Billy Graham was quoted as saying that the biggest surprise he's had has been the brevity of life. And he turned ninety last year!

The closest I've come to Heaven so far happened several years ago when I was jetting home from a race in Loudon, New Hampshire, with eight other people. We had reached cruising altitude and I had just begun dozing when a loud bang woke me up. I was sitting behind Jimmy Makar, our crew chief at the time, and I remember seeing his arms shoot up and the oxygen masks drop down.

The pilots began a steep dive, and I could hear them shouting, "Mayday! Mayday!" Soon the fuselage was full of hot air, and I was sure the aircraft was going to burst into flames. When I looked around at my friends, their faces all hidden behind oxygen masks, their eyes were bugging out with fear, as I'm sure mine were.

We came hurtling out of the clouds, and the young team member next to me looked out the window. "We're over water!" he shouted, which sounded better to me than being over hard ground, though it wouldn't have made much difference at the speed we were going. I was sure we were all going to bite the dust that day.

But when we got down to a few thousand feet, the pilots were able to level off, and I heard them talking on the radio. There was still a flutter in their voices, but no more Maydays. Turns out a valve had broken loose, which made the loud noise, and the system had compensated for the possibility of frigid air filling the plane by releasing the heat. To our great relief, we were able to limp all the way home.

That was about as scared as I've ever been. I was a Christian and assured of Heaven, but I had to ask myself, Was I ready to be face-to-face with my Maker? Believers in Jesus Christ are going to live forever, but we don't put our stock in things on this earth. We don't know how long we have on earth.

When a driver approaches speeds of almost 200 mph on a super-speedway like Daytona or Talladega, he's taking a calculated risk. Sure, we have extensive safety features in our race cars to minimize harm to the driver in case of an accident, but the fact is you can't control everything that happens when a car wrecks. Your real focus is on the driver. What is going to happen to the man inside the car? When it stops rolling, will he be able to walk away?

I was in the infield at Daytona when Dale Earnhardt's fatal crash occurred on the last lap of the Daytona 500. In fact, earlier in that same race, our driver Tony Stewart, in the #20 Home Depot car, was in a wreck in which he actually got airborne and landed on our #18 Interstate Batteries car, driven by Bobby Labonte. Watching that collision was heart-stopping.

After Tony tumbled to a stop in the grassy infield, there was a long pause before both he and Bobby, badly shaken, got out of their cars. Their lives had been spared. Dale's wasn't. You never know what's going to happen, so you want to be prepared for eternity.

I think you'll enjoy Randy Alcorn's description of Heaven. It will give you a clear picture that should be encouraging. If you are not yet on the winning team, my prayer would be that this chapter will help you think about making that important decision—one that will have eternal consequences.

Randy Alcorn served as a pastor for fourteen years before founding Eternal Perspective Ministries in 1990, a nonprofit organization dedicated to teaching biblical truth and drawing attention to the needy. He has spoken around the world and has taught on the adjunct faculties of Multnomah University and Western Seminary in Portland, Oregon. Randy is the author of more than thirty books, with more than four million copies in print, including Heaven, *which has been acclaimed as one of the most comprehensive studies on what the Bible has to say about the subject. He produces a quarterly issues-oriented magazine,* Eternal Perspectives, *and has been a guest on more than six hundred radio and television programs. This guy has dramatically changed my view of Heaven. Randy was the first guy we called when launching this project, and he gave me and the team great insights and wisdom.*

Where Will I Spend Eternity?
RANDY ALCORN

Tired of the way things are? Or the way *you* are?

Maybe you're stressed, discouraged, or depressed. You've lost a loved one; a family member has a terminal illness; or you're jobless and can't pay the bills.

Maybe your marriage is hurting, or your children are struggling. Your dreams have crumbled.

Perhaps you've been betrayed—or worse, you've betrayed someone.

The mirror screams, "You're past your peak." Most of the sand has dropped to the bottom of your hourglass.

Or maybe you're still young, but you're floundering and disillusioned.

I have good news: Understanding the truth about Heaven can forever change the way you look at your future *and* your present.

It can give you reason to hope. Reason to be happy. Reason to be excited about where your life is headed.

Focus on the Shore

Some years ago, a woman named Florence Chadwick stepped into the Pacific Ocean off Catalina Island, planning to swim the twenty-one-plus miles to California's mainland.

The weather was foggy and cold, and the water was icy. Through the fog, Florence could barely see the team of small boats that accompanied her. Still, she swam for nearly sixteen hours until, physically and emotionally exhausted, she finally gave up and begged to be pulled from the water.

Once aboard the escort boat, she discovered the shore was less than half a mile away. She had been 98 percent there! At a later news conference, Florence said, "All I could see was the fog. If I could have seen the shore, I think I would have made it."

I know that feeling; don't you? As we face difficulty and discouragement, surrounded by life's fog, it helps if we can get a clear glimpse of the shore. We need to see where we're headed.

God's people once saw the shore more clearly. Night after night, like experienced sailors, they peered through the clouds, looking at Heaven as their North Star—a fixed point to chart their homeward course through perilous waters.

Is Heaven your reference point? Perhaps you heard something about it as a child; but now, as for most people, it has fallen off your radar screen.

More than Harp Strumming

"Whenever I think about Heaven," a pastor told me, "it makes me depressed. To float around in the clouds with nothing to do but strum a harp. . . . It sounds terribly boring."

Where did this Bible-believing, seminary-educated pastor get such a dismal view of Heaven? Certainly not from Scripture, where the apostle Paul—the writer of much of the New Testament—says that to be with Christ is *far better* than remaining here.[2]

Does the idea of Heaven excite you? Or would you rather watch a stock car race or a football game or just hang out with your friends? Maybe you relate to the Far Side cartoon depicting an angel-winged man with a halo, sitting on a cloud and saying, "Wish I'd brought a magazine."

It's become popular for people to say they don't even believe in an afterlife. But Heaven is a real place. Jesus said, "In my Father's house are many rooms. . . . I am going there to prepare a place for you."[3]

Jesus, the carpenter from Nazareth, knows how to build. The Bible says that even before man was created, Jesus created the heavens and the earth. If Jesus is preparing a place for me, I want to see it.

One man told me, "I really want to be with Jesus, but I'd like to be with Him here on earth, not up in Heaven floating like angels." He'd attended church for many years, but had never heard the Bible's good news—that God's people *will* live with Him forever on a New Earth. (I'm capitalizing New Earth—though Bible translations usually don't—because it's a real place, like New England.)

God says, "Behold, I will create new heavens and a new earth."[4] He refers to the New Earth again in Isaiah 66:22. And in the New Testament, the apostle Peter says, "In keeping with his promise we are looking forward to a new heaven and a new earth, the home of righteousness."[5]

Don't you agree that it's time we stop worrying that Heaven might be boring? Nothing else God created is boring. I'm looking forward to that new universe.

The Best Is Yet to Come

If you haven't already done so, let me urge you to read all the chapters in this book because Joe Gibbs was careful to invite his friends—experts on these things—to make clear how you can be assured of going to Heaven when you die. Joe's story gives reasons why you can be certain of your own future. He's asked me to explode the myths about Heaven and tell you what the Bible says it will really be like.

Luke 6:20-24 promises future rewards for present difficulties. Think about that. If you've put off becoming a believer in Christ—or admitting that

WHAT MANY ASSUME ABOUT HEAVEN	WHAT THE BIBLE SAYS ABOUT HEAVEN
Non-Earth	New Earth
Unfamiliar	New, with old improved
Disembodied	Embodied
Foreign (won't be like the home we know; utterly different)	Home (all the comforts of home, with many innovations)
Leaving behind what we love	Retaining the good; finding the best ahead
No time and space	Time and space
Static, unchanging	Dynamic, developing
No art, culture, or progress	Art, culture, and progress
Neither old (like Eden) nor new and earthlike; just unknown and unhuman	Both old and new, familiar and innovative; nostalgia and adventure
Nothing to do but float on clouds, strum harps; old life and relationships forgotten	God to worship and serve; friends to enjoy; universe to rule; purposeful work to do
Instant and complete knowledge; no curiosity, learning, or discovery	An eternity of exciting learning and discovery of God and His creation
Boring	Fascinating
Unhuman; no individuality; desires lost	Fully human individuals; desires fulfilled
Absence of the terrible (but presence of little we desire)	Presence of the wonderful (everything we desire and nothing we don't)
Story over	Story continuing forever

Adapted from *Heaven* by Randy Alcorn (Tyndale, 2004)

you're one, because you are afraid of what your friends might think (or say), consider this: We're told that when we suffer for following Christ, we're to "rejoice in that day and leap for joy, because great is your reward in heaven."[6]

And really, if you happen to be a reader from America or somewhere else in the West, the worst you might face for being known as a Christian is some teasing or criticism. Imagine what it's like for people in parts of the world where being known as a Christian can endanger their very lives.

Jesus said, "Blessed are the poor in spirit, for theirs is the kingdom of heaven. Blessed are those who mourn, for they will be comforted. Blessed are the meek, for they will inherit the earth."[7]

On the New Earth, life's troubles and tragedies will be reversed.

God will remove your heartbreaks and make up for them. You will feast instead of hunger; be rich instead of poor; be at peace rather than persecuted.

Have financial problems, poor health, war, or lack of time prevented you from pursuing your dreams? Life isn't over—there's a new world coming. And what a world it will be!

God promises a planet without evil, suffering, war, tragedy, frustration, anxiety, injustice, or oppression—"a new earth, in which righteousness dwells."[8]

Those who die young, are disabled, or have bad breaks in this life won't miss out on the best life. Our present minds, bodies, cultures, and relationships are only temporary. Those on the New Earth will be far better.

God, the Happy-Making Sight

Now, I recognize that outside of a church service or a seminary class, the following might sound like nonsense, but stay with me. We're told that "the throne of God and of the Lamb" is in the New Jerusalem, which will be brought down to the New Earth.[9] Let me try to unpack that. The throne of God is just what it sounds like: the place where God Himself resides. The Lamb is Jesus, and He's called that because He became our sacrificial lamb, shedding His blood for our sins, taking our punishment so we are no longer separated from a holy God.

Can you see from this that we have been made for a *person* and a *place*? Jesus is the person, and Heaven is the place.

Maybe you've had the experience of striving for happiness and satisfaction by moving on to the next person or place. It seems we're always trying for something new and different, believing it will somehow satisfy some deep inner longing. But we'll never really be satisfied with any person less than Jesus, or any place less than Heaven.

The apostle John reveals a vision God gave him (in a New Testament book naturally called *Revelation*). He describes God's final judgment of the earth, and then goes on to say, "I saw a new heaven and a new earth. . . . I saw the Holy City, the new Jerusalem, coming down out of heaven from God. . . . And I heard a loud voice from the throne saying, 'Now the dwelling of God is with men, and he will live with them. They will be his people, and God himself will be with them and be their God.'"[10]

I don't know about you, but I find that thrilling! God will actually dwell with us! Sometimes, even for devout believers, God can seem distant and remote. We long to see Him. Well, the New Earth will fulfill God's ancient promise: "My dwelling place will be with them; I will be their God, and they will be my people."

So that will be Heaven: God's throne and His presence on the New Earth.

When Jesus was sent to earth by God to become a man, He was called *Immanuel,* which means "God with us." So instead of God taking us up to live with Him in His place (which is what happens now when a believer dies), one day God will come down to live with us in our place (on the New Earth).

Ancient theologians spoke of the "beatific vision," from the Latin phrase meaning "a happy-making sight." That sight was God Himself. Revelation 22:4 says of God's people on the New Earth, "They will see his face." Though seeing God's face was once a frightening thought—because Scripture says that to see Him in our present state would result in death—seeing God in Heaven will prove incredibly joyous for His children, because we'll be completely without sin and able to delight in seeing His face. You may have been raised to believe that God is an angry master, condemning you for anything you do wrong. The truth is, He is the source of all good, the fountainhead of all joy and delight. To dwell with God will be to experience unending goodness. "In your presence is fullness of joy, at your right hand are pleasures forevermore."[11]

Had my pastor friend understood that, *boring* is the last word he'd have used for Heaven!

No More Death, Crying, or Suffering

In Revelation 21:4, John says, "[God] will wipe every tear from their eyes. There will be no more death or mourning or crying or pain, for the old order of things has passed away."

Imagine that! No more death, suffering, or sin. The best the earth has to offer, with none of the worst.

The Bible says this earth will be destroyed, but that a New Earth is coming.[12] At first glance, that's confusing. How can a destroyed earth exist again? But the Bible says our destroyed or decayed bodies will also be made alive again when we are resurrected.[13] No doubt you've heard that Jesus was resurrected, and maybe you're familiar with the story of Lazarus, whom Jesus raised from the dead. But if you're a true believer in Jesus and what He did for you by dying for your sins on the cross (as the sacrificial Lamb), one day you will be resurrected too.

If we were to live forever in an angelic realm, we wouldn't need bodies. Our spirits or souls would simply reside there. But we're going to need our bodies, because we're going to live on the New Earth.

You might think it would make more sense for God to just destroy His original creation and put it all behind Him, starting over. But he won't. After creating the heavens and earth, He called them "very good."[14] He won't abandon His creation; He'll restore it.

An entire biblical vocabulary makes this point clear. Though some of these terms may sound foreign, others you'll recognize: *Reconcile. Redeem. Restore. Recover. Return. Renew. Regenerate. Resurrect.* Each word begins with *re-*, indicating a return to an original condition that was ruined or lost.

Redemption means buying back what was formerly owned. *Reconciliation* means reestablishing a lost friendship. *Renewal* means restoring to an original state. *Resurrection* means becoming physically alive again.

These words emphasize that God plans to restore us to our best, and the earth to its best.

God's perfect plan is "to bring all things in heaven and on earth together under one head, even Christ."[15]

No Boredom in Heaven

Everything good, enjoyable, refreshing, and fascinating originates with God. That's why He says to His faithful servants, "Come and share your master's happiness!"[16]

Outside God's presence, there is no joy—nothing good. Consequently, Hell is a place of isolation, where friendship and good times don't exist. Aside from the torment, it will be eternal boredom.

Any thought that Heaven might be boring implies that God Himself is boring. That's nonsense. He handcrafted our taste buds, adrenaline, sex drives, and the nerve endings that convey pleasure to our brains. Our capacity and desire for pleasure comes from God.

Satan's strategy, first used with Adam and Eve, is to convince us that sin brings fulfillment. False! For whatever temporary thrill it brings us, sin robs us of fulfillment. Sin doesn't make life interesting; it makes life empty and boring. When we see God as he is—an inexhaustible reservoir of fascination—boredom disappears.

Addicts are convinced that without drugs they can't be happy. But the truth is—as everyone else can see—drugs make them miserable. Those who believe there can't be excitement without sin are thinking with sin-poisoned minds. They believe a lie.

Freedom from sin means freedom to be what God intended; freedom to find far greater joy in everything good.

Many people believe this life is all there is. "You only go around once, so grab all the gusto you can."

But if you're a child of God, you do *not* just go around once. As an undying person on an undying Earth, you'll live forever in vigorous and enthusiastic enjoyment with the Lord you treasure and the people you love. Talk about all the gusto you can handle!

Living between Eden and the New Earth

Adam and Eve's fall into sin didn't catch God by surprise. He had a plan in place to redeem mankind—and all Creation—from sin and death.

Because the earth was damaged by our sin, we've never known a world without corruption, suffering, and death. But still we long for such a place, don't we? When we see a roaring waterfall, a beautiful hillside, happiness in our pet's eyes, or when we enjoy a good workout or a delicious meal, we sense this world was meant for us. We're homesick for Eden.[17]

Will Eden return? Will it have familiar, tangible features and physical people? The Bible answers emphatically: *Yes!* In the New Jerusalem, the tree of life, not seen since Eden, will be a forest of life, surrounding a magnificent river.[18]

In the greatest story ever told, the unfolding drama of redemption in the Bible, the ending ties up all the loose ends. In it, we see the extraordinary parallels between our past and our future. In the first two chapters of Genesis, God plants a garden on Earth; in the last two chapters of Revelation, he brings the New Jerusalem, with a garden at its center, to the New Earth.

In Eden, there's sin, death, and a curse; on the New Earth, no more sin, death, or curse.

In Genesis, the Redeemer is promised; in Revelation, the Redeemer returns.

Genesis tells the story of paradise lost; in Revelation, paradise is regained.

In Genesis, humanity's stewardship of the earth is squandered; in Revelation, it's restored by the God-man, King Jesus.

These mirror images demonstrate the perfect symmetry of God's plan. We live in between, hearing both the distant echoes of Eden and the approaching hoofbeats of the New Earth. A better world is coming—the world made for us; the world for which we were made.

Ready to Feast?

God promises he will "transform our lowly bodies so that they will be like his glorious body."[19] The older I get, the more I long for that. Jesus' resurrection body was physical. He said to his disciples, "It is I myself! Touch me and see; a ghost does not have flesh and bones, as you see I have."[20]

After His resurrection, Jesus asked His stunned disciples for something to eat. "They gave him a piece of broiled fish, and he took it and ate it in their presence."[21]

Will we eat and drink in Heaven? God promises we will! Jesus said to His disciples, "I confer on you a kingdom, just as my Father conferred one on me, so that you may eat and drink at my table in my kingdom."[22]

He said, "Many will come from the east and the west, and will take their places at the feast with Abraham, Isaac and Jacob in the kingdom of heaven."[23]

Feasts in Heaven are referred to repeatedly: "Blessed are those who are invited to the wedding supper of the Lamb!"[24]

Imagine those meals! Conversations, storytelling, relationship building, and fun and laughter happen at meals. Don't we love to eat and drink together?

"On this mountain the Lord Almighty will prepare a feast of rich food

Three Eras of Earth and Mankind

Past	Present	Future
GENESIS 1–2	GENESIS 3–REVELATION 20	REVELATION 21–22
Original mankind	Fallen mankind; some believe and are transformed	Resurrected mankind
Original Earth	Fallen Earth, with glimmers of original	New (resurrected) Earth
God delegates Earth's reign to innocent mankind	Disputed reign with God, Satan, and fallen mankind	God delegates Earth's reign to righteous mankind
Mankind given dominion, with intended stewardship of Earth	Mankind's dominion thwarted, frustrated, and twisted	Mankind's dominion fulfilled; redeemed stewardship of Earth
God in Heaven, visiting Earth (walking in Eden)	God in Heaven, cut off from fallen mankind (indwells believers by his Spirit)	God's face gloriously seen, as He dwells with mankind on New Earth
No Curse	Sin and the Curse	No more Curse
No shame	Shame	No shame or potential for shame
Tree of life in Eden (mankind can eat)	Tree of life in Paradise (mankind cut off from)	Tree of life in New Jerusalem (mankind can eat again)
River of life in Eden	Rivers and nature, with glimmers of past and future	River of life flows from God's throne in city
No death	Death permeates all	Death forever removed
Mankind created from the earth	Mankind dies, returns to the earth; new life to some	Mankind resurrected from the earth to live on New Earth
First Adam reigns	First Adam falls; mankind reigns corruptly, with glimpses of good; second Adam comes	Last Adam reigns as God-man, with mankind as co-heirs and delegated kings
Serpent, Satan, on Earth	Satan judged but still present on Earth	Satan forever removed from Earth, thrown into eternal fire
Creation and mankind perfect	Creation and mankind tainted by sin	Creation and mankind restored to perfection
Mankind names, tends, rules the animals	Animals and mankind hurt each other and suffer	Animals and mankind live in complete harmony
Ground fertile, vegetation lush	Ground cursed, vegetation diseased	Ground fertile, vegetation thrives
Abundant food and water	Hunger and thirst, toil for food and water	Abundant food and water
Restfulness, satisfaction in labor	Restlessness, toil in labor	Enhanced restfulness, joy in labor
Paradise	Paradise lost, sought; glimmers seen, foretastes	Paradise regained and magnified
Mankind in ideal place	Mankind banished; struggles and wanders in fallen place(s)	Man restored to ideal place, but much improved
Mankind able either to sin or not to sin	Mankind enslaved to sin, empowered not to sin	Mankind unable to sin, permanently empowered
One marriage (Adam and Eve)	Many marriages (designed to reflect Christ and church)	One marriage (Christ and church)
Beginning of human culture	Contamination and advancement of culture	Purification and eternal expansion of culture
Mankind learns, creates, in purity	Mankind learns, creates, in impurity (Cain, Babel)	Mankind learns, creates, in wisdom and purity
God's plan for mankind and Earth revealed	God's plan delayed and enriched	God's plan for mankind and Earth realized

Adapted from *Heaven* by Randy Alcorn (Tyndale, 2004)

for all peoples, a banquet of aged wine—the best of meats and the finest of wines."[25] If God himself prepares the feast, it's sure to be good!

On the New Earth, we'll not only eat, but also drink together.[26] Any reason to suppose we won't drink coffee or tea there? Who created coffee beans and tea leaves?

Can you imagine having coffee with Jesus, tea with Mary, or even lemonade with Joe Gibbs on the New Earth? Why not?

Or how about sitting around a dinner table talking and laughing with the great heroes of the faith? And those aren't limited to Augustine, C. S. Lewis, Martin Luther, John Calvin, and Billy Graham. Imagine getting to know the humble Sunday school teacher no one knew, but who faithfully taught for decades without fanfare and will now be honored by Jesus.

What about the Old Testament saints? Could there be a second of boredom chatting with Abraham, Ruth, Esther, or David? And what about the apostles? The biblical teachings of the resurrection and New Earth give me every reason to believe we'll enjoy these wonderful meals and have these fascinating conversations.

Culture and Sports?

Can you imagine Earth without rivers, mountains, trees, and flowers? Neither can I. So why imagine the New Earth without them? Bible verses that talk about the New Earth speak of animals, mountains, flowing water, and trees, as well as buildings, dwelling places, and streets.

Heaven is called a city.[27] Since ancient times, cities have had structures, transportation, goods and services, art, music, drama, and athletic events. People gather and engage in activities and conversations.

Revelation 22:3 says that on the New Earth, "his servants will serve him." Servants have things to do and places to go. The New Earth will have all the best that cities have to offer without the bad—no crime, poverty, or pollution.

The Bible also calls Heaven a country.[28] Countries have territories, rulers, culture, national pride, and diverse yet united citizens.

In describing the New Jerusalem, the apostle John writes, "The kings of the earth will bring their splendor into it," and "the glory and honor of the nations will be brought into it."[29]

Still worried about being bored? The prophet Isaiah mentions the cultural products of once-pagan nations—ships of Tarshish, trees of Lebanon, camels of Ephah, and the gold and incense of Sheba—which will be brought in by its people "proclaiming the praise of the LORD." I get the impression there will be plenty to do, see, and enjoy, don't you?

Life on the New Earth will apparently include *many* redeemed cultures, and likely some ancient civilizations not seen today.

As God's image-bearers, we are creative. We love music, art, drama, and writing. Would we expect to be less creative on the New Earth?

What about sports? Some people think sports are a waste of time, even evil. Of course, if you're reading this book, you probably don't fall into that camp. Joe Gibbs has made his living in two major sports. I love sports. My wife, Nanci, is a rabid NFL fan. Fortunately for us, Scripture compares the Christian life to athletic competitions.[30] If sports were evil, they wouldn't be used as positive examples.

God invented playfulness. He made otters that play all day on their water slides. Enjoying sports is good. Sports suit our minds and bodies. They're an expression of our God-designed humanity. I play and coach tennis, and I won't be surprised to play tennis on the New Earth.

Olympic champion Eric Liddell said, "He made me fast, and when I run I feel God's pleasure." I have to believe that will be all the more true in Heaven.

Given God's promise of our having real bodies and residing in an earthly community, there's every reason to believe the same activities we enjoy here will be on the New Earth. Your favorite sport may be one not yet invented. (And you may not yet have tasted your favorite food or met your best friend.)

In your resurrection body, how would you like to play golf with Payne Stewart or basketball with David Robinson? Go running with Eric Liddell or Joni Eareckson Tada? (Joni broke her neck in a diving accident as a teenager and has been a quadriplegic for more than forty years. You can imagine how she longs for her new body.) Want to kickbox with Chuck Norris? Play football with Reggie White or Matt Hasselbeck? There'll be no injuries in resurrection bodies. Hey, maybe Joe Gibbs or Tony Dungy will be your coach!

Heaven on Earth—for Animals Too?

Will Rogers said, "If there are no dogs in Heaven, when I die I want to go where they went."

Some people say that only beings with souls or spirits will go to Heaven, and from this they conclude that animals won't make it. Well, if you enjoy animals, there's good news. Two Old Testament prophecies about the New Earth are cited in Revelation 21–22, and they clearly refer to animals.[31]

God speaks of the "whole creation"—not just human beings—groaning in suffering, and awaiting redemption.[32] What part of Creation besides human beings suffers most? Animals.

Romans 8 suggests that some of the same animals now groaning will be delivered from suffering and will live again!

Jesus spoke of the future "renewal of all things."[33] Peter preached of a day when "the time comes for God to restore everything, as he promised long ago through his holy prophets."[34]

Christ proclaims from His throne on the New Earth: "Behold, I am making all things new."[35] So "all things"—including horses, cats, dogs, lions, and zebras—will be made new when Christ restores the earth.

If God will re-create some animals, might our pets be among them? Scripture doesn't say, but there's certainly no reason to tell a child— grieving over a departed pet—that he'll never see it again. I believe we can say with confidence that it would be simple for God to re-create a pet on the New Earth. He's far better than we are at giving good gifts to His children.[36] Certainly, if it would make us any happier in Heaven, God would restore a pet.

By finding pleasure in God's creation—whether in animals, music, drama, sports, or study, now and in eternity—we find our pleasure in Him.

Will We Know Everything?

People often say, "We don't understand now, but in Heaven we'll know everything."

Not true.

God alone is all-knowing. When we die, we'll see more clearly and know more than we do now, but we'll always be finite, so we'll *never* know *everything.*

Ephesians 2:6-7 says that God saves us "in order that in the coming ages he might show the incomparable riches of his grace." The word that's translated *show* means "to reveal." The phrase "in the coming ages" indicates an ongoing revelation, in which we'll continually learn about God's grace. Some people, and I'm one of them, love to study. But even if you don't like working at it, surely you enjoy learning new things. Imagine the joy of never-ending discovery! Who knows what we may discover in the far reaches of the new universe, revealing new depths of God's character?

I often give books to people I meet in passing, hoping they'll be drawn to Christ. I can't wait to hear the rest of their stories if I see them on the New Earth. How many tales are waiting to be told by people influenced by our prayer, kindness, and financial giving?

Overflowing with Laughter

Martin Luther said, "If you're not allowed to laugh in Heaven, I don't want to go there."

God created all good things, including humor. If He didn't have a sense of humor, human beings—his image-bearers—wouldn't either. And there wouldn't be aardvarks, baboons, platypuses, and giraffes!

As I said, my wife loves pro football. She opens our home to family and friends for Sunday night dinner and football. Week after week, there are stories and heart-to-heart talks—all surrounded by laughter. God made us to love laughter. If you can't picture Jesus teasing and laughing with His disciples, why not? I'll bet His laughter was loudest.

The new universe will ring with laughter. Jesus said, "Blessed are you who hunger now, for you will be satisfied. Blessed are you who weep now, for you will laugh."[37] *You will laugh*—words just as inspired as "For God so loved the world."

When facing discouragement, recite Christ's promise for the new world, a promise that echoes off the distant galaxies: *You will laugh!*

Is Your Name on the List?

In Scripture, Jesus says more about Hell than anyone else does.[38] He describes it in graphic terms, including raging fires. He says the unsaved "will be thrown outside, into the darkness, where there will be weeping and gnashing of teeth."[39]

Jesus taught that in Hell the wicked suffer terribly, are conscious, retain their memories and reasoning, long for relief, cannot be comforted, and are bereft of hope.[40] He couldn't have painted a bleaker picture.

For those who don't know Christ, this present life is the closest they'll come to Heaven. For those who know Him, it's the closest they'll come to Hell. That should bring comfort to believers and sober warning to unbelievers.

Revelation 21:27 says, "Nothing impure will ever enter [the New Jerusalem], nor will anyone who does what is shameful or deceitful, but only those whose names are written in the Lamb's book of life." Heaven is not for good people or even perfect people; it is reserved for only the forgiven.

Vocalist Ruthanna Metzgar was asked to sing at a wealthy man's wedding. The reception was on the top floors of Columbia Tower, Seattle's tallest skyscraper. Ruthanna and her husband, Roy, were excited to attend.

To begin the reception, the bride and groom ascended a beautiful glass and brass staircase to the top floor, followed by their guests.

Outside the door to the great banquet room, the maitre d' stood holding a bound book.

"May I have your name, please?"

"Ruthanna Metzgar. This is my husband, Roy."

He searched the book. "I'm not finding it." Ruthanna spelled her name slowly. The maitre d' looked up. "I'm sorry, but your name isn't here."

"There must be some mistake," Ruthanna said. "I'm the singer!"

"It doesn't matter who you are. Without your name in the book, you cannot attend the banquet."

On their way out, Roy said, "Sweetheart, what happened?"

"When the invitation arrived, I was busy," she said. "I never bothered to respond. Besides, I was the singer. Surely I didn't have to return the RSVP to go to the reception!"

Ruthanna had missed the most lavish banquet she'd ever been invited to. But what struck her most was the taste of what it will be like for people who have not put their faith in Jesus Christ as they stand before Him and discover the awful truth that their names aren't written in the Lamb's book of life.

You're Invited—Have You Said Yes?

Countless people are too busy to respond to Christ's invitation to his wedding banquet. Many assume the good they've done—attending church, being baptized, singing in the choir, giving a donation, doing volunteer work, or just not being too bad a person—will be enough to earn entry to Heaven. But all that will matter is whether their names are in the Lamb of God's book of eternal life. If you haven't responded to God's invitation, you'll be turned away. And that won't mean simply being left out. It will mean being cast into Hell.

People say, "How could a loving God send people to Hell?" The sad truth is, they send themselves there by not responding to His invitation. The Bible says that Jesus is not willing that any should perish but wants all of us to repent and place our faith in Him.[41]

Forgiveness is not automatic. We must admit our sin: "If we confess our sins, He is faithful and just and will forgive us our sins and purify us from all unrighteousness."[42]

"In him we have redemption through his blood, the forgiveness of sins, in accordance with the riches of God's grace."[43]

Jesus Christ took upon Himself the punishment for our sins.[44] We get no credit for salvation: "For it is by grace you have been saved, through faith—and this not from yourselves, it is the gift of God—not by works, so that no one can boast."[45]

Christ offers everyone the gift of forgiveness and eternal life: "Whoever is thirsty, let him come; and whoever wishes, let him take the free gift of the water of life."[46]

That free gift to us was incredibly costly to God's Son. Imagine—He went to Hell on the cross for us, rather than live in Heaven without us.

If you think you can enter Heaven without responding to Christ's invitation, or you're putting off your response, one day you will deeply regret it.

But if you've said yes to Christ's invitation to join him at the wedding feast and spend eternity with Him, you can rejoice—your name is in His book, and Heaven's gates will be open to you!

Death, the Doorway to Life

For believers in Jesus, death is the doorway to His presence. Strange as it sounds, heading toward death is heading in the right direction—but only if you have the right game plan. That means believing in and trusting Jesus, and therefore knowing where you're going.

Jesus came "so that by His death He might destroy him who holds the power of death—that is, the devil—and free those who all their lives were held in slavery by their fear of death."[47]

When five-year-old Emily Kimball was hospitalized and heard she would die, she cried. Emily loved Jesus and wanted to be with Him, but she didn't want to leave her family.

Emily's mother asked her to step through a doorway into another room and closed the door behind her. Then, one at a time, the entire family entered the room. Her mother explained that this was how it would be when Emily died. She would go ahead to Heaven, and then the rest of her Christian family would follow. This was a great encouragement to Emily.

In light of the coming resurrection, the apostle Paul asks, "Where, O death, is your victory? Where, O death, is your sting?"[48]

Understanding the future should radically affect our view of deteriorating health. The elderly and disabled should recognize that life on the New Earth will be far better than the best they ever knew here.

"Therefore we do not lose heart. Though outwardly we are wasting away, yet inwardly we are being renewed day by day. For our light and momentary troubles are achieving for us an eternal glory that far outweighs them all. So we fix our eyes not on what is seen, but on what is unseen. For what is seen is temporary, but what is unseen is eternal."[49]

As people age, they tend to look back at when they were at their best, knowing they'll never regain those days. But if you're a Christ-follower, you don't look back to your peak. You look forward to it.

When we feel our bodies shutting down, let's remind ourselves, "The strongest I've ever felt is just a hint of what's to come."

C. S. Lewis ends the Chronicles of Narnia as the characters enter Aslan the Lion's country, Heaven:

> But for them it was only the beginning of the real story. All their life in this world and all their adventures in Narnia had only been the cover and the title page: now at last they were beginning Chapter One of the Great Story which no one on earth has read: which goes on forever: in which every chapter is better than the one before.[50]

The Ultimate Adventure

To endure life's cold waters and fog, remember Florence Chadwick's lament: "If I could have seen the shore, I would have made it." Consider

Paul's words: "Set your hearts on things above, where Christ is seated at the right hand of God."[51]

Anticipating a New Earth, full of righteousness, Peter writes, "So then, dear friends, since you are looking forward to this, make every effort to be found spotless, blameless and at peace with him."[52]

Thinking about the fact that it is our destiny to live on a righteous Earth with our righteous God should be a powerful incentive to live for Him today, with the strength He supplies.

Remember, on the New Earth, God "will wipe every tear from their eyes. There will be no more death or mourning or crying or pain. . . . 'I am making everything new!'" Perhaps knowing that this promise might sound too good to be true, Jesus added, "Write this down, for these words are trustworthy and true."[53]

That's the promise of King Jesus, sealed with His blood. Count on it. Take it to the bank. Live every day in light of it.

If you know Jesus, a great reunion awaits you with believers who've gone before you. I'll see you in Heaven, as will the other authors of this book. Someday we'll populate that wondrous New Earth together, to God's glory. What great times we'll have!

With the Lord we love, and with family and friends we cherish, we'll embark on the ultimate adventure in a spectacular new universe.

Jesus will be the center of everything.

Joy will be the air we breathe.

And just when we think, *It can't get any better than this,* it will.

JOE'S TWO-MINUTE DRILL
Heaven: Where Will I Spend Eternity?

Many people today, when they think about Heaven, imagine people sitting around strumming harps up in the clouds. I don't know about you, but that sounds really boring to me! According to Randy Alcorn, this perspective is simply not true of God's game plan. Let me recap some of the truths about Heaven that Randy points out for us:

- ✓ Heaven is a real place. The earth as we know it will be destroyed but made new again by God. God will dwell among us on the New Earth.
- ✓ Heaven will not be boring. We will not be sitting around strumming harps. Heaven is a place we should look forward to and be excited about.
- ✓ We will keep our physical bodies in Heaven. The decayed or worn-out ones we have now will be restored and made even better.
- ✓ We will eat, drink, laugh, listen to music—and maybe even play football in Heaven.
- ✓ We will see friends and family in Heaven.
- ✓ Hell is also a real place—one of eternal suffering and isolation from God. There will be no joy, friendship, or good times in Hell—only torment.
- ✓ To get into Heaven, you must have a relationship with Jesus. Heaven is not a place for perfect people; it is reserved only for the forgiven. Forgiveness is found in Jesus.

CHAPTER 14

Still Battling

One thing you need to know: I'm still a work in progress. Don't be misled by my desire to put together this *Game Plan for Life*. I need it just as much as you do.

I'd like to be able to say that, in my sixties, I've mastered the game plan for life. But I haven't. I guess you might call me a life learner. Maybe you are too.

When Dan Snyder asked me to coach the Redskins again, he offered me a five-year deal. In 2007, the year we faced so many challenges—chief among them the death of Sean Taylor—I was going into the end of the fourth year of my contract. I needed to make a call as to whether to keep coaching or not.

A few factors that affected my decision weighed heavily on my mind.

Our two sons have eight kids between them, and as you can imagine, Pat and I love them all deeply.

In January 2007, when J.D. and Melissa's fourth son, Taylor, was just two years old, he became seriously ill. The doctors feared leukemia. I'll never forget waiting for the final diagnosis and seeing older kids in the hospital who were suffering from what we dreaded Taylor might have. We paced and prayed and cried and hoped. And even though we had been warned to be prepared, when the leukemia diagnosis was confirmed, we were devastated.

Precious Taylor has since undergone operations and chemotherapy. If anything will test your faith or make you want to question God, it's when a little loved one suffers like that. I can't say I understand it, and I sure don't like it. But I've learned the true meaning of intercessory prayer. It isn't just praying for someone; it's being willing to trade places with him or her and wishing you could. *If only I could . . .*

My diabetes was no doubt triggered by my lifestyle, my eating habits, my age, and maybe some genetics. Half of those I could have controlled. When a toddler gets a horrific disease, you just have to trust the Lord and deal with it, that's all. It has brought our whole family together in a very special way.

My head knows that God is all-powerful and all-knowing, and that He loves us with an everlasting love. But I ache for my grandson. To hear him, despite all he's been through, sing in his little tiny voice, "God is so good," well, it just tears my heart out. He has the sweetest personality.

On one of my visits to Charlotte during the 2007 season, Taylor's mom, Melissa, put together a big party to celebrate Taylor's third birthday. At the same time, she and J.D. wanted to honor all of those faithful friends and acquaintances who'd stepped up to the plate to help them get through the first year of Taylor's cancer treatment. They showed a video they had made, featuring clips of everyone who had helped.

As I watched the video, I saw that an awful lot of people had encircled J.D. and Melissa to support their family and Taylor. I wasn't one of them. "Coach" had been gone a lot of the time.

I'll be honest with you; it didn't make me feel very good.

Earlier, I mentioned that I regret missing so much of my two boys' childhoods. I have been trying to rectify that with them, working together and spending more time together. By 2004, J.D. and I had worked together at the race team for twelve years, and he was doing a great job. One of the reasons I had gone back to the Redskins was to have more time with Coy. Having played linebacker at Stanford, he was considering going into coaching. He could coach on our staff with the Redskins.

I've also tried to spend a lot of time with my grandkids. Outside my office at the race shop are a bunch of plastic #11, #18, and #20 cars for the smaller grandkids to pedal around the office. And I catch as many of the older kids' games as I can.

But now, here I was, once again away from the family at a time when

I might have been really helpful. Between Sean Taylor and Taylor Gibbs, I saw how fragile life can be.

By this point, Coy had decided to try a different career path and was no longer with me at the Redskins. My whole family was living their lives in Charlotte, and I was in Washington, coaching. That is not what I had envisioned.

That video of Taylor and later interactions with Pat, J.D., and Coy had a huge impact on me. I decided I needed to opt out of my fifth year with the Redskins and get back home.

That final season turned out to be tough.

We had started out 2–0, then went to 3–1, 4–2, and 5–3 before we lost three straight games, all by eight points or less. Our chances of making the postseason were next to none.

That's when a head coach is really put to the test. How do you stay prepared, keep your guys motivated, and try to put a win streak together? We had good personnel and had lost close games, but something had to give. We were heading into December and had just five games to go in the regular season. I figured we had to win them all to make the playoffs.

Two days after that third straight loss, I was awakened by the call from Dan Snyder with the news about Sean Taylor. Dan had been right, and now Sean was gone. I had never had anything like that happen in all my years of coaching. The team was deeply shaken, yet somehow we had to get ready for the next Sunday's game at home. I had no idea what to expect. We were one emotionally rocked team.

That game was the one against Buffalo I told you about earlier. We lost it by a field goal because of my bad call. Silently, I was praying, "God, I want to finish this season well. I want to be able to keep a strong testimony so I can continue to reach people for You."

As I continued to suffer, I had to face myself and ask the tough questions. Did I really want to turn things around for God's sake—or for my own sake? Didn't I want a great year just so it would be another feather in my cap? I finally confessed to the Lord and asked His forgiveness, because I recognized that this was more about me and my embarrassment, and my fear that nothing positive would be said about my coaching again. Isn't it amazing the way God can take the toughest experiences in our life and use them to shape and mold us?

The next day, the entire team traveled to Miami to attend a celebration of Sean's life. Then it was straight back to Washington for a short work week, as we were scheduled to play the Bears at home on Thursday night. We were 5–7 with four games to play, pretty much on life support. I had no idea whether the players could even get up for the game, as gut-wrenching as the previous week had been.

And then everything went from bad to worse for us. Our quarterback was knocked out of the game, and soon injured guys were going and coming from the locker room like it was a fire drill. One of our defensive backs, Fred Smoot, got hit so hard he was throwing up blood. In the locker room, he saw on the TV monitor that the Bears were throwing into his coverage area, taking advantage of his replacement. He knew the trainer would never let him go, so he asked the guy to go get him a towel, and then slipped out and came back to play.

Somehow we were able to beat a really good Bears team, 24–16, and now we were 6–7.

Ten days later, we played the New York Giants, the team that would go on to win the Super Bowl. They had beaten us three times in a row at their stadium in the Meadowlands, and it's a tough place to play. The wind was strong and frigid, but we went after them from the get-go and won 22–10. Now we were 7–7, but we had to face the Minnesota Vikings the next Sunday in their dome, and no one gave us a chance. You can't hear yourself think in that place. Plus they had a real shot at the playoffs, so they were motivated.

What an emotional game! Our guys played their guts out, up and down that field, and it turned out to be one of the biggest upsets I've ever been a part of. We won 32–21, and all of a sudden we were 8–7 and knocking on the door of a wild card spot. The only thing standing in our way was our archrivals, the Dallas Cowboys. At least we got to play them at home.

The Cowboys were already 13–2 and had locked up their playoff berth, but they didn't make it easy for us. They started their first string, and you know they didn't want to lose to us. But we would not be denied, and we beat them 27–6. We had followed four straight losses and a horrible tragedy with four straight victories to get into the playoffs.

I could hardly believe it. From Sean's death and the Buffalo fiasco—the lowest point in my coaching career—just four weeks earlier, tragedy and misfortune were turning into something of a triumph. The media were actually starting to say positive things about my coaching and the Redskins again. That couldn't help us get over Sean's death, but at least there was some good news for a change. Only God could have done that.

But you know what? If no one said another positive thing about my coaching career or the team, it ultimately wouldn't matter, past hurting my pride. What will last is what I pass on to my sons, my grandchildren, and others.

At this writing, our Taylor continues to undergo extensive treatments—some lasting a full day—and I have worked out my schedule to be part of the extended family that is helping in this trial.

Like I said, I can be a slow learner, but I am a life learner. And as I write to you about the game plan for life, I am once again reminded that I'm playing to an audience of one.

God never ceases to amaze me. My own life is a testimony to His faithfulness. I can point to my setbacks, shortcomings, and failings, and show how He has lifted me back up when I've reached out to Him and confessed and moved on with what He's called me to do with my life. It's a never-ending process.

As I near the end of my sixties, I'm still working on a lot of the areas we cover in this book. I hope and pray that you can learn from the mistakes I've made and make God your coach and the Bible your playbook in the game of life.

JOE'S TWO-MINUTE DRILL
Going for Two, to Win the Game of Life

Now that you've read *Game Plan for Life,* I hope you realize that the central point of the book is to make sure you're part of God's team. If you haven't yet made that decision, God has made it so simple that all you have to do is accept His offer of salvation. If you'd like to do that, pray this prayer:

> Lord, I recognize that you have created me, and I confess that I am a sinner. I know that you sent your Son, Jesus Christ, to die on the cross for my sins. I want you to come into my life, forgive me of my sins, and be my Lord and Savior.

If you sincerely acknowledge Jesus as your Lord, you will be on God's team—the one team that is guaranteed victory.

Resources for Further Reading

The Bible

New Evidence That Demands a Verdict by Josh McDowell (reliability of the Bible)

The Case for Christ by Lee Strobel (reliability of the Bible)

More Than a Carpenter by Josh McDowell (authenticity of Jesus Christ)

I'm Glad You Asked by Kenneth Boa and Larry Moody (apologetics)

I Don't Have Enough Faith to Be an Atheist by Norman L. Geisler and Frank Turek (apologetics)

20 Compelling Evidences that God Exists by Kenneth Boa and Robert M. Bowman Jr. (apologetics for seekers)

The Reason for God by Timothy Keller (apologetics for seekers)

Jesus: Fact or Fiction (an interactive DVD exploring the evidence about Jesus)

www.rzim.org (Web site on apologetics)

Vocation

The Call by Os Guinness (vocation)

Wisdom at Work by Kenneth Boa and Gail Burnett (vocation)

Business by the Book by Larry Burkett (work)

Business for the Glory of God by Wayne Grudem (biblical view of vocation)

Your Work Matters to God by Doug Sherman and William Hendricks (meaning and calling in the workplace)

The 9 to 5 Window by Os Hillman (how faith transforms the marketplace)

Creation

Darwin's Black Box by Michael Behe (evolution)

Darwin on Trial by Phillip E. Johnson (intelligent design)

The Privileged Planet by Discovery Institute (DVD on intelligent design)

Unlocking the Mystery of Life by Illustra Media (DVD on intelligent design)

I Don't Have Enough Faith to Be an Atheist by Norman L. Geisler and Frank Turek (scientific support of Scripture)

Why the Universe Is the Way It Is by Hugh Ross (scientific evidence for intelligent design)

The Case for a Creator by Lee Strobel (scientific evidence that points to God)
Icons of Evolution by Jonathan Wells (errors in evolutionary arguments)
www.discovery.org/csc (Web site on intelligent design)

Finances

Faith-Based Family Finances by Ron Blue and Jeremy White (overall financial reference)
Money, Possessions and Eternity by Randy Alcorn (biblical teaching on finances)
The Treasure Principle by Randy Alcorn (generous giving)
Your Money Counts by Howard Dayton (financial principles)
A Life Well Spent by Russ Crosson (investing yourself and your money in your family)
Your Money after the Big 5-0 by Larry Burkett and Ron Blue with Jeremy White (Nashville: Broadman & Holman, 2007).
Your Kids Can Master Their Money by Ron and Judy Blue and Jeremy White (Carol Stream, IL: Tyndale, 2006).
Splitting Heirs: Giving Money and Things to Your Children without Ruining Their Lives by Ron Blue with Jeremy White (Chicago: Northfield, 2004).
www.masteryourmoney.com (Web site on finances)
www.crown.org (Web site on finances)

God

Knowing God by J. I. Packer (knowing God)
The Knowledge of the Holy by A. W. Tozer (knowing God)
Conformed to His Image by Kenneth Boa (knowing God)
Making Sense of the Trinity by Millard J. Erickson (reader-friendly text on the Trinity)
The Holiness of God by R. C. Sproul (the awesome nature of God)

Health

10 Essentials of Highly Healthy People by Dr. Walt Larimore and Traci Mullins (personal health)
God's Design for the Highly Healthy Person by Dr. Walt Larimore and Traci Mullins (personal health)

The Wounded Heart by Dr. Dan B. Allender (sexual abuse recovery)
Fit after 40 by Don Nava (keys to looking good and feeling great)
A Resilient Life by Gordon MacDonald (developing inner and outer resources)
www.drwalt.com (Web site on health)

Heaven

Heaven by Randy Alcorn (Heaven)
Heaven for Kids by Randy Alcorn (Heaven)
Heaven: Your Real Home by Joni Eareckson Tada (Heaven)
One Minute after You Die by Erwin W. Lutzer (death)
Sense and Nonsense about Heaven and Hell by Kenneth Boa and Robert M.
    Bowman Jr. (what the Bible reveals about Heaven and Hell)
Heaven: The Heart's Deepest Longing by Peter Kreeft (Heaven)
www.epm.org (Web site on Heaven and eternity)

Relationships

Two Becoming One by Don and Sally Meredith (marriage)
The Five Love Languages by Gary Chapman (loving your spouse)
Love and Respect by Emerson Eggerichs (marriage)
The Friendship Factor by Alan Loy McGinnis (cultivating lasting friendships)
The Mystery of Marriage by Mike Mason (marriage)
Intended for Pleasure by Ed Wheat (sex)
The Language of Love by Gary Smalley and John Trent (developing relational
    understanding)
Shepherding a Child's Heart by Tedd Tripp (parenting)
Love and Respect by Emerson Eggerichs (DVD on marriage)
www.2becoming1.com (Web site on marriage)
www.familylife.com (Web site on marriage and family)

Purpose

The Kingdom Agenda by Tony Evans (God's purposes)
Desiring God by John Piper (living for God's glory)
The Purpose-Driven Life by Rick Warren (purposeful living)
The Man in the Mirror by Patrick Morley (solving twenty-four problems men
    face)
The Pursuit of God by A. W. Tozer (developing a heart for God)

Conformed in His Image by Kenneth Boa (biblical purpose)

www.desiringgod.org (Web site for John Piper's Desiring God ministry)

Salvation

Born Again by Charles W. Colson (personal testimony)

The Cross of Christ by John R. W. Stott (the Cross)

Mere Christianity by C. S. Lewis (saving faith)

Salvation by Earl D. Radmacher (salvation)

So Great Salvation by Charles C. Ryrie (what it means to believe in Jesus Christ)

Why I Am a Christian, Norman L. Geisler and Paul K. Hoffman, eds. (seventeen leading thinkers explain why they believe)

Sin and Addiction

The Screwtape Letters by C. S. Lewis (spiritual warfare)

The Game Plan by Joe Dallas (a men's guide for attaining sexual integrity)

The Purity Principle by Randy Alcorn (principles for sexual purity)

Legislating Morality by *Frank Turek and* Norman L. Geisler (how the law can be used to promote good and curtail evil)

Freedom from Addiction by Neil Anderson and Mike & Julia Quarles (breaking the bondage of addiction)

www.purelifealliance.org (Web site for sexual purity)

My Team

Randy Alcorn, chapter 13, Where Will I Spend Eternity?

In 1990, Randy founded Eternal Perspective Ministries, a nonprofit organization dedicated to teaching biblical truth and drawing attention to the needy.

Prior to that, he served as a pastor for fourteen years. He has spoken around the world and has taught on the adjunct faculties of Multnomah University and Western Seminary in Portland, Oregon.

Randy is the author of more than thirty books, with more than four million copies in print, including *Heaven* and several best-selling novels. He produces a quarterly issues-oriented magazine, *Eternal Perspectives,* and has been a guest on more than six hundred radio and television programs.

Ron Blue, chapter 9, How Do I Master My Money?

Ron founded a CPA firm in 1970 that has grown to become one of the fifty largest such firms in the United States. In 1979, he founded a biblically based financial planning firm that has grown to manage more than $4 billion in assets for more than five thousand clients, with a staff of more than 175 people in fourteen regional offices.

Ron retired from financial planning in 2003 in order to lead Kingdom Advisors, an international effort to equip and motivate Christian financial professionals.

He is the author of sixteen books on personal finance, including the bestseller *Master Your Money* (now in its thirtieth printing).

Dr. Ken Boa, chapter 4, Who Is God?

Ken is engaged in a ministry of evangelism and discipleship, teaching, writing, and speaking. He earned a B.S. degree from Case Institute of Technology, a master's of theology from Dallas Theological Seminary, and doctoral degrees from New York University and Oxford University.

Dr. Boa is president of Reflections Ministries and also of Trinity House Publishers. He has written dozens of books and is a contributing editor to *The Open Bible* from Thomas Nelson, and consulting editor to the *NASB Study Bible* from Zondervan.

Ken's free monthly teaching letter, "Reflections," is available from www.
KenBoa.org or (800) DRAW NEAR (800-372-9632).

Charles Colson, chapter 7, How Do I Get on God's Winning Team?

Chuck was special counsel to President Richard M. Nixon from 1969 to 1973
and later served prison time for obstruction of justice related to the Watergate
scandal. After his release from prison, he founded Prison Fellowship
Ministries, a nonprofit organization that uses fifty thousand volunteers to
minister to prisoners and their families in nearly ninety countries.

He is also founder and chairman of the Wilberforce Forum, the Christian
worldview thinking, teaching, and advocacy arm of Prison Fellowship.
Chuck's daily radio broadcast, *BreakPoint,* is heard on more than a thousand
stations. He is the author of several books, including *Born Again,* the story of
his life and conversion to Christ.

Dr. Tony Evans, chapter 12, How Do I Get the Most Out of Life?

Tony was the first African-American to earn a doctorate in theology from
Dallas Theological Seminary. He has also received two honorary doctorates. He serves as senior pastor of Oak Cliff Bible fellowship in Dallas and is
founder and president of The Urban Alternative, a national organization that
seeks to bring about spiritual renewal in the inner city. *The Alternative with
Tony Evans* is broadcast daily on more than five hundred radio stations in the
United States and in forty other countries.

Tony has served as chaplain for both the Dallas Cowboys and the Dallas
Mavericks. In 1989, he was named Father of the Year in Dallas.

He is the author of nine books.

Dr. Os Guinness, chapter 10, How Do I Build a Successful Life and Career?

Os is the great-great-grandson of Arthur Guinness, the Dublin brewer.
His parents were medical missionaries to China during World War II. He
studied at the University of London and earned his doctorate in philosophy
in the social sciences from Oriel College, Oxford.

Os was a freelance reporter with the BBC before coming to the United
States in 1984. He has been a guest scholar and visiting fellow at the Brookings
Institution and was for many years a senior fellow at the Trinity Forum.

Os has written and edited more than twenty-five books, including his latest, *The Case for Civility: And Why Our Future Depends On It.* Os is a frequent speaker and seminar leader at political and business conferences in the United States and Europe.

Dr. Walt Larimore, chapter 11, How Do I Achieve True Health?
Walt earned his medical degree at Louisiana State University and completed his family medicine residency at Duke University. He practiced medicine for more than twenty years before becoming vice president and family physician in residence at Focus on the Family in Colorado Springs, where he worked until 2004.

Walt has appeared on countless radio and television shows, including hosting more than 850 live, daily episodes of the national cable TV show *Ask the Family Doctor.* One expert said that he had "more actual on-air TV experience than any physician in the history of television."

Dr. Larimore has published eighteen books and more than six hundred articles. He is now a full-time author, educator, and journalist.

Dr. John C. Lennox, chapter 5, How Life Begin?
John has a master's in bioethics and three doctorates, and serves as professor of mathematics at Oxford University. He is also a fellow in mathematics and philosophy of science at Green College, Oxford, where he serves as pastoral advisor.

He speaks Russian, French, and German and is the author of several books on the relationship of science with religion and ethics.

John has debated Professor Richard Dawkins (*The God Delusion*), Christopher Hitchens (*God Is Not Great*), and Michael Shermer (*Skeptic* magazine).

During the Cold War, Dr. Lennox made repeated visits to the Communist bloc over a span of twenty-five years. Since the collapse of Communism, he has often visited Russia to speak in universities and academies of science. He teaches at Christian conferences around the world, showing how Scripture engages with worldview questions in contemporary society.

Josh McDowell, chapter 3, Can I Believe the Bible?
Josh earned a bachelor's degree from Wheaton College and graduated magna cum laude from Talbot Theological Seminary with a master's of

divinity. In 1964, he became a traveling representative of Campus Crusade for Christ International and remains closely associated with the organization today.

He is best known for his seminars, debates, and books on the subject of Christian apologetics (or defense of the faith). Josh is founder of Josh.org and of Operation Carelift, an international humanitarian aid ministry run by the Global Aid Network, a branch of Campus Crusade.

Evidence that Demands a Verdict and *More than a Carpenter,* the best known of the 112 books Josh has authored or coauthored, blend historical arguments with legal arguments concerning both eyewitness and circumstantial evidence for Jesus' life and resurrection.

Don Meredith, chapter 8, What Does God Say about Marriage and Sex?

In 1976, Don was asked by Campus Crusade for Christ to help start the FamilyLife Ministry, teaching marriage principles in churches across America. For three years, he worked with the original speaker teams, eventually turning over the helm of that great ministry to cofounder Dennis Rainey.

Church planting is another ministry dear to his heart, and to his wife, Sally. The Merediths were instrumental in planting the first Fellowship Bible Church in Dallas in 1972, and another in Little Rock in 1977. Don has gone on to help start six more churches in Virginia and North Carolina.

In 1983, Don relocated to Washington, D.C., to work with congressional couples in the areas of marriage and Bible studies. There, he helped Redskins coach Joe Gibbs start a home called Youth for Tomorrow for at-risk boys. It is a 24/7 residential facility with an on-site school located on two hundred acres.

In 1991, Don helped Joe Gibbs start a NASCAR team, which now employs more than 450 people. Don and Joe have worked side by side in ministry, racing, and marriage ministry for more than twenty-five years.

Don is also the founder and director of Christian Family Life, Inc.

Ravi Zacharias, chapter 6, How Do I Deal with Sin?

Ravi is widely regarded as one of the great thinkers of this generation. His Ravi Zacharias International Ministries is headquartered in Atlanta, with offices in six other countries.

Born in India, Ravi immigrated to the West at age twenty and was educated at Trinity International University (Illinois) and Cambridge University (England). He has honorary doctorates from Houghton College (New York), Tyndale College Seminary (Toronto), and Asbury College (Kentucky).

He is currently a visiting lecturer at Wycliffe Hall at Oxford University (England).

Ravi's weekly program, *Let My People Think,* airs on more than seventeen hundred radio outlets worldwide. He has authored or edited more than twenty books, several of which have been translated into many languages. His most recent book is *The End of Reason: A Response to the New Atheists.*

About the Authors

Joe Gibbs is a National Football League Hall of Famer, having served as head coach of the Washington Redskins from 1981 to 1992, and again from 2004 to 2007. During his sixteen years with the team, Gibbs led the Redskins to ten playoff appearances, four NFC Championship titles, and three Super Bowl victories. He also owns a NASCAR team, Joe Gibbs Racing, and has won three national championships in that sport. Joe and his wife, Pat, live in North Carolina, where he works with their sons, J.D. (married to Melissa) and Coy (married to Heather). Joe and Pat have eight grandchildren.

Jerry B. Jenkins is a widely published author, best known for the *New York Times* best-selling Left Behind series, which he wrote with Tim LaHaye. Jerry has written many biographies, including the stories of Walter Payton, Hank Aaron, Orel Hershiser, Meadowlark Lemon, Mike Singletary, and Nolan Ryan, among others. He also assisted Billy Graham with his memoirs, *Just As I Am*. Jerry currently serves as chairman of the board of trustees of the Moody Bible Institute of Chicago. He and his wife, Dianna, live in Colorado and have three sons and four grandchildren.

Notes

2: MY OWN JOURNEY
1. John 3:16.

3: THE ULTIMATE PLAYBOOK/CAN I BELIEVE THE BIBLE?
1. Jason Reid, "A Kick to the Gut," *Washington Post* (3 December 2007).
2. 2 Kings 3:16-18.
3. See Deuteronomy 13:1-18; 18:20-22.
4. See Genesis 12:1-3; 15:1-21; 17:8; Deuteronomy 30:1-10; Isaiah 11:11–12:6; 43:5-7; Jeremiah 30:7–31:40; Ezekiel 20:33-44; 36:16–37:28; Amos 9:11-15; Romans 11:25-27.
5. Peter Stoner, *Science Speaks* (Chicago: Moody, 1963), 107.
6. 2 Timothy 3:16-17.
7. Acts 1:3.
8. See Mark 14:50.
9. See Luke 24:11.
10. See John 20:24-27.
11. Luke 1:1-2, emphasis added.
12. 1 John 1:3, emphasis added.
13. 2 Peter 1:16, emphasis added.
14. Acts 4:20, emphasis added.
15. Acts 2:22, emphasis added.
16. Acts 26:25-26, emphasis added.
17. W. F. Albright, *Recent Discoveries in Bible Lands* (New York: Funk and Wagnalls, 1955), 136.
18. Adapted from Josh McDowell and Thomas Williams, *The Relational Word* (Holiday, FL: Green Key Books, 2006), 219.
19. F. J. A. Hort and Brooke Foss Westcott, *The New Testament in the Original Greek, vol. 1* (New York: Macmillan, 1881), 561.
20. Norman L. Geisler and William E. Nix, *A General Introduction to the Bible* (Chicago: Moody, 1968), 386.
21. Ravi Zacharias, *Can Man Live Without God?* (Nashville: Word, 1994), 162.
22. Frederic G. Kenyon, *Our Bible and the Ancient Manuscripts* (London: Eyre and Spottiswoode, 1939), 38.
23. Geisler and Nix, *General Introduction to the Bible*, 430.
24. William F. Albright, *The Archaeology of Palestine,* rev. ed. (Baltimore: Penguin, 1960), 127–128.
25. John Elder, *Prophets, Idols, and Diggers* (New York: Bobbs Merrill, 1960), 159–160; Joseph P. Free, *Archaeology and Bible History* (Wheaton: Scripture, 1969), 285. See also Luke 2:1-7.
26. John Garstang, *The Foundations of Bible History: Joshua, Judges* (New York: R. R. Smith, 1931), 146.
27. See Joshua 6:20.

28. Norman L. Geisler, *Baker Encyclopedia of Christian Apologetics* (Grand Rapids: Baker, 1998), 50–51. See also Genesis 19:23-29.
29. Portions of this chapter were adapted from Josh McDowell, *Evidence that Demands a Verdict* (Nashville: Thomas Nelson, 1993); Josh McDowell, *More than a Carpenter* (Wheaton, IL: Tyndale, 1977); Josh McDowell and Bob Hostetler, *Beyond Belief to Convictions* (Wheaton, IL: Tyndale, 2002); Josh McDowell and Thomas Williams, *The Relational Word* (Holiday, FL: Green Key, 2006).

4: THE COACH/WHO IS GOD?

1. A. W. Tozer, *The Knowledge of the Holy* (New York: Harper & Row, 1961), 9.
2. Howard E. Mumma, *Albert Camus and the Minister* (Brewster, MA: Paraclete, 2000), 86–87.
3. David Servan-Schreiber, *Anticancer: A New Way of Life* (New York: Viking, 2008), 91.
4. C. S. Lewis, *Mere Christianity* (New York: Macmillan, 1960), 118.
5. See Genesis 1:27.
6. John 3:16.
7. Augustine, Confessions 1.1.
8. Deuteronomy 6:4.
9. For references to the Spirit, see for example 1 Samuel 11:6; Isaiah 63:10-11; Ezekiel 11:24. For "angel of the Lord" examples, see Numbers 22:22-35; Judges 13:13-21.
10. See Matthew 28:19; John 10:30; 1 Corinthians 12:4-6.
11. 1 John 4:8, 16.
12. Wayne Grudem, *Systematic Theology: An Introduction to Biblical Doctrine* (Grand Rapids, MI: Zondervan, 1994), 198.
13. Ephesians 1:3.
14. Ephesians 1:5, NLT.
15. 1 John 4:10.
16. Romans 5:8.
17. John 3:16.
18. John 8:12.
19. John 9:5.
20. John 15:15.
21. See Psalm 19:1-6; Romans 1:19-20.
22. John 1:18.
23. John 4:24.
24. See John 16:7.
25. John 16:13.
26. Ephesians 1:13-14.
27. See 1 Corinthians 13:8.
28. "Top 10 Hitters in the NFL," http://sportsillustrated.cnn.com/multimedia/photo_gallery/0707/top10.hitters.today.nfl/content.10.html.

5: CREATION/HOW DID LIFE BEGIN?

1. Psalm 19:1.
2. Romans 1:20.
3. Francis Crick, *The Astonishing Hypothesis: The Scientific Search for the Soul* (New York: Touchstone, 1995), 3.

4. David Brooks, "The Neural Buddhists," *New York Times*, May 13, 2008; http://www .nytimes.com/2008/05/13/opinion/13brooks.html.

5. John Gray, *Straw Dogs: Thoughts on Humans and Other Animals* (London: Granta Books, 2002), 33.

6. Arno Penzias, interview by Malcolm W. Browne, "Clues to the Universe's Origin Expected," *New York Times*, March 12, 1978.

7. I'm not convinced that these mechanisms support all the weight that is often put on them. But that is a separate point. What we are emphasizing here is that, whatever you think about evolution, you cannot deduce atheism from it. For further information, see my book *God's Undertaker: Has Science Buried God?* (Grand Rapids, MI: Kregel, 2007).

8. Psalm 19:1.

9. Sir Ghillean Prance, "The Dying Planet?" http://www.cis.org.uk/assets/files/Resources/ Articles/gprance.pdf.

10. See also Rodney Stark, *For the Glory of God* (Princeton, NJ: Princeton University Press, 2004).

11. John 1:1-3, KJV.

12. Francis S. Collins, *The Language of God: A Scientist Presents Evidence for Belief* (New York: Free Press, 2006), 3.

13. BBC Radio 4 interview, December 10, 2004. See also Antony Flew, *There Is a God* (New York: Harper Collins, 2007).

14. Hebrews 11:3

15. Roger W. Sperry, quoted in *Brain Circuits and Functions of the Mind: Essays in Honor of Roger W. Sperry,* Colwyn Trevarthen, ed. (Cambridge: Cambridge University, 1990), 385.

16. Romans 1:20.

17. The text of Genesis 1 is highly sophisticated in that it uses the word *day* in several different ways, so that dogmatism about its meaning is, in my opinion, unwarranted. It should also be noted that interpreting Genesis 1 in terms of an ancient earth is not a recent approach designed to accommodate the findings of contemporary science. It was the view, for instance, of both Augustine and Origen.

18. Genesis 1:1.

19. Genesis 1:2, KJV.

20. Paul Davies, *God and the New Physics* (London: J. M. Dent and Sons, 1983), 179.

21. Arno Penzias, "Creation Is Supported by All the Data So Far," *Cosmos, Bios, Theos: Scientists Reflect on Science, God, and the Origins of the Universe, Life, and Homo sapiens,* Henry Margenau and Roy Varghese, eds. (Chicago: Open Court, 1992), 83.

22. Revelation 4:11, emphasis added.

23. Genesis 2:7.

24. Genesis 3:6.

25. Richard Dawkins, *The God Delusion* (Boston: Houghton Mifflin, 2006), v. See also Douglas Adams, *The Hitchhiker's Guide to the Galaxy* (New York: Ballantine, 1997), 107.

26. See Genesis 2:15–3:24.

27. Immanuel Kant, *The Critique of Practical Reason*, trans. Thomas Kingsmill Abbott (Radford, VA: Wilder, 2008), 111.

28. Though the phrase, "If there is no God, then everything is permitted," does not appear

in any of Dostoyevsky's works, it most likely derives from dialogue between characters in his masterpiece *The Brothers Karamazov*. For example, at one point, Rakitin quotes his brother Ivan: "If there is no immortality of the soul, then there is no virtue, and therefore everything is permitted." And later in the novel, Mitya asks, "How will man be after that? Without God and the future life? It means everything is permitted now, one can do anything?" (Fyodor Dostoyevsky, *The Brothers Karamazov*, trans. Richard Pevear and Larissa Volokhonsky [New York: Farrar, Straus and Giroux, 1990], 82, 589.)

29. Richard Dawkins, *Out of Eden* (New York: Basic Books, 1992), 133.
30. See Genesis 1:31.
31. See Romans 1:18-32.
32. John 1:11-12.

6: SIN AND ADDICTION/HOW DO I DEAL WITH SIN?

1. 1 John 1:8-9.
2. John 14:19, RSV.
3. Romans 1:18-25, NLT.
4. Luke 20:20-26, NLT.
5. John R. W. Stott, *Basic Christianity* (Downers Grove, IL: InterVarsity, 1971), 62.
6. Mark I. Pinsky, *The Gospel According to Disney: Faith, Trust, and Pixie Dust* (Louisville, KY: Westminster, 2004), 231.
7. See http://www.youtube.com/watch?v=31ZevWuxrNE.
8. Oscar Wilde, *The Picture of Dorian Gray* (Oxford: Oxford University Press, 1998), 128–129.
9. Habakkuk 2:18-20, NLT.
10. Isaiah 29:7-8.
11. Matthew 6:22-23, NLT.
12. Romans 1:29-32, NLT.
13. "Marion Jones' e-mail to family and friends," *The Daily Telegraph*, October 6, 2007, http://www.news.com.au/dailytelegraph/story/0,22049,22541801-5001021,00.html.
14. NLT.
15. John Newton, "Amazing Grace," first appeared in *Olney Hymns* (London: W. Oliver, 1779).

7: SALVATION/HOW DO I GET ON GOD'S WINNING TEAM?

1. John 14:6
2. C. S. Lewis, *Mere Christianity* (New York: Harper Collins, 2001 edition), 49.
3. John 10:30.
4. Matthew 16:25.
5. Romans 3:23.
6. Romans 6:23.
7. 1 Corinthians 1:27-29.

8: RELATIONSHIPS/WHAT DOES GOD SAY ABOUT MARRIAGE AND SEX?

1. Proverbs 17:17.
2. Mark 12:30-31.
3. Genesis 1:26-27.

4. See John 17:20-21; Ephesians 5:31-32.
5. Joshua 1:6-9.
6. Ephesians 6:11.
7. See Genesis 3:8-10.
8. Genesis 2:18.
9. Genesis 2:19-20.
10. Genesis 2:23.
11. Romans 3:23.
12. Genesis 2:24-25, KJV.
13. Matthew 19:4-6, NKJV.
14. See such passages as Proverbs 5 and Song of Solomon.
15. 1 Corinthians 6:18.
16. See 1 Corinthians 6:18-20.
17. 1 Corinthians 6:20, NKJV.
18. See 1 Corinthians 6:18-20; 1 Corinthians 7:1-4.
19. 1 Corinthians 7:5.
20. See Malachi 2:16; 1 John 1:9.
21. Hebrews 13:8.

9: FINANCES/HOW DO I MASTER MY MONEY?

1. Proverbs 22:26, NASB.
2. Matthew 25:21, 23.
3. Philippians 4:11-12.
4. Luke 16:11-12.
5. See Ephesians 2:10; Deuteronomy 8:16-18; Proverbs 22:2.
6. See 1 Corinthians 3:13-15; Hebrews 11.
7. See Ecclesiastes 5:10; Philippians 4:11-13.
8. See Jeremiah 9:23-24.
9. Proverbs 3:9, NASB.
10. 1 Corinthians 16:2, NASB.
11. Romans 13:7, NASB.
12. Matthew 22:21, NASB.
13. Proverbs 6:6-8.
14. Psalm 37:21, NASB.
15. 1 Timothy 5:8, NASB.
16. Peter F. Drucker, *The Effective Executive* (New York: HarperCollins, 1967), 134.
17. Ecclesiates 5:10, NASB.

10: VOCATION/HOW DO I BUILD A SUCCESSFUL LIFE AND CAREER?

1. John 10:10.
2. Homer, *The Illiad,* trans. Robert Fagles (New York: Penguin Classics, 1998) 21.119.
3. Luke 12:20.
4. Matthew 16:26.
5. Abraham Joshua Heschel, *Who Is Man?* (Stanford, CA: Stanford University, 1965), 53.
6. "Art Monk's Enshrinement Speech Transcript," Official Site of the Pro Football Hall of Fame, http://www.profootballhof.com/history/release.jsp?release_id=2798

11: HEALTH/HOW DO I ACHIEVE TRUE HEALTH?

1. See Leviticus 11; 13; 14.
2. See Luke 10:30-37.
3. John Wilkinson, *The Bible and Healing: A Medical and Theological Commentary* (Grand Rapids: Eerdmans, 1998), 7.
4. "Constitution of the World Health Organization," 45th ed., supplement, October 2006; http://www.who.int/governance/eb/who_constitution_en.pdf.
5. D. Dean Patton, M.D., personal communication, January 10, 2001.
6. Romans 10:17, NLT.
7. Psalm 29:11, NLT.
8. John 17:3.
9. Matthew 22:37-39, NLT.
10. Proverbs 3:7-8, NLT.
11. NLT.
12. 1 Corinthians 6:19; see also 1 Timothy 4:8.
13. Proverbs 17:22, NLT.
14. 3 John 1:2, NLT.
15. Psalm 32:3-4, NLT.
16. 1 Corinthians 11:29-30, NLT.
17. Michael Freeney, personal communication, January 6, 2001.
18. 1 Timothy 4:8-9, NLT.
19. See John 10:10.

12: PURPOSE/HOW DO I GET THE MOST OUT OF LIFE?

1. Adapted from "By and about Hank Aaron," ESPN Classic, http://espn.go.com/classic/s/000727hankaaronquote.html; and "About Yogi," on YogiBerra.com; http://www.yogiberra.com/about.html.
2. Luke 12:15, 21.
3. 1 Corinthians 10:31.
4. See 1 Samuel 13:14; Acts 13:22.
5. Matthew 5:16.
6. See Genesis 12:1-3.
7. "Many Needlessly Died on Titanic; Lifeboats Launched Only Half-Filled," *New York Times*, April 20, 1912; http://query.nytimes.com/search/sitesearch.
8. See John 2:17; Romans 15:20; Jeremiah 20:9.
9. See James 1:13-15.
10. Genesis 39:2, 23.
11. See Genesis 50:19-21.
12. See 2 Corinthians 2:12.
13. See Romans 8:28.
14. See John 17:4.
15. Psalm 128, NASB.
16. Hebrews 10:25, NKJV.

13: HEAVEN/WHERE WILL I SPEND ETERNITY?

1. Ecclesiastes 3:11.

2. See Philippians 1:23.

3. John 14:2.

4. Isaiah 65:17.

5. 2 Peter 3:13.

6. Luke 6:23.

7. Matthew 5:3-5.

8. 2 Peter 3:13, NKJV.

9. See Revelation 21:1-3; 22:1.

10. Revelation 21:1-3.

11. Psalm 16:11, NKJV.

12. See 2 Peter 3:10-13.

13. See 1 Corinthians 15:19-54.

14. Genesis 1:31.

15. Ephesians 1:10.

16. Matthew 25:21.

17. See Genesis 3:17.

18. See Revelation 22:2.

19. Philippians 3:21.

20. Luke 24:39.

21. Luke 24:40-43.

22. Luke 22:29-30.

23. Matthew 8:11.

24. Revelation 19:9.

25. Isaiah 25:6.

26. See Luke 22:30; Revelation 21:6.

27. See Hebrews 11:10; 13:14.

28. See Hebrews 11:16.

29. Revelation 21:24, 26.

30. See 1 Corinthians 9:24, 27; 2 Timothy 2:5.

31. See Isaiah 60:6; Ezekiel 47:7-12.

32. Romans 8:19-23.

33. Matthew 19:28.

34. Acts 3:21.

35. Revelation 21:5, NASB.

36. See Matthew 7:9-11.

37. Luke 6:21.

38. See Matthew 10:28; 13:40-42; Mark 9:43.

39. Matthew 8:12.

40. See Luke 16:19-31.

41. See 2 Peter 3:9.

42. 1 John 1:9

43. Ephesians 1:7.

44. See 2 Corinthians 5:21.

45. Ephesians 2:8-9.

46. Revelation 22:17.

47. Hebrews 2:14-15.

48. 1 Corinthians 15:55.
49. 2 Corinthians 4:16-18.
50. C. S. Lewis, *The Last Battle* (New York: HarperCollins, 2000), 210-211.
51. Colossians 3:1.
52. 2 Peter 3:14.
53. Revelation 21:3-5.